LAST LIGHT

ALSO BY TERRI BLACKSTOCK

LAST LIGHT

A RESTORATION NOVEL I *BOOK ONE*

TERRI BLACKSTOCK

ZONDERVAN·
.com

ZONDERVAN.com/
AUTHORTRACKER
follow your favorite authors

ZONDERVAN

Last Light
Copyright © 2005 by Terri Blackstock

This title is also available as a Zondervan ebook product.
Visit www.zondervan.com/ebooks for more information.

This title is also available as a Zondervan audio product.
Visit www.zondervan.com/audiopages for more information.

Requests for information should be addressed to:
Zondervan, *Grand Rapids, Michigan 49530*

Library of Congress Cataloging-in-Publication Data

Blackstock, Terri, 1957–
        Last light / Terri Blackstock.
            p. cm. — (A restoration novel ; bk. 1)
        ISBN 978-0-310-25767-7
        1. Regression (Civilization) — Fiction. I. Title.
    PS3552.L34285L37 2005
    813'.54 — dc22   2005016639

Published in association with the literary agency of Alive Communications, Inc., 7680 Goddard Street, Suite 200, Colorado Springs, CO 80920. www.alivecommunications.com

Interior design: Beth Shagene

ISBN 978-0-3103-3778-2 (2013 repackage)

Printed in the United States of America

HB 09.13.2022

*This book is lovingly
dedicated to the Nazarene.*

DEAR READER

THANK YOU FOR READING MY RESTORATION SERIES. I GOT the idea for these books as the world was preparing for "Y2K." The world was expecting a huge catastrophe as the clocks turned from 1999 to 2000. Computers were expected to crash, power grids to shut down, and the world as we knew it might come to an end. We all sat around our televisions the night of New Year's Eve, bracing ourselves for darkness. That darkness never came, and the catastrophe didn't happen. But the thought of what might have happened continued to germinate in my brain.

I asked a physicist friend of mine what kind of event could knock out our power grid and fry all our technology, and he told me to research electromagnetic pulses. These pulses could be caused by different things—solar flares, celestial events, E-bombs, and nuclear weapons exploding in our upper atmosphere. As I read and studied these situations and their repercussions, I became more and more aware that these things were real threats to our way of life.

At the same time, I was troubled spiritually by the cultural decline in America. Families (including my own) seemed to be eating most meals in their cars between ballet and soccer practice, the children were glued to video games and television, and parents were distracted by their smart phones. Our comfort had numbed us to the things God wanted to do in our lives. I became convicted that He was going to have to do something drastic to America to get our attention. What would that be? Would it be war? Famine? A nuclear attack?

That's when I decided to flesh out the idea for the Restoration Series and challenge a spoiled American family with a massive global power outage. The Brannings, who'd been used to fast food and take-out, now have to grow their own food and find water. Their cars don't run, their jobs are gone, the banks are closed, there's no communication . . . and this family has to decide if they will hoard what they have or share with their neighbors, when sharing might lead to their own starvation. All around them are desperate people, some willing to kill for food or the opportunity to get ahead.

Since I wrote these books years ago, there have been variations of this theme in television series and books by other authors. Mine are different because I chose not to focus on the military aspect, but on the changing character of the people suffering through this disaster. I fell in love with these characters as I wrote the four-book series, and so did many of my readers. Several years since the series was first released, people are still buying the books and sharing them with their friends. For that reason, we've decided to give the series a second life with new covers and a re-launch that will give new readers an opportunity to discover them. It's my hope that "rehearsing" this catastrophe with my characters will help prepare readers for catastrophes in their own lives. And if it gets the attention of God's people *before* He has to give us a wake-up call . . . well, that would be my idea of true success.

If you like the books, please tell others about them. And if you enjoy the way I tell a story, there are many other books where these came from. Learn more about all of them at http://www.terriblackstock.com/books.

Thanks again for reading my books!
Terri Blackstock

ONE

DENI BRANNING STEPPED DOWN ONTO THE TARMAC, PULLED out the handle of her carry-on, and glanced back up at her dad. He was just exiting the commuter plane as he chatted over his shoulder with the man who'd sat next to him on the flight. Doug Branning had never met a stranger, which accounted for his success as a stockbroker. He'd snagged some of his best clients on flights like this.

The oppressive Birmingham humidity settled over Deni like a heavy coat. *It's temporary*, she told herself. She wouldn't have to spend the summer here. Just this last week of May, and then it was back to D.C., her new job, and the fiancé she'd dreamed of for all of her twenty-two years. Yes, it was hot in the nation's capital, too, and probably just as humid. But its fast-paced importance made it easier to bear.

As her father reached the bottom step, his small bag clutched in his hand, the loud hum of the plane's engine went silent. A sudden, eerie quiet settled over the place, as if someone had muted all the machinery around them. The conveyor belt purging the cargo bin of its luggage stopped. The carts dragging the luggage carriers stalled.

She smelled something burning.

Her father seemed oblivious to the sudden change, so she fell into step beside him, rolling her bag behind her.

"Look out! It's coming in too fast!"

She turned back to see the airline employees gaping at the sky. An airliner was descending too steeply from the sky, silently torpedoing toward the runway. "Dad—!"

She screamed as the plane shattered into the runway, the impact vibrating through her bones. Time seemed to stop in a nightmarish freeze-frame, then roll into slow-motion horror as the plane tumbled wildly across the pavement and spun into a building.

Her dad tried to pull away. "In the building, Deni! Now! Let's go!"

Before she could get her feet to move, the plane exploded, flames bustling around it like a parachute that had finally caught wind. The blast of rippling heat knocked her off her feet, and before she could scramble up, her dad was over her, sheltering her with his body.

"Stay down, honey!"

She struggled to see through the shield of his arms. The fire conquered the broken fuselage, swallowing it whole. She imagined the people inside that plane, crawling over each other in a desperate effort to escape, slowly perishing in the murderous heat. Panic shot through her.

Her father got up and pulled her to her feet. "Come on, we're going inside!"

"But the people! Dad, the people—" She looked back, feeling the heat on her face.

"*Now*, Deni!"

"They're burning," she screamed. "Somebody has to get them out!"

"They're trying." His voice broke as he got back to his feet and grabbed up her suitcase. "There's nothing we can do."

She got up, staring toward the wreckage. The crowd of employees who ran to give aid stood helpless, unable to get close. Her father put his arm around her and moved her toward the building. They ran up the steps to their arrival gate.

They were greeted by darkness.

They hurried through the terminal to a window that provided some light. A crowd of people clustered around it, watching the plane burn.

Doug headed for two Delta clerks who stood talking urgently. "Where are the fire trucks? Has anybody called them?"

A distracted employee shook his head. "The phones aren't working. Everything's out."

He grabbed his cell phone out of his pocket, and Deni watched him try to dial 911. But the readout was blank. He shook his head. "It's dead. My battery must have lost its charge. Try yours, Deni."

She dug her phone out of her purse and hit the *on* button. Hers was dead, too. Had both their batteries died on the plane?

She looked back out the window. The plane continued to burn … engulfed in a conflagration that wouldn't be quenched. Helpless airport employees stood back, looking around for help. Someone had pulled out a fire extinguisher and was shooting white foam, but it was like squirting a water pistol at a towering inferno.

Deni thought of herself and her dad sitting on the plane just moments ago. It could have been *them* out there, trapped in a burning metal coffin.

Gritting her teeth, she pounded her fists on the window. "Where are the stupid fire trucks?"

"I don't know." Doug's whisper was helpless, horrified.

She watched the chaos on the tarmac as employees ran in different directions, looking confused and defeated, shouting and gesturing wildly for help. Some started pointing up to the sky …

"Another plane!" someone next to her shouted.

She followed the man's gaze to another airliner coming in. The others started to scream as that plane dropped too fast, too steep.

She couldn't watch as it hit the ground, but she heard the deafening sound of another crash, felt the impact shake the building. Screams crescendoed.

Shivering, Deni looked up. The plane was spinning and tumbling across the grass separating the runways.

"Daddy!" She glanced at him, saw the horror in his eyes. She followed his gaze to the sky. Was something shooting the planes down? Were there more to come? Deni slipped her hand into his and felt his trembling. For the first time in her life, she was aware of her father's fear. And though his strong, protective grip held her tight, she knew everything had changed.

TWO

Doug Branning's mind raced to understand — planes falling out of the sky, crashing, burning, people dying ...

There was a power outage, but that wouldn't have caused planes to crash. Maybe there was some kind of battle going on in the air that they couldn't see. If someone was shooting the planes down, maybe they'd also knocked out the power on the ground. Was it some kind of terrorist attack?

In all his uncertainty, he knew one thing. He had to get his daughter to safety. The airport felt like a target for whatever evil hovered above them. He put his arm around Deni and pulled her from the window. He hoped she couldn't feel his trembling. "Come on, Deni, we're getting out of here."

For once in her life she was compliant as he pulled her up the long dark hall, past the empty gates. Several Delta ground clerks came running past them.

"Excuse me," he called out. "Can anyone tell me what's going on?"

"Power's out," one of them called back. "Nothing's working."

"Did the planes crash because the tower's electricity is down?"

"May have. We can't say for sure."

Doug frowned. That didn't make sense. Didn't pilots have emergency procedures for situations like this? Couldn't they land the planes without an air traffic controller talking them through it?

He walked Deni past another window and saw the ball of fire, still burning. The other plane hadn't caught fire, and men rushed toward it, fighting to get the door open. Still no fire trucks had come.

"Dad, what's going on? What would make two planes crash?"

He shook his head. "No power outage, that's for sure. One of the planes must have hit a power line."

"No, the power shut down *before* the crashes. That's why things went quiet. I heard our plane's engine power off at the same time everything else stopped. The luggage belt, the maintenance cars ..."

Dozens of people were at the second plane now, but they couldn't seem to get inside. He bit his bottom lip. The passengers had all probably died in the impact. How could anyone have survived? He didn't want Deni to see them pulling the bodies out.

"Let's go to the car." Still carrying Deni's suitcase, he headed to the exit. "Maybe we can get a signal on our phones after we leave the airport, and call your mother. She's probably heard about it on the news and can tell us what's happening."

Deni followed him at a trot, hiccuping sobs. He reached the front door, but it didn't open.

"Power's out, Dad," she reminded him.

He turned and found a manual door. As they pushed through it, he was struck with the silence in the street. No cars moved through, and the security guards were probably helping the rescue effort. Doug and Deni hurried across the street into the big parking garage. They'd parked on the fourth level, so they found the stairs and trudged up.

Doug was damp with sweat by the time they reached their level and made their way to his new Mercedes. He used the remote on his key chain to pop the lock on the trunk, but when he got to the car, the trunk was still closed. He pressed the button again, but it still didn't open. Frustrated, he jabbed the key into the lock, and opened it. He threw their two bags in, slammed the trunk, then tried to open his driver's door. It hadn't come unlocked with the trunk, so he manually unlocked it and got in, punching the power locks button to open Deni's door.

But Deni just stood there, knocking on the passenger window.

He frowned at the door lock. The power locks weren't working—how could *that* be? The power outage couldn't extend to his car, could it? He leaned across the leather seat, and opened the passenger door.

As Deni got in, he put the key into the ignition and turned it ... but nothing happened.

Deni just looked at him. "The car's dead, too? Dad, this is like the *Twilight Zone*. What could cause this?"

"Got me."

Doug looked around. Usually cars circled everywhere, competing for parking spots. But not today. He got out and walked to the edge of the garage, looked over to the roads that took them out of the place. There were a few cars lined up at the pay booth, but they weren't moving. No cars ran on the streets leading to the interstate, though several seemed stalled in the middle of the road. People stood outside their vehicles, opening the hoods ...

Doug went back to his car and tried turning the key again, to no avail. He tested the radio. Still nothing. "I don't believe this."

Deni found a Kleenex and blew her nose. "This is just great! Are we going to have to stay in this creepy place with planes crashing all around us? I want to go home."

He turned to the backseat and saw a Walkman one of the kids had left there. He grabbed it, shoved the headphones on, and tried to get a station.

All he got was silence.

"Nothing?" Deni asked.

"Nothing."

"Maybe it's all the metal in the garage, blocking the radio waves."

He got back out of the car, took it to the edge of the garage, and tried again. Still nothing.

Slowly, he removed the headphones as the stark realization took hold of him. Everything was dead. Electricity, phones, cars, radio waves ... even planes in midflight.

As he got back into his useless car, Doug Branning felt the world spinning out of control.

And he was powerless to stop it.

THREE

"OH, NO! TELL ME THIS ISN'T HAPPENING." A BRAND-NEW CAR wasn't supposed to die in rush hour traffic. But one minute Kay Branning was sitting in line at the red light, cranking up the air conditioner so her kids would stop complaining, and the next minute the engine had cut off and stubbornly refused to start again.

Panicked, she turned the key, but nothing happened. Soon the light would change, and people lined up for miles behind her would start honking their horns if she didn't get out of the way.

"Come on, Mom!" Jeff, her sixteen-year-old jock who'd just pitched a no-hitter, banged on the dashboard. "I've got a date tonight and I have to get a shower!"

"Calm down." Kay tried to think. Maybe the air conditioner and radio were putting too much strain on the battery. She cut them all off.

The car still wouldn't start.

"I didn't even want to come to this stupid game," Beth, her twelve-year-old, cried. "Dad and Deni are going to be home before we are. Why did you even make me come?"

Kay ground her teeth. "Because it's your brother's game, and we support each other in this family!"

"Don't do me any favors, Beth," Jeff said. "I didn't need you there, pouting like a four-year-old."

"Why don't you shut up?" Beth snapped.

9

"Mom, I told you to buy the Tahoe," Jeff went on, unscathed. "But no, you had to have the Expedition."

"I'm dying of thirst." This whimper came from the backseat, as Kay's nine-year-old stood up and leaned over the seat in front of him. "It's hot. Can't you turn the air conditioner on?"

"No, Logan, I can't."

"The car's dead," Beth said. "As in, no power." As she spoke, she grabbed the Game Boy that he'd laid on the seat.

"Give that back!" he shouted. "Mom!"

Kay gave up trying to start the car. She popped the hood and opened her door to get out.

"What are you doing?" Jeff asked.

"Looking under the hood."

He started to laugh. "For what? Do you even know what you're looking for?"

"No, but if you do, why don't you get out and help me?"

"That's right, genius," Logan snapped. "Go help her."

Kay looked at the line behind her, hoping they'd be patient with her. Maybe someone who knew cars would come to her aid.

But no one was focused on her. Others were getting out of their own cars, popping their own hoods. An eerie silence hovered over them—no engines running, no horns beeping, no radios playing. Just the sound of the hot breeze sweeping through the trees.

And she smelled something burning, but there was no sign of a fire or smoke anywhere.

"What is this?" Kay whispered.

Jeff got out and looked around, his eyes as big as quarters. "Way cool. They're all dead. Everybody's car died at the same time."

Beth got out of the car, and Logan climbed up to the front. "Everybody's?" he said. "Why?"

Kay shook her head. "I have no idea, but I'm calling your father." She grabbed her cell phone out of the car, flipped it open ...

But it was dead, too. "It's not working, either."

"What?" Jeff took her phone. "Let me see."

Kay went to the man standing at the pickup in front of her. He, too, was trying his cell phone.

"Excuse me, do you have any idea what's going on?"

"None," he said. "The cars are dead, my cell phone doesn't work, my PDA won't come on, even my watch has stopped."

Kay looked down at her own watch. The digital readout was blank. "What in the world would knock out our cars and our watches?"

Jeff came around the car. "There's a store at the Exxon station on the next block. Why don't we walk there and see what we can find out?"

Kay turned back to her Expedition. "I can't abandon the car here. I have to move it when it starts again."

"Then I'll go by myself."

Kay couldn't explain the feeling of uneasiness weighing on her. "Okay, but be careful."

"Why?" Jeff chuckled. "Not like I'm gonna get hit by a car."

"Use the pay phone to call your dad. He and Deni should have landed by now. Maybe he knows something."

She watched as Jeff trudged off in his baseball uniform and dirty cleats.

"Mom, it's hot!"

"Then get out of the car, Logan."

"It's hotter out there."

Kay was already starting to sweat. "What would you like me to do?"

"I don't know."

"Unless you have a solution, stop whining." She looked down the street at all the cars stalled in rush hour traffic and told herself to calm down. There was a perfectly reasonable explanation for this. Something had happened to cause it, and soon they would know what it was and how to fix it.

People came out of the insurance office next to them, and a woman hurried toward her. "What's going on with the cars?"

"They're all dead," Kay said. "No reason. They just stopped running at the same time."

The woman looked stunned. "And all our power went out."

"Really?"

"Has to be an electromagnetic pulse." The man from in front of her seemed to be thinking aloud. "That would knock out everything electronic."

"But what would cause something like that?"

"An e-bomb, maybe."

"A bomb?" Kay caught her breath and looked out over the sky. "Then we could be under attack?" She searched for a sign of smoke indicating a bomb had hit somewhere. The sky was a radiant blue, and there was no sign that anything catastrophic had happened. She looked back at her Expedition, and saw Beth walking up the street to talk to a friend three cars up.

"Beth, come back!"

Her daughter turned around.

"Don't go anywhere. Stay right here with me."

"Why?"

She couldn't tell her that she feared something worse might be about to happen, that there could be radiation in the air, or toxins, or bombs about to drop ... "Just do what I tell you."

Logan picked that moment to come out of the car. She grabbed his arm and shoved him back in. "Get back in the car!"

"But you said to get out! It's hot in there!"

"Do it!" she shouted. "Now!"

Both kids muttered as they got back in. Kay stood there a moment, trying to get a grip on herself. Why was she yelling at them? It didn't make any sense.

None of this did. All she knew was that she was scared. She just didn't know of what.

FOUR

SWEAT TRICKLED DOWN DOUG'S NECK AND SOAKED INTO THE
collar of his button-down shirt as he sat with Deni inside
the airport. They'd gone back inside after realizing the car
wasn't taking them anywhere. As they'd come in, they'd seen
firefighters running to the scene on foot. Through the glass,
he saw the planes still on fire, caught the smell of burning
metal and fuel working its way into the terminal. The firefighters worked at the wreckage with handheld fire extin-
guishers in a desperate attempt to quench the flames and
pull survivors from the planes.

There was more activity at the second plane than the
first. There hadn't been an explosion on that one, and even
though the plane had spun and tumbled after landing, it
looked like there could be survivors. The emergency crews
worked quickly, as if anticipating an explosion, and finally
got the doors open.

Deni erupted out of her seat and rushed to the window.
"Dad, look! Someone's alive."

Doug joined her, watching as they carried out a man in
uniform. "It's one of the pilots."

They placed the man on a gurney, but where would
they take him? They couldn't put him in an ambulance and
whisk him to the hospital. Doug wished he were a doctor
and could treat him on the spot. He prayed that there was
one out there already, someone who knew exactly what
needed to be done.

Doug watched, breath held, as a few others came out of the wreckage, some walking, others carried.

Deni reached for his hand as she kept her gaze glued to the site. He didn't know when she had last done that before today. Ten years? Twelve? At twenty-two, Deni was fiercely independent. He closed his hand around hers, offering shallow reassurance. The crew started bringing the survivors in the door close to Doug and Deni, and the cluster of people at the window moved to get a look.

They waited until the pilot was carried in, and Doug tried to see if he was conscious. A man ran alongside the gurney, keeping pressure on the pilot's bleeding head wound. He saw the pilot bring a bloody hand to his face. The man was conscious.

Another passenger walked in behind him, smudges from smoke marring the skin around her nose and mouth. Coughing, she limped through the crowd.

Deni let go of Doug's hand and threw herself at the woman. "Ma'am, did your plane get shot down?"

Doug grabbed Deni's arm, wishing she had waited for someone who wasn't injured.

The woman coughed, then answered in a raspy voice. "I don't know what happened. All I know is that the lights shut off in the plane, and we started dropping. No announcement, no nothing. Next thing we know we're rolling across the runway."

Deni turned back to Doug. "That pilot is awake, Dad. I bet *he* knows what happened."

Doug nodded. "Let's follow and see if we can find anybody who spoke to him."

They followed the gurney up the concourse and to the small Crown Room. Doug caught up with one of the disheveled crew members who'd helped get the pilot out.

"Excuse me, did the pilot say what happened?"

The man's eyes darted from the victims to the window. "He's as much in the dark as we are. Said his power just shut off, and nothing worked. Not even the radio. All four engines died. He had to glide the plane to the nearest airport and land it manually. If it had been a bigger, newer plane, they'd have fallen like a lawn dart—just like the first plane. It's a miracle there were any survivors."

Doug stared after the man as he disappeared into the Crown Room, running the words through his mind. Plane engines dying midair, cars stalling, electricity failing ...

"Dad, I'm scared. Planes don't just fall out of the sky."

He swallowed and rubbed his jaw. It was war. Had to be. Someone had attacked them, just like on 9/11. Maybe it was a nuclear attack in the atmosphere, powerful enough to knock out everything electronic, but not to destroy the buildings and cities ... or people.

He supposed he should be grateful there was no more human fallout. But what if their safety was just an illusion? What if the bomb, if there was one, had somehow released deadly bacteria or viruses or toxins that would wipe out the whole region in a matter of hours? If not that, then radiation could be rippling on the air right now, slowly working on the cells of their bodies ...

"Dad, I want to go home." Panic rippled on Deni's voice.

The same panic lodged itself in his throat. He took a deep breath, and tried to draw his thoughts back. *Get a grip, man. Deni needs strength from you, not paranoia.*

He didn't have enough information to form any solid conclusions. It wasn't necessarily a nuclear or atomic attack. It could be just a weird weather front, like all those hurricanes in Florida last year, or the tsunami that hit Sri Lanka. Some kind of unexpected electrical force that flashed through the sky. Or something else none of them had even thought of.

He had to stay calm. "Yeah, I think we need to go home. Doesn't look like the power's coming back on in the next few hours."

Her lips quivered. "But how will we get there?"

He crossed the floor to the other side of the building, looking out the window to the parking lot. People were hiking up the road that circled the terminals. "We'll have to walk." He looked down at the four-inch heels on his daughter's feet. How on earth did she walk in those things? "Deni, don't you have some tennis shoes in your bag?"

"No, I didn't anticipate having to hoof it for forty miles."

He ignored the petulance in her tone. "It's not forty. It's more like sixteen. But you still won't make it in heels."

"So what do we do? Just stay here?"

No, that wasn't an option. They had to get home. He wanted to be with his family, make sure everything was all right.

"Tell you what," he said. "There's a Wal-Mart a few miles away. Let's walk there and buy a bicycle and some more comfortable shoes."

Her eyes lit up. "Okay, let's hurry before other people get the same idea. But what about our bags? We won't be able to carry them on bikes."

"We'll leave them in the car. Come back for them in your mom's car."

"Okay." She pranced along in her designer pants and silk blouse. "But I need to get some stuff out of my suitcase."

"Deni, we'll have to travel light."

"I know. Just a few necessities." They reached his car, and he opened the trunk and watched, irritated, as she opened her suitcase and pulled out her Chanel makeup pouch, and the 5x7 framed portrait of her fiancé, Craig, who lived in D.C. He'd made a big deal yesterday of giving her a "special gift," and Deni got all excited trying to guess what it was. When she finally opened the package and saw that it was an 8x10 of Craig, Doug felt like slugging him and saying, *You think that's a prize, bud? A lousy picture of you? It's about as exciting as that pitiful excuse of a diamond you gave her.*

Doug suspected since she'd come home with that one-carat rock that it was cubic zirconia. He supposed, with Craig's position in Senator Crawford's office, the kid could afford the real thing. But Craig Martin didn't strike him as the type who would spring for a diamond that size. For himself, maybe, but not for Deni.

He bit his tongue as Deni pulled that picture out of her suitcase, like it was her most cherished possession. Next came her flat iron.

"Deni, until the power comes back on, you can't even use that."

"But what if it's on at home?"

Doug shook his head. "You can't carry all that stuff on a bike."

She started to argue, then sighed. "I guess you're right." She jabbed the flat iron under the wadded clothes and put the picture back. "Okay, there."

He slammed the trunk shut. "Let's go."

Deni walked next to him at a fast clip, her heels clicking on the asphalt. They crossed the garage and stepped out into the sunlight. It was only five thirty p.m., and the sun blazed down with merciless heat. His shirt would be soaked by the time they reached Wal-Mart.

Already, dozens of people walked ahead of them, winding their way out of the airport maze. Unless something changed, hundreds of others would follow them soon.

As they made their way around Messer Airport Highway, they saw cars stalled in the middle of the road. Some were abandoned, though most still had people sitting on hoods or milling around them in the street. The atmosphere seemed almost festive.

He looked over at Deni, wondering how her feet were holding up. She walked with her head held high, that slight air of superiority floating around her as she clomped through the people, her purse swinging from her shoulder.

His daughter was pretty and she knew it, and if her feet ever hurt in those ridiculous shoes, she would die before admitting it. He wondered exactly what image she hoped to convey. Professional? Career woman? Very Important Person?

Glamour Girl?

Didn't she realize how silly that persona was when her hair was wet with sweat and her mascara streaked on her face? And she still had fifteen miles to go before they were home.

A mile into the walk, Deni kicked off her shoes and walked barefoot on the hot pavement. Her face blotched, and he didn't know if it was sunburn or heat that colored it.

They were both drenched with sweat by the time they reached the Wal-Mart parking lot. He prayed there hadn't been a run on bicycles.

The parking lot was full of stalled cars. Their owners stood around them, some with their heads under the hoods, trying to make sense of things. As they reached the front door, Doug saw that it was only partially opened. When the power had gone out, the door had apparently frozen.

Deni turned sideways to slip through the opening, and Doug followed.

The power was out inside, too, but hundreds of people milled about. The ceiling had skylights every few feet, which allowed some natural light into the otherwise dark building. Lines of thirty or more people waited at each cash register, and the clerks looked frazzled and stressed as they tried to take money with no registers working.

"Cash or checks only!" a worker yelled over the people. "Our credit card machines don't work! Cash or checks, please!"

Doug pulled his wallet out and checked his cash. Twenty bucks—not nearly enough to pay for a bicycle. He looked toward the ATM machine. A crowd gathered around it, and a man was kicking it and cursing. Clearly, it was dead, too.

"Deni, we've got a problem. I don't have enough money."

She grunted. "Don't you have checks?"

"No, your mother has the checkbook. All I carry is my debit card."

Deni dug through her purse. "I have checks for the account I just opened in Washington, if they'll take an out-of-state check. There's not much in my account, but we can transfer some money into it before the check clears."

"Great. Somehow we'll convince them to take it. Come on."

Deni ran behind her father, her bare feet slapping on the tile floor. "I'm going to the shoe section."

"Okay, I'm in the bikes."

He got to the bike section, and saw that most of them had already been taken.

He grabbed the first one he came to, a red ten-speed woman's bike, and lifted it free. Rolling it beside him, he went for a bigger one for himself. He grabbed a cheap model ten-speed.

A man who looked like Hulk Hogan's big brother grabbed it out of his hands. "I had this one first, pal. Hands off. You already got one."

"You didn't have it first! You were ten feet away."

"I was reaching for it, okay?"

Anger flared up inside him, but it wasn't worth a fight. He let the bike go, almost pushing it over. The man hurried away with it.

He turned to find another, but they were already gone, except for a retro banana seat children's bike. *At least it rolls*, he thought, so he reached for it, but a woman lunged for it at the same time. "Please, I have to get home! My child is there alone!"

He had no choice but to let it go.

Deni came running up with a box of tennis shoes in one hand, and her high heels in the other.

"I can only get one," Doug said. "We'll both have to ride this one."

"But, Dad, there isn't a second seat. Where am I gonna sit?"

He scanned the aisles and found a flat backseat attachment. "Here. We'll use this."

She huffed out a sigh, but apparently realized there was nothing else they could do. "I can't believe this hick town can't do better than this in an emergency."

There she went again, putting her hometown down. "I doubt they ever imagined this happening. Bicycles aren't typically what people go for in emergencies. And Birmingham's not a hick town. You're a product of it and you're no hick."

"I had it educated out of me."

Her typical response. He never should have agreed to send her to Georgetown University to study Broadcast Journalism. She'd developed such arrogance there that she was sometimes a pain in the neck.

He blamed it on the boyfriend.

As they made their way to the checkout lines, Deni grabbed two bottled waters.

"Good thinking," Doug said.

They went to stand in line, and Deni put the new tennis shoes on. He liked the way they looked on her. So much better than those cloppity-clops she bent her feet into. The shoes made her look more like the girl he remembered—the one who used to play tennis with him. The one who screamed like a wild kid at the UA football games.

He often wondered how different she would have been if he'd insisted she go to college closer to home, instead of shipping her off halfway across the country. Would she still be as arrogant, or as proud?

"It smells like a gym in here," she muttered. "Some of these people need to be introduced to the concept of deodorant."

"Deni, don't look now, but I think we're reeking with the best of them."

She gave him a half-amused smile. "Speak for yourself."

He grinned and shook his head. Man, when she started that television job next week, her head would swell even bigger. So what if she'd just be an intern at NBC's D.C. affiliate? She was already strutting around like she thought she was Katie Couric.

And if he knew Deni, she'd have Katie's job before the decade was over.

Part of him was so proud of her that he wanted to burst. The other part half hoped she'd be knocked down to size. Gently, of course ...

He'd gone with her to Washington to find her new apartment and get her set up. Though she'd only live there for four months—until her wedding, when she'd move into Craig's townhouse—he made sure she was choosing a safe apartment complex in a good part of town. As she milked him for every penny he was worth for her furniture and "necessities," he realized he'd spoiled her. Doing without—or doing with less—was going to shock her system. But once she had paychecks coming, he had no intention of keeping her on the family dole.

"Come on. How hard can this be?" Deni said under her breath. "All they have to do is add it up. Surely they have calculators."

"Looks like they're doing it on paper."

"That clerk must have missed the day they taught addition."

Again, the arrogance.

They waited in the line, quiet among the hot, irritated customers. The line was moving slowly, and the nervous clerk added up items as best she could. Tempers flared as customers demanded answers these hourly employees didn't have.

By the time Doug and Deni worked their way to the front of the line, the clerk looked as if she wanted to break and run.

Deni pulled out her checkbook and started to write the check.

"That an out-of-state check?" the woman asked.

Deni turned her prideful face up. "Yes. It's a new account in Washington, D.C."

The woman wasn't impressed. "We can't take out-of-state checks. Local checks or cash only."

Deni grunted. "Come *on*! We've stood here for forty-five minutes!"

"I'm sorry. We're doing the best we can."

Deni turned back to Doug. "Now what?"

Doug felt helpless. "All I have is twenty bucks."

"Then get out of the way, mister." The man behind him reached for the bike. "I'll take that."

As the man grabbed the back wheel, Doug threw his leg over the seat and sat on it. He felt like a child on the verge of a tantrum, but there wasn't time for shame. Addressing the sweating clerk, he said, "Please, she's my daughter. The check will be good. I'm local, and we can put my address and phone number on it."

"Sorry, sir, but I can't do it." She turned to the man behind him.

"Wait!" Doug looked down at himself, trying to think of anything he had that he could use to pay. "My watch!" He worked it off of his arm. "It's a Rolex, worth ten thousand dollars."

The girl looked up at the ceiling as if praying for patience. "I can't take your watch, sir."

"Please. Just this once, make an exception with her check and you can keep the watch."

The girl hesitated, then took the watch. "It doesn't even work."

"It's a Rolex," he said again, as if she hadn't heard. "When all this is over—whatever it is—it'll work again. You can sell it on Ebay and make a fortune. Please, I have to get home."

The clerk glanced over her shoulder, as if looking for the manager. He was too busy, running from cashier to cashier solving problems.

"Hurry up, lady!" someone down the line yelled.

She sighed. "All right, but put your local address on the back of the check. I'll probably get fired."

Doug gushed gratitude, then rolled the bike out into sunlight. Quickly, he assembled the backseat and put it on, using a dime as a screwdriver. Tightening the screws the best he could, he got the seat on and shook it to make sure it would support Deni.

Something rammed him from behind, knocking him over with the bike. As the bike clattered to the ground, his knee skidded on the pavement, shredding his skin. The attacker scrambled to get the bike out from under Doug, but he held on and grabbed the man by the collar. Slinging his assailant back, he became eight years old again, reeling with the sense of righteous indignation over the school bully's unwarranted attack, vicious with the need to right a wrong.

He got his footing as the man came at him, trying to mount the bike. Doug swung and hit the man in the chin with the heel of his hand, knocking the bike out from under him.

The man fought to keep it, but suddenly Deni was there, swinging the bag with her bottled water, knocking him in the head.

It stunned him enough that he lost his grip.

"Get on, Deni!"

She jumped on back, clutching the bag.

"Hold on!" Doug took off, rolling slowly at first, then, not looking back, he managed to pull away from the would-be thief and across the parking lot.

"Way to go, Dad!" Deni slapped him on the back. "Wooo-hooo!"

"Hush, Deni." He was not in the mood for gloating or theatrics. This was serious. He had fought like a barroom brawler over a stupid bicycle he wouldn't have paid a quarter for two hours ago. And he wasn't proud of it.

He pulled out into the street, dodging pedestrians and stalled cars, and headed for the interstate.

He tried to remember the last time he'd been in a fight. Must have been the tenth grade, when he'd given his brother a black eye for tripping him in the school assembly. They'd both gotten a three-day suspension after that. His dad grounded them both for a month. What would he think of him now?

Doug made it a mile down the road and saw the interstate overpass crossing up ahead of them.

"Oh, my gosh!" Deni's fingers gripped his shoulders. "It's like when the power went out in New York City, and all those people were walking home."

He looked toward the overpass, but instead of the people, the steep on-ramp caught his attention. How would he pedal the bike uphill, with his weight and Deni's? They might have to get off and walk it. He should have been using the stationary bike he had in the exercise room at home. There was no excuse for him being this out of shape. He headed for the ramp, and stood on the pedals, pumping with all his might.

"You okay, Dad? Want me to get off 'til you're on the road?"

"Might be a good idea."

He felt her slide off, and was relieved at the lighter weight. She walked beside him as he pulled uphill.

"I should have used my gym membership," he panted. "Everyone's thinking I'm in the shape of an eighty-year-old man."

"No, they're not, Dad. They're too busy envying your bike."

He reached the top and merged onto the interstate, then stopped behind a stalled car and let Deni get back on.

He hugged the road's shoulder, every push of the pedals sending fire through his thighs. Sweat dripped into his eyes, and he breathed like an asthmatic.

Cars were stalled almost bumper to bumper, and hundreds of people walked in both the east- and westbound lanes. He stayed on the shoulder, hoping to bypass the hiking crowds and avoid the stalled vehicles.

Deni's hands on his waist made him sweat more. "Maybe in a mile or so we'll see that the power is back on. It can't be the whole city. Maybe then we can get a ride the rest of the way."

Doug didn't answer. He panted like a thirsty dog, and his soaked clothes clung to his body. His legs strained to keep moving the bike forward, but his scraped knees were beginning to sting with every push.

He wondered if his attacker had been a thief before today, or had the man's actions been out of the ordinary, as Doug's had? Maybe the man was a deacon in his church, just like Doug. Maybe he had kids at home he was trying to get to. Maybe he was worried about his wife.

They couldn't be blamed for reacting to this bizarre situation the way they had, could they?

He wanted to think that there was some very interesting explanation for what was going on here, and that it wasn't far-reaching. But he feared that was wrong. Nothing he knew of that could cause such an event would be short-lived.

Along the road, hundreds of people still sat on their cars, unwilling to abandon them just yet. A stalled beer truck had its back doors open, and the driver was apparently selling beer to anyone who had cash.

Another hill. Doug made his way over it, gritting his teeth with the effort. At forty-seven, he'd never felt old until today. Now when he needed his muscles they rebelled like lazy teenagers.

He got over the hill, then saw with almost ecstatic relief that the next few miles were downhill or level, so he could move more quickly.

"Dad, do you see that smoke up ahead?"

He scanned the horizon, saw the plume of smoke. "Yeah, I see it."

"What do you think that is?"

"No idea."

"Maybe it's a plant of some kind that knocked out the power grid."

"Wouldn't knock out cars and watches." His tone was almost sarcastic, though he knew it didn't help. But the stupidity of this whole situation was beginning to get to him. What in the world was going on?

He kept looking toward that plume as he rode, trying to avoid the pedestrians in the street and spilling off onto the shoulder.

Then, from out of nowhere, something whacked him from the side. His tires slid out from under him, and they went over.

Deni screamed as they fell, and his flesh scraped across asphalt again.

He was getting tired of this.

A man with a shaved head and a goatee grabbed the bike and pulled it out from under them.

Doug yelled and shot to his feet. He swung at the man, but the thief kicked him in the chest, knocking the breath out of him, and got his leg over the bike.

"Oh, no, you don't!" Deni got up, her arm bleeding, and tried to wrestle the bike away. But she wasn't strong enough. The man slipped out of her grasp and pulled out of reach.

Doug launched out after him, racing beside him, grabbing the bike, trying to stop him. The man kicked him again, this time doubling him over.

"Thanks for the ride, bud!" he shouted back.

"Dad, he's getting away! Go after him!"

Pain shot through his stomach, but he forced himself to rise up. Breathless, he shook his head. "He's too far. There's nothing I can do."

He dropped to the grass on the side of the highway, draped his arms over his knees. "Are you all right?" he asked Deni.

"*No*, I'm not all right. I'm bleeding!" She kept staring after that bike. "Why did you let him take it?"

Had she missed that Chuck Norris kick that almost took him out? "I tried to stop him."

"But you didn't fight hard enough!"

He ground his teeth. "Deni, I really don't need your attitude right now. A bicycle is not worth killing someone over."

"I didn't say *kill* him. But you practically handed it over."

He didn't want to talk about his defeat. "Walking won't kill us. It's better than a knock-down-drag-out over something I didn't even care about three hours ago." He looked down the long road. It was growing crowded as more and more people abandoned their cars and joined the exodus to the suburb. "It's only another six miles or so."

Her face twisted. "Come on! That's absurd!"

"No, it's not. Do you have any better ideas?"

"Yeah," she said. "Let's trade a $10,000 Rolex for a bike, and then hand it over to some thug."

He wanted to throttle her. "How about some of that water?"

She grunted and pulled the bottles out, thrusting one of them at him. He took it and gulped the water down.

Deni stood there, staring in the direction of home. She opened her own water and began to drink. "This stinks," she grumbled between gulps. "We should have just stayed in D.C."

Doug's mind wandered back to the flight they'd been on a couple of hours ago. Ten minutes later, and they would have fallen out of the sky like the other planes. They might be dead. He looked back at that plume of smoke. Was it another plane that had missiled into the ground?

He supposed they had a lot to be thankful for. Even if there had been a terrorist attack of some sort, knocking out the power was a lot better than a nuclear explosion that killed millions.

Trying to take solace in that, he drew in a deep breath, got back up, and dusted himself off. "Come on, Deni, let's go."

They abandoned their bag with the empty bottles and Deni's high-heeled shoes, and joined the thick stream of people heading east.

They walked at a brisk pace, people around them laughing and talking like comrades.

"Remember everyone crossing the Brooklyn Bridge when New York's power grid went out?" Deni asked again.

"Yeah, but the cars still ran."

"I know, but it's similar. It'll probably make national news. I bet NBC is already covering it. I'll be an authority. Maybe I could contact the affiliate here and they could let me do the report."

"They have their own reporters at the affiliate here."

"Well, yeah. But I could try."

"Deni, what makes you think the TV stations have power?"

She trudged onward for a moment, not answering, then finally said, "Maybe they do. They did in New York."

He decided to stop shooting her down. Let her dream. What would it hurt?

"That smoke is a small plane that crashed," someone next to them was saying to his walking partners. "I talked to someone back a ways who watched it fall out of the sky."

Deni jumped in. "My dad and I just came from the airport. We saw two planes crash right after our plane landed."

The group around her slowed, captivated by her story of what the surviving pilot had told them about the power going out. There she was, a reporter in tennis shoes.

Speculation bred around them as they walked, but no one knew what had happened. No one had a clue.

At least the conversation helped Deni as they walked, distracting her from the drudgery, keeping her from grumbling and taking potshots at her father's poor excuse for courage.

Doug used the time to mentally work through the different possible scenarios. He kept going back to war—or some major terrorist attack.

Whatever had caused this, he feared it was only the beginning.

FIVE

A TWO-HOUR WALK LATER, KAY REACHED THE ROAD TO THEIR subdivision in the small suburb of Crockett, her children in tow. Jeff had finally convinced her to leave the car. They'd put it in neutral and pushed it onto the side of the road. She prayed it would still be there, intact, when they went back.

As they walked home, they saw a plume of smoke coming up over the trees several miles away. Someone on the road claimed they'd seen a small plane go down just as his car had stalled. Kay had quenched the urge to bolt off toward the smoke, to make sure it wasn't Doug and Deni's commuter airliner. They could be lying there dying, waiting for help to come.

But she didn't know how to get there, and it wouldn't pay to frighten her children that way. Still, as she walked, she kept looking back toward that smoke, praying that God would come to their aid.

Most of those walking home had reached their neighborhoods long before the Brannings. Those last three miles, she had rued the day they decided to live so far out in the country. But Oak Hollow was a neighborhood in high demand, its beautiful new homes beckoning those who could afford them. They'd tried to get one of the homes on the small lake at the center of the subdivision, but those had all been taken. Still, they were thrilled to find the home of their dreams, never yet lived in. And the extra driving time was worth it.

Living so far from town, she worried a bit about her children's safety driving home at night down the long, dark road. Doug convinced her they would be all right, and Deni and Jeff had agreed. But in her wildest dreams, she never anticipated *walking* here. The long country road seemed to stretch farther with each step. Pastureland stretched for miles on one side of the road, nothing but forest on the other.

Even though she knew the cars were dead, she couldn't escape the sense that everything would power back on as they journeyed up this road, and some teenager's car would come flying by and take out her children. She kept them on the side of the road as they walked, something they thought absurd.

Others walked up ahead of them, and some walked behind them. Most of them she recognized to be her neighbors, even though she didn't know them by name. They'd lived in the neighborhood for six years now, but she had yet to meet more than a few of her closest neighbors.

Beth and Logan trailed behind her, their hair wet with sweat and their cheeks mottled red. Jeff hurried ahead, refusing to be encumbered by his embarrassingly out-of-shape family.

When they finally reached the entrance to Oak Hollow, she looked up the street to their house—fifth from the entrance—and saw that Jeff already waited in the driveway. She wondered why he hadn't gone inside.

"Mom, do you have a key?" he called as she approached. "The code doesn't work."

Her heart sank. "Oh, no. I didn't even think of that." It was *her* bright idea to set the burglar system with an outside code for opening the garage door. That way the kids would never have a key to lose—all they had to do was punch in the code to get in. The door that led into the house from the garage was unlocked at all times. It had worked out perfectly.

Until now.

She hadn't carried a key in years, so had no means of getting in. She trudged up the driveway. "Can we pull it up?"

"No way. If you could do that, any doofus out there could break into our house."

"But there must be some way."

"There is," Jeff said. "It's called a key. You remember what a key is, don't you, Mom? It's one of those things that you were always afraid I'd drop into the hands of a serial killer? Like Logan and Beth haven't given the code out to all their friends."

Kay decided not to bite. Jeff had a habit of picking fights with her when he was tired, hungry, and hot, but she had more important things to do than worry about who had their code. As soon as this crisis passed, she'd ream her kids, change the code, and threaten their lives if they ever so much as uttered it again.

"Don't tell me we can't get in!" Beth came up the steep driveway and threw herself down on the grass. "It's a thousand degrees out here! I want to go in and get cool."

"It's not cool in there, Bozo," Jeff said. "The air conditioner is out, too."

Logan didn't have the energy to join in the banter. He just went to the hose on the side of the house and turned on the water. A small stream trickled out. He took a drink, then turned back to Kay. "Is the water going out, too? I turned it on full blast."

Kay grabbed the hose and tried the faucet again. He was right—full blast, but only a trickle. She twisted it off to save what was in the pipes. "Okay, nobody else use any water until we get in. Everybody spread out and check the windows to see if one's unlocked."

The kids did as they were told for once, and Kay prayed there would be one open, in spite of the fact that she rarely opened windows for fear of letting out the valuable air-conditioning. There was also the security issue. Two houses in the neighborhood had been broken into in the last three weeks. Both times, the burglar had gone in through an open window. She hadn't allowed anyone to unlock their windows since.

She heard Jeff yelling from the backyard and ran around the house.

"My window's open!" he shouted.

She looked up to the second-floor window and saw that it was open about six inches. "Thank goodness. Now if we could just get up there."

"I can do it," Jeff said. "All I have to do is climb the lattice on the side of the house where the roof is a little lower, then I can walk up onto the steeper roof and slide down to the landing below my window."

Kay just stared at him. "You sound like you've done this before."

He grinned. "Nah. Just thought about it. You know, when I was grounded and stuff."

She didn't have time to deal with this, so she put it on her growing list of things to discuss later. "All right. Do it."

They went around to the lattice, and she watched him climb it deftly, as if he'd had plenty of practice. No wonder a couple of the slats were broken. She'd thought the weather had worn them out.

As he maneuvered his way onto the roof, she wondered how many nights he'd sneaked out this way after she and Doug had gone to bed. She couldn't wait to tell Doug when he got home. He would know what to do about this revelation.

Jeff disappeared through his bedroom window, then after a few moments, he opened the back door. "Yeah, I'm the hero!" He raised his hands in a victory wave. "No applause, please."

"Don't worry." Beth pushed past him into the dark house.

Logan came in and went straight to the refrigerator.

"Honey, close that. We don't want the food to go bad."

"Mom, I'm dying of thirst, okay? I need a drink."

Kay reached past him and pulled out the pitcher of tea and a six-pack of Cokes. The icemaker in the door was dripping as the ice melted, but she decided to leave it in the freezer in hopes it would keep the food from thawing.

She poured herself a glass of cold tea as the kids tore the six-pack apart. As she drank it down, she tried to think. The water ... that was the next crisis to address. If the water was going out, then she needed to save what she could in case this lasted longer than a few hours.

She went to the bathroom off of the guest room and bent over the tub. Turning the faucet on, she watched, disheartened, as water trickled out.

This was ridiculous. Their water flow had nothing to do with electricity, did it? She thought back to that time her parents had been in a hurricane down in Florida. Their power was out for two weeks, and they'd been warned not to drink the water because it could be contaminated.

But at least it had run.

Maybe the power outage had affected the treatment plant, and it had stopped pumping it through the system, if they indeed pumped it to begin with. That had to be it, didn't it?

She sat on the edge of the tub, watching the trickle as though she could help it along. At least water was coming. She didn't know why she was collecting it, really, except somewhere in the back of her mind she remembered someone saying that it was helpful. Besides the obvious reasons, they'd need it to flush the toilets.

What a pain! It was the last thing she needed when Deni was home for just a few days before embarking on her new postcollege life. They had wedding details to see to, and tomorrow they were meeting with the florist and the cake decorator. They were having a tasting at the caterer the next day. A power outage didn't fit into any of Kay's plans.

She left the faucet running and went back into the kitchen. Logan was standing at the sink wetting a dish towel with a trickle of water.

"Logan, no! Don't waste the water." She rushed to the sink and turned it off.

"Sorry, Mom, but nobody's told me the rules. I just wanted to wash my face."

He'd gotten the dish towel sufficiently wet, so she took it from him and wet his face, red from the sun and blotchy from the heat.

"So what do we do now?" he asked her. "There's nothing to do."

"I don't think that will kill us, do you?"

"It might," he said.

She sighed. "I'm sure it'll be over before we know it."

"Can I go next door and play with Drew?"

Nine-year-old Drew and his little brother rode the bus home from school in the afternoons, then stayed alone until their parents got home from work. She doubted Judith had been able to get home from the hospital already, since it was about twenty miles away. And their father, a Birmingham attorney, never made it home before seven, even when things were running well.

"Good idea. Go over there and see if they're all right. If they're alone, bring them back here and they can stay with us until their parents get home. Tell them to leave their folks a note."

Logan ran out, suddenly energized.

"Mom, nothing's working," Jeff said. "Even the stuff that doesn't use electricity isn't working. And the phones are still out. That really stinks. Mandy's gonna think I stood her up. I was supposed to be there a half hour ago."

"Well, you can't go now. I need your help. We have to gather up all our candles while we still have some light, and look for our flashlights. And we need to start the generator to keep the refrigerator going. Everybody needs to help."

She had the candles in a million places. Some were in the boxes in the storage room where she kept the Christmas decorations. Others were on the top shelf of her kitchen cabinets, and some lay lined up in the top drawer of the buffet in the dining room. Two candelabra were in her china cabinets, with half-burned candles from the last time she'd had guests over. She put at least one candle in every room.

Jeff came in from the garage with two flashlights he'd found. "These batteries are old. They're not gonna last long. What about those Y2K kerosene lamps we had?"

Kay tried to remember. She had bought four of them before the great Y2K scare, and never even took them out of their boxes. Where had she put them?

"I'll have to find them. Do you know where they are?"

"In your closet," Beth said. "Back behind the suitcases."

She shot her a look. "And how do you know that?"

Beth grinned. "I was kind of looking for my birthday presents last month and I saw them."

"Fooled you, huh? They weren't in there."

"Nope. They were in Daddy's trunk."

Kay set her hands on her hips and recalled her daughter's ecstatic surprise when she'd opened her new camera cell phone. Had it been faked?

It hardly mattered now. Kay headed back to her room, found the boxes with two lamps each, and took them into the kitchen near the big bay window. She got Beth busy putting the lamps together, then led Jeff out to the garage to pull out the portable generator they'd bought before the Y2K scare. It had never been taken out of its box. She hoped she could figure out how to make it run.

Jeff unhooked the mechanism keeping the garage door locked, and raised the door, letting the light in. He got the generator out of the box, and they sat on the concrete floor, reading the instructions.

It ran on gas, so Kay found the lawn mower gas in a jug in the utility room and emptied it into the generator.

"So do you think Dad and Deni made it to town? That could have been their plane, you know."

Kay thought of that smoke, and a knot formed in her throat. "We won't think about that, okay? They said it was a small plane. I'm thinking like a little two-seater or something, not the kind of plane Dad and Deni would be on. They're fine, okay? They have to be."

Jeff didn't look convinced.

"Besides, I talked to them when they boarded their flight, and it was on time. If they were on time, then they probably landed just before the power went out."

"Wish we could find out for sure. How would we even know? They wouldn't be able to get home if they were stranded at the airport."

"They'll figure out a way to get home."

She looked for the next step on the instructions, and saw that it called for engine oil. "Great. It says to put engine oil in, but I don't think we have any. Do you know where your dad might keep some?"

Jeff shook his head. "Sorry."

She sighed. "I guess we'll have to wait until he gets home. Maybe he's got some stashed somewhere."

As they went back inside, Logan dashed in through the back door, his friend Drew and his seven-year-old brother, Jeremy, on his heels. The two African American boys looked as if they'd been crying.

Kay went over and hugged each of them. "Hey, boys. Some adventure we're having, huh?"

"Our mama isn't home," Jeremy said as tears welled up in his dark eyes. "And we couldn't call her, and it's dark in our house, and we're not allowed to go outside until she gets home."

"Just stay over here, guys. I'm sure it'll be okay this once. They'll be along eventually. Did you leave a note?"

Drew nodded. "Is it true the cars aren't working?" The older boy was doing his best to look brave, but his wide eyes gave him away.

"Yes, it's true. We walked home from Lakeview."

"Then how will they get here?"

"Trust me. Your parents will get home somehow. They may have to walk, but they're strong and healthy and they can do it. And if they don't get here until tomorrow morning, you'll stay here with us all night. Okay?"

Neither of them looked happy with that prospect.

"You guys go keep each other company, and forget about all this. Pretend you're in *Little House on the Prairie* or something, before they even had electricity."

"Yeah!" Thankfully, Logan caught the vision. "Let's go play."

As they shot out the door, Kay got up and went to stare out after them. "Don't leave the yard, guys."

Even as she said the words, she wondered if she should call them back in and keep them all sheltered, windows shut tight. But it was probably too late. Wouldn't they all have been saturated with radiation on the way home, if it lingered in the air?

Again, she wanted to sit down and cry, but there was too much to do. It was time for supper, and the kids needed to eat. She had bread, thankfully, and the bologna couldn't have gone bad yet. There were some chips in the pantry. Enough for a makeshift feast.

Since she had a plan, she decided to go change out of her sweat-drenched clothes and get off of her aching feet. She closed her bedroom door, and darkness swallowed her. Quickly, she opened the curtains and let dusk paint its gray hues on the room.

She went to Doug's side of the bed, grabbed his pillow, and hugged it against her stomach. "Please, God, let them be all right. Help them get home."

As she prayed, she started to cry. The frustrations of the day avalanched upon her, but she tried to rein in her emotions. She had so much to be thankful for. Three of her children were with her, safe and in their home. So what if they didn't have lights?

What if Jeff had been out of town at an away game? What if Beth had been at the mall? What if Logan had been on a Boy Scout camping trip?

Oh, but where were Doug and Deni?

She sat down on her bed, praying that they were safe and would soon make their way home. Then she prayed this event would be short-lived.

Finally, she asked God to give her the strength to handle whatever lay before her. She felt certain she was going to need it.

SIX

THAT DARK ROAD LEADING UP TO THEIR NEIGHBORHOOD
seemed three times longer than Deni remembered—the
longest stretch yet of their walk home. The heat had finally
lifted as night set in, but she would have killed for a glass of
cold water or a meal.

Neither she nor her father had spoken much for the last
hour or so. Their minds were set on getting home, and all of
their concentration went into meeting that goal.

Most of the hikers glutting the interstate had gone
another way when Deni and Doug passed through Crockett
and turned toward home. Only a few walkers trudged down
this country road—and none spoke, probably for fear they'd
be mugged or attacked in the oppressive darkness. Deni was
glad her father was at her side, even if he *had* handed their
bike over to that thug.

As they made that last stretch home, Deni thought about
the absurdity of the day's events. She was willing to bet this
had happened because some technology that might have
prevented it—whatever *it* was—had been put on some
Southern politician's back burner. Everyone would find out
it could easily have been prevented, probably *had* been prevented in other states that kept up technologically.

That was why she was dead-set on starting her new life
on the East Coast, where everything was cutting edge and
state of the art. But she couldn't say that to her dad. He took
things so personally. He'd rattle on about how she needed

to appreciate her home and realize that it was as advanced as any other place in the country. Then he'd launch into a list of medical advances coming from the Deep South, technology invented by those who lived here, and she'd wind up wishing she'd never even brought it up.

She picked up her step as they got closer to the entrance of Oak Hollow. "I can't believe we're here."

"Finally." Her father's one-word statement came out on a breath of relief as they turned into the neighborhood.

Deni saw it with new eyes. She had never come here on foot before, and whenever she'd driven here at night, the road approaching it had been illuminated with streetlights. Lights in the windows of the homes always gave the sense that families lived here and were busy inside those houses. Now, with all the lights out, it looked like a ghost town, and gave her an unwelcoming sense of trepidation.

"I hope Mom has something to eat."

"I hope she's here," Doug said.

That thought worked its way into her soul. Wherever her mom had been when the power went out, she couldn't possibly have been farther than Deni and Doug. Surely she was home.

The garage door was closed, so Deni couldn't tell if the car was here. They went to the front door and knocked on the mahogany.

Finally, the door flew open. "Oh, thank God!"

Her mother threw her arms around her dad, almost knocking him down, then grabbed Deni and pulled her into a hug. "I thought your plane might have crashed. Oh, you're all right!"

Deni wasn't in the mood for hugs. "I need to sit down. We've walked sixteen miles."

"Not all the way," Doug said. "We rode part of the way on a bike; otherwise it would have been even later before we got home."

"Yeah. Some jerk fought with Dad over our bike, and Dad lost."

"Fought with you?" She looked him over. "Are you all right?"

"I'm fine. It wasn't as bad as it sounds."

They went into the great room as her father gave a weary recounting of all that had happened. The living room was lit by candles and a kerosene lamp that cast a warm glow on the room. Deni had never been so glad to be home in her life.

"Hey, they made it!" Jeff leaped off the staircase, looking genuinely glad to see her, and she heard Logan and Beth pounding down the stairs.

"Dad! Deni!"

Another round of hugs, then Deni dropped down on the sofa and examined her scraped elbows. "I can't wait to get a bath."

"No baths," Beth said. "Water's out."

Deni looked up at her sister. "What? Why?"

"We don't know why," Kay said. "I guess maybe the treatment plant has no power, so the water couldn't be pumped."

"That's just great. I trekked sixteen miles home. A stupid bath is not too much to ask for!"

The two boys from next door followed her sister and brother into the great room. They looked disappointed when they saw her.

"Did you see my mom or dad?" Jeremy asked.

Deni shook her head. "No, sorry. There were millions of people walking home on the interstate. Your folks are probably on their way."

But her optimism did nothing to change the worry and fear on their faces.

DOUG WENT TO HIS FAVORITE RECLINER, KICKED OFF HIS SHOES, and pulled the footrest up. Kay ran into the kitchen and brought back two lukewarm Sprites. She handed one to him, the other to Deni. "Nothing works, Doug. Nothing. Not even radios. The flashlights work, but we don't have extra batteries, so I'm afraid to use them for long."

Doug wished he'd thought of grabbing batteries at Wal-Mart, but he'd only been focused on the bike. He took a long sip, then laid his head back.

"Daddy, are we at war?"

Beth's question surprised him.

All faces turned to him, and he realized he was going to have to pull something out of his hat. "No, I don't think so. It's probably no big deal. Doesn't look like anyone was hurt except for the people in those planes. We still have our house, and we're all home. I'd say we're blessed."

"Do you think the power will come back on soon?" Kay asked.

He bottomed his Sprite, then set the can down on the table. "I'm not gonna lie to you guys. I think it could be off for a while. If it was just the electricity, it would be one thing. But with the cars failing, the planes, the phones, even the water ... I'm afraid this could go on for several days at least. We need to just brace ourselves for that."

"No way!" Logan cried. "I can't *stand* this. There's nothing to do. I *hate* it!"

"You'll live."

"Yeah," Deni said. "Not like you had to walk sixteen miles."

Logan threw himself dramatically on the sofa. "I can't take any more of this. It's the worst day of my entire life."

Doug met Kay's eyes in semi-amusement. "What about that time you fell out of the tree and broke your arm?"

"At least I wasn't bored. When I got home I still had my computer and TV. I could talk to my friends."

Doug didn't want to hear it. "You have two friends over right now. Go play with them and stop whining."

"In the dark? We can't see anything."

"You have candles. Get a board game or something."

As the boys left the room, Doug looked up at Kay. "Is there anything to eat?"

"I have sandwiches and chips. Just stay right there and I'll bring you a plate."

Kay seemed to beam with contentment as she hurried out of the room. It was nice to know she was so glad to see him.

How bad could things be, now that the whole family was together?

SEVEN

JUDITH CAME A LITTLE WHILE LATER TO GATHER HER children, and cried as she kissed their faces. Still wearing her nursing scrubs, she told of a twelve-car pileup she'd been caught in on the interstate when the power died. She had walked home, worried sick about her children, and was grateful to see that they'd been safe and cared for.

When the Caldwells were gone, Kay found Doug in the garage with Jeff. They were kneeling on the floor, examining the generator.

"Did you find some oil?" Kay asked.

"Yeah, I had some. But it hardly mattered." Doug's voice was dull. "It doesn't work, either."

"What? I thought generators *always* worked in power outages."

"Not this one. We started it up, and after a couple of seconds, it died, just like everything else."

"What?" She stepped closer and saw that they had taken the housing off of the generator. Jeff held the flashlight as Doug worked. "Dad, do you even know what you're looking at?"

"No, I don't." Frustration rippled in his tone. "But I thought maybe I could see something that would give us a clue why it isn't working. Some common denominator that would make all these things go out."

Kay stooped down behind them. "Do you?"

He was quiet for a moment as he probed with his screwdriver, studying the wiring and the motor. Finally, he threw the screwdriver down and sat back on the concrete floor. "No. I'm a stockbroker, not an electrician."

Kay started to rub his shoulders. They were so tense ... his head and neck had to be aching. "Don't be so hard on yourself, honey. Even the electricians are probably baffled tonight. Why don't we all just go to bed? Maybe by morning it'll all be over."

He rolled his head back as she managed to relax his muscles. "That's just it, Kay. I don't think it will be over by morning. This looks to me like something that might last awhile."

She stopped rubbing and moved around him so she could see into his face. "What would make you think that?"

He took the light from Jeff. "An EMP would irreversibly damage electronic equipment. So if that's what happened, it's not likely that things will be up and running again right away. But it doesn't seem to *be* that. An EMP shouldn't knock out a generator, should it?" He shook his head. "Whatever is causing this might have done even more damage than an EMP. Which means the outage could last a lot longer than we think."

"No way!" Jeff said.

Kay stared at her husband. "Doug, you can't be serious."

"I hope I'm wrong," he said. "But strange things can happen in the atmosphere. I remember reading about something like this happening in the late eighties after a geomagnetic storm on the sun. Solar flares shut down Tibet and caused a massive blackout in Canada. Power transformers overheated because of the solar activity."

Kay frowned. "Then it could be some kind of solar event? Something in space?"

"It could be," Jeff said, eyes rounding. "I mean, if you think about it, what do scientists really know about the stuff out in space? I heard that the space station has been dumping its garbage out for years, and it's just floating around in outer space. Who knows what that could mean to the balance of the universe?"

Doug shone the light on Jeff's excited face. "Orbital debris didn't do this, Son."

"Dad, *something* caused this."

Doug got up and dusted his shorts off. "Yeah, but only God knows what it was. Let's go back inside."

They followed him in, and as they stepped into the light of the kerosene lamp, Kay saw the fatigue casting shadows on her husband's face, making him look much older than he was. "We need to plan for the long term just in case. And if I'm wrong, great. The lights will come back on, and our cars will start, and everything will go back to normal. But if I'm right, and this thing lasts for days or weeks — "

"That can't happen, Doug. We're not prepared!"

"No one is. But we have to think realistically. We need to ration our food. Eat the frozen stuff tomorrow after it thaws, then make the pantry stuff last as long as we can. We have a little charcoal. We can cook the meat out on the grill."

Kay opened the pantry, let her eyes sweep over the contents. She'd needed to go to the grocery store for the last few days, but hadn't gotten around to it. Why hadn't she made the time?

Jeff slid up onto the counter. "No way you're right, Dad. This can't last. We're probably making a big deal about nothing."

Kay wished she could agree, but as she looked into her husband's eyes, fear took a tighter hold.

And she dreaded seeing what tomorrow would bring.

EIGHT

As the family prepared for bed, Doug stepped outside and looked up at the night sky. There was no evidence that he could see of any kind of cataclysmic solar event. The stars were as clear as they'd ever been—clearer, now that the lights of the city weren't competing with them. The crescent moon glowed white against the black sky, casting off little light.

He heard voices somewhere in another yard. Were other neighbors sitting outside staring at the sky, wondering what had happened? Were weary travelers still walking home from their long commutes from the city?

The breeze whispered through his hair, cooling his face, and he let himself sink for a moment into the peaceful quiet. But then his soul grew uneasy again, and he began to wonder if this was just the calm before the storm, the false sense of security before the terror began. What dangers lurked outside this yard, this neighborhood? Would militant terrorists come riding in on the back of pickup trucks with machine guns pointed at his children? If something like that happened, would Doug and his family have any recourse?

Of course they would. They had guns, and determination, and a love for freedom. Would they be called to die for it?

The thought destroyed his sense of peace, and he went back in to his study, to the gun safe he kept there. He opened it for the first time in a year, and saw his three firearms—two rifles and a shotgun.

Jeff came and leaned into the doorway as Doug got the .12 gauge out.

"What are you doing, Dad?"

He opened the action to make sure it wasn't loaded. "I don't know if we're going to have to defend our property, but I want to be ready if we are."

Jeff's face twisted. "What? You think people might attack us now that our guard's down?"

"I don't know what's gonna happen." He went to the closet across the room and checked the shelf where he kept the ammunition. He never kept the cartridges in the same place as the guns, in case, someone didn't close the safe well enough, and Logan and his friends got into it.

"We're low on ammo, so we'll have to conserve it. No big deal. Probably nothing's going to happen. But just in case ..."

He saw the color draining from his son's face, and let out a heavy sigh. "Look, I know this sounds crazy to you. I'm not trying to be an alarmist. You know that's not how I am."

"I know, Dad. That's why you're freaking me out."

"It's just that there are a lot of unknowns right now. This has never happened before. Watches going out? Generators not working? Cars dying in the road? It just doesn't make any sense, and such massive damage makes it seem intentional. All I'm saying is that if all this is because of some hostile act by terrorists or an enemy nation, then we need to be prepared. As the men of this house, we have to protect our family and our home."

He handed Jeff the shotgun, then got out his own rifle, a Remington .30/06.

Jeff took the .12 gauge and stared down at it. He swallowed, and brought his troubled eyes back up to Doug. "So how far are you gonna go with it, Dad? Do you want me out back and you out front all night, like we're soldiers guarding our camp?"

"No, I don't think that'll be necessary. We just need to keep the guns close by."

The shadows cast by the kerosene lamp magnified the worry lines on Jeff's face.

"Son, it's probably nothing at all." He took the .22 out and checked it.

"Should I load it?"

Doug looked at the gun in Jeff's hand. When had he last fired it? Two years? Three? He'd gotten Jeff his own shotgun when they used to go deer hunting. That was a great time of bonding for him and the boys—until he got so busy with work that he didn't have time anymore.

Respect for their weapons was the first thing he'd taught his boys, and the number one rule was to keep their gun unloaded when they weren't hunting. "Why don't we keep them unloaded, but carry some ammo around with us just in case?"

Jeff's eyes had grown darker, more serious. "Okay, Dad. Logan's gonna want his."

Doug shook his head. "Just you and me for now. That should be enough. Here, give it back to me and I'll clean it. It's been a long time since it's been used."

"Yeah, a long time. I was thinking about taking Logan myself this deer season if you can't go. Shame for him to miss freezing in a deer stand eating beef jerky and Starbursts if he doesn't have to. Kid needs a little nature."

Doug smiled. "How about I make a point of going this year?"

Jeff shrugged. "Said that last year."

Doug knew Jeff wasn't just talking about their hunting trips. It was a commentary on his parenting—or lack thereof. The blessing of having a capable wife came with curses also. It made you forget you were needed.

He mumbled more promises that he hoped he would keep. Seemingly satisfied—and slightly amused—Jeff left his gun for Doug to clean and went up to his room. Doug took all three guns, his cleaning kit, and the kerosene lamp, and set them out on the patio table. The breeze was cool now, sweeping through his hair.

Kay stepped out and joined him. "You okay?" she asked.

"Yeah, I'm fine."

She sat down next to him. "You really think you need those guns?"

"Probably not," he said, shoving the swab down the barrel, "but I've got them if I do."

She looked up at the mysterious sky. "Beth is sleeping with Deni tonight, because she doesn't want to be alone. I thought I might hit the sack, too, if you don't need me for anything."

Doug was silent for a moment. "We should have prayed together."

Kay looked at him. "What?"

"We should have prayed together as a family before everybody started going to bed. We should have gathered in the family room, holding hands, asking God's blessing and protection on our family tonight."

She studied his face. "You're really scared, aren't you?"

"Not scared. Cautious ... thoughtful."

Kay leaned forward, putting her face inches from his. "That's why I always feel so safe with you. You think ahead, figuring out every possible scenario that might threaten our family, while we go on about our business."

He breathed a laugh, glad she'd noticed.

"Honey, I think it's okay that we didn't pray together," she said, taking his hand. "If we made a big deal out of it, sitting around in a circle praying together for what—the first time ever?—the kids would be even more disturbed. We want to keep them calm. It may be no big deal at all."

Shame heated Doug's face for the second time that night. Here he was, the supposed leader of his family, and the most he'd ever prayed with them was a hurried prayer before meals—*if* they ate together at the table. He and Kay prayed together sometimes, but not nearly enough.

"Besides," she said, "I think we're each praying on our own."

Doug wondered if the silent, hurried prayers of frustration were even close to what they needed.

"Mom, Dad?"

Deni stepped out on the patio. She looked young again, four-teen maybe, with her hair pulled up in a ponytail and her face scrubbed clean of makeup. The sight of that lifted his heart a little. She'd changed so much in the last few years that Doug often longed for the sight of his little girl in old shorts and a big T-shirt, her hair swept back instead of fluffed and teased like a model's.

"I don't think I can sleep." Deni pulled up a chair in the dark-ness, sat down facing her parents. "I know this outage has left a lot of people inconvenienced, but I think this could actually mess up my whole life."

The self-centered assessment almost amused him. "Deni, it's gonna be all right. Whatever happens."

"No, Dad, you don't understand. I *have* to report for work next Monday. I worked too hard for this job. There were eighty-three people up for it, and they hired me. If I don't show up, they'll find someone else. I have to be there."

Kay sighed. "Can we cross that bridge when we get to it? We'll know more tomorrow. You've got plenty of time—a whole week."

"But I need to get in touch with Craig. He'll want to hear from me. It's crazy that we have no communication. We don't even have the news. This is the twenty-first century!" She got up and paced across the patio as she ranted. "We ought to be able to do better than this. I'm gonna be panicked if I can't get back east. My job is important. They need me."

Doug made a point not to roll his eyes. As proud as he was of his daughter, and as excited as he was about her internship, it was just that. An internship. It wasn't like she was going to be cohosting the news with Brian Williams. If she was a few days late, it would hardly matter.

He tried to keep the apathy out of his voice. "Deni, there's no use sitting around and complaining and whining over what can't be. Especially tonight. We'll know more tomorrow, I'll guarantee you."

"It just stinks!" She plopped back into her chair. "Here I am on the brink of the rest of my life, ready to start making a living and being on my own, and this has to happen."

Kay touched her daughter's knee. "Honey, I wish you'd count your blessings. You could be dead right now. That plane might not have landed today."

Deni stared at her as if her cluelessness couldn't be tolerated. "But it *did* land, and I have to move on. I have to think about the future, and this could be messing it all up. Nobody in this family is as affected by this as I am."

Kay met Doug's eyes, and he could see the aggravation there. *Don't say it, Kay.*

Too late. "I hate to break this to you," she said, "but this is not just about you."

Their daughter grunted. "That was a mean thing to say. I never said it was all about me."

Kay closed her eyes. "There are people all over this city without electricity. Every one of us was inconvenienced in some way. We all have plans, and none of us is thrilled about what's happened."

"And you think I don't realize that?"

"You don't sound like it."

She sprang up again. "Well, that's just great. I thought I could be honest with my parents. I thought I could share my concerns with them. Vent a little."

"Venting's okay," Doug said, "but what your mother's trying to point out is that there are people in a lot more trouble than you right now. Think of the hospitals. Think of the people with pacemakers. The nursing homes. Think of people who can't get to their medications. Families who are separated—"

"Just forget it." Deni threw up her hands and started for the door. "I should have known I couldn't talk to you anymore. This is why I'm leaving home. I'm going someplace where people don't automatically think the worst of me."

Kay began rubbing her forehead, and her words came out through her teeth. "Nobody's thinking the worst of you, Deni. Just don't filter everything through how it affects you. We're all going through stuff. So you delay your career for a few days. It won't hurt anything. And you may actually get there on time anyway."

Doug closed his eyes. Why did they have to have this conversation right now? He was just too tired. "If you don't make it, you need to consider the fact that Washington may not have electricity either. This could be across the whole country. We don't know."

Deni breathed a laugh. "No way. That whole area is more secure and more advanced than we are. They've got the Pentagon. I don't believe that everything is shut down there."

"Well, if it's just our area, then we'll know soon enough when cars that run make it here."

Deni stood there a moment, staring at both of them as if she wanted them to fix it and was crushed that they couldn't. "I'm going to bed," she said finally. "And if Beth kicks me or snatches the covers, I'm shoving her onto the floor."

"Oh, now that's mature," Kay said. "She's scared, Deni. She wants to sleep with her big sister. Is that so awful?"

"I'm just saying . . ." With that she stormed into the house.

Kay sat there for a moment, staring up at the sky and shaking her head. "We spoiled her, and now it's coming back to haunt us."

"We spoiled all of them. And we're spoiled, too. Maybe that's why this happened."

"Stop being so doomsdayish." Kay got up, went to the post and leaned against it. "You're talking like this is an act of God that's going to last forever. It can't. We're too smart for that."

"Who's too smart for that? You think if God wanted to teach us a lesson, we could stop Him?"

"God isn't doing this. He doesn't send power outages. The electric company does."

"Then why does God say that He's the One forming light and creating darkness, causing well-being and creating calamity?"

"The Bible doesn't say that."

"Yes, it does. It's in—" He laid his head back and looked at the night sky, trying to remember where it was. "Somewhere in one of the prophets. We had to learn it when my accountability group studied God's sovereignty."

"I'm impressed."

He breathed a laugh. "Don't be. It's the only thing I was really accountable for. Out-reciting that know-it-all Dan Milner. Wonder what he's doing tonight."

"Probably cleaning his guns, too."

"The bottom line, Kay, is that God does do things like this. And look at all the stuff that's been happening in the world—war, hurricanes, tsunamis—it's like He's been trying to get our attention."

She looked out at the night, and he could almost see the wheels turning in her mind. She had to know he was right.

Finally, she leaned over and kissed the top of his head. "I've never seen you like this. You need to just come on in and come to bed. You've had a very long day."

"I will, in a minute."

"All right, then I'm going to bed. Glad you're home. Things could be so much worse."

"Yep, they could. Sleep well. I'll be along in a minute."

He kissed her, then watched her go inside, aware that she thought he was overreacting. He hoped she was right. But if she wasn't, things were about to get bad. And he'd have to hold it all together.

If only he were more certain of his strength as a husband and father ... a protector and provider, and didn't just feel like a forty-seven-year-old guy who'd gotten his bike stolen today.

Maybe God was about to show him what he was made of.

NINE

THE POWER WAS STILL OUT THE NEXT MORNING, AS DOUG HAD predicted. He got his own ten-speed down from its hook in the garage. He hadn't ridden it in at least three years, and it needed some air in the tires and a little lubrication on the chain. After getting it into shape, he slung his rifle over his shoulder and rode out of the neighborhood, struck by the number of cars stalled in the street. It seemed strange, somehow, that the sun still shone and the wind still blew. The flowers grew bright and fragrant, reaching up to the sky in praise. Birds went about their daily business, oblivious to the mess the humans were in.

He rode about five miles through town to the Kroger store on Keisler Street, and saw the other bikers there who'd had the same idea. The store was closed, and as he peered in, he saw that the shelves had been almost cleared. Hundreds of people had probably stopped by to get what they needed during the exodus home last night. Why hadn't he had the forethought to do that? He'd just been so anxious to get to the house that he hadn't thought of it. Besides, it would have been difficult to carry anything that far.

He rode through town, checking convenience stores and fast-food restaurants, but nothing was open. Finally, he decided to go to the street where Kay had left their car. He turned onto the main thoroughfare through the town, and saw the bumper-to-bumper traffic stalled there.

Kay's Expedition was several cars down the line, and as he approached it, he realized the driver's side door was wide open. Had she left it open? What had she been thinking?

He got off his bike and looked inside. And then he understood.

The CD player had been ripped from its hole, and the speakers gouged from the doors. He got out of the car and looked up and down the street. About ten cars back, he saw some boys climbing out of a van, arms full of stuff that they threw into a wagon. His stereo was probably in there, too.

"Hey! What are you doing?"

The boys looked back at him, then took off running, rolling the overflowing wagon behind them. Doug jumped on his bike and tried to follow them, but they dashed into the woods, maneuvering their wagon with skill and dexterity.

Behind him, he heard another car door slam. He turned and saw a man sitting in a Cadillac, digging through the glove box.

"That your car, mister?" he yelled.

The man just kept working.

Doug rode his bike toward him. "Hey, get out of that car!"

The man stuffed some items into his pockets, got back on his own bike, and rode off.

Doug thought of chasing him, but what would he do if he caught him? Shoot a man over a car stereo? It wasn't like he could stay here all day, guarding the cars. There was really nothing he could do.

If only there were a police station in Crockett. But since it hadn't yet been annexed, they were under the county sheriff's care. It was only ten miles to the sheriff's office. Surely someone had reported for duty today. He could ride there and tell them what was happening. If they knew criminals were having a field day with the parked cars, they could surely stop it.

By the time he reached the sheriff's office he ached from the exertion. His muscles already hurt from yesterday's strain, and his rump felt bruised from the triangle the manufacturers called a seat. Breathing hard, he rode his bike to the curb, then carried it up the steps. The door was open, so he pushed inside.

The office had few windows, so very little light graced the place. "Help you?"

He had to look for the origin of the voice. A chubby deputy sat fanning himself at one of the back desks.

"Oh, good. I was worried the law had shut down, too."

"Depends on how you look at it, I guess."

The man looked like Wilford Brimley, but his name tag read ED GRAY. "Look, you need to get over to Fairview Street. My car was broken into and the stereo was taken, and there are people stealing everything they can carry."

The deputy, who looked way past retirement age, seemed unimpressed. "We know. We're on it."

Doug just looked at him. "You are? What are you doing about it?"

The man pulled out a handkerchief and wiped his neck. Sweat rings the size of pizza pans had formed under his armpits. "It's hard to patrol without the cars running, but we've got every available man out on bikes today. Even so, our hands are tied. If we round up the thieves and vandals, how do we get 'em back here? Walk 'em in handcuffs for four or five miles? We got a whole jail full of convicts we can't feed now, and we'll probably get sued for holdin' 'em in dark cells—cruel and inhuman punishment and all that—if we don't have an out-and-out riot."

And Doug thought he had problems. "I understand, but you can't just let the thieves get away with this. It could get dangerous."

The man threw his handkerchief on his cluttered desk. "I told you, we're on it. But we can't be everywhere. I'm here to keep the office open and take complaints. You want to file a complaint, sit down and I'll get you the paperwork. Or if you want to put on a uniform and go after 'em, be my guest."

Doug didn't think he'd take him up on the offer. "No, I have my family to take care of."

"So do most of our guys. But they're out there busting their bums. And for what? They can't even cash their paychecks, with the banks closed."

Doug quelled the sarcasm on the tip of his tongue. He didn't want to upset him more. "Listen, do you know what caused the outage?"

"Not a clue."

"You're not in communication with any government authorities?"

"How could I be?"

Deputy or not, the guy had a real attitude. "I don't know. I just thought that maybe government and law enforcement had some kind of plan for a crisis like this."

"We got plans, pal. We got plans for explosions and tornado warnings and school shootings and about a zillion other things. But we never planned for this. Everything going out at once. It's like a fluke of nature."

"Has anybody come in from out of town?" Doug asked. "Some place where there's still power?"

"Nobody yet. I've been all over this morning, and I haven't seen one moving vehicle. Even if somebody came, they probably couldn't pass through our streets with all the cars blocking the way. One thing you can do is tell everybody to come push their stalled cars off the road to make room for any moving vehicles that might make their way here. You want to help, you can find some men and get started on that."

"But there are thousands of cars. There's no way we could put a dent in that. And that would invite even more thefts, having people moving cars that weren't theirs."

"You come up with a better idea, then," the man said. "What are you? Some kind of computer jockey, I bet."

He didn't know why he felt insulted. "No. I'm a stockbroker."

The man grimaced. "Like I thought. Talks on the phone all day and thinks he can tell me how to do my job."

This was going nowhere. Doug could sit around bantering with this man all morning, or he could get back to his family and try to do something constructive. He thanked the officer and left, feeling as useless as the deputy thought he was.

TEN

KAY WIPED THE SWEAT FROM HER BROW AND BROUGHT THE last of the cooked meat in from the barbecue pit. It was much more than they could eat—six steaks, a dozen pork chops, ten hamburger patties, and a whole chicken. The freezer had kept the meat cold as it thawed last night, but she had no choice but to cook it all today or let it go to waste.

"I'm not eating that," Beth said, bringing the last platter into the house. "I'm a vegetarian."

"Since when?"

"Since I felt like barfing the minute you started cooking spoiled meat."

"It's not spoiled. It was still cool this morning."

"You hope. It's not like you can get us to the hospital when we start croaking of food poisoning."

Clearly, her younger daughter had a bright future in theatre. "There's too much to eat all by ourselves anyway. I was thinking we could take some to the neighbors. I need to check on Eloise. You can come with me."

Beth shook her head. "I don't want any part of that. Feeding spoiled food to a woman who's already sick?"

The seventy-year-old widow across the street had inoperable liver cancer and had been taking chemo treatments every three weeks.

"It's not spoiled, I told you. Stop saying that."

Deni came in, hauling a bucket of water she'd gotten at the lake, and sloshed it up onto the counter. "Slave labor.

56

We should have a pool, Mom. If we did, we wouldn't have to drag that nasty water back from the lake, and we could wash off our grime. It's just crazy that we don't have one. You know we can afford it."

"We don't have one because I didn't want to take care of it, your father doesn't have time, and I knew I couldn't get any help from the four of you."

"And now look," Deni said. "No water, no bath, no nothing. What are we going to do about the wedding plans? This may be the last week I'll be home before then, since I won't have vacation time."

"I don't know," Kay said. "If the power doesn't come back on in the next few days, I guess I'll have to do the planning myself."

"No way. I want to plan my own wedding. I want to see the flowers, taste the cake, hear the music. I have no intention of being denied that."

"Deni, the wedding is five months away. We're fine. We don't have to decide that today." She thrust a plate of pork chops at Deni. "Here, while I take some of these to Eloise, why don't you take a plate to the Caldwells next door? And then take some chicken to the Rowes."

"Right," Beth said. "Poison the babies, too."

Kay ignored her. With three kids under three, the young couple next door probably had their hands full and would be happy to have the food. "While you're there, Deni, ask them if they have any matches they can spare. Then hurry back so we can eat before it cools."

Kay found Eloise sitting on her front porch, looking pale and sickly, her bald head hidden beneath a bandana tied neatly at the nape of her neck. She took the pork chops thankfully, then invited Kay into the dark, hot house.

Kay followed her into the lonely living room. Eloise's son, a big-shot trial lawyer up in Boston, had bought his widowed mother this house five years ago, and hired a decorator to deck it out. Kay had mentioned once how moved Eloise must have been by the gift.

The older woman's eyes welled with tears. "It *was* a lovely gift, but to tell you the truth, I'd rather have stayed in the house I raised my children in and have them come visit me once in a while. My son's never even seen the house he bought me."

Now the woman's loneliness seemed even more stark.

Eloise had lost more weight in the last few weeks, and her skin looked paper-thin. "Has anyone been in touch with the power company?" she asked.

Kay just looked at her, wondering if she was unaware of the extent of the problem. "Uh ... no. The phones don't work. Even the cars are dead."

Eloise stared at her for a moment. "So that's why my car didn't start. I thought I must have a problem with my battery. And the water ... It's out, too. I know I paid my water bill."

"I'm afraid no one has water, Eloise. Crazy, isn't it?"

Her bare eyebrows lifted. "You wouldn't be pulling an old woman's leg, would you?"

Kay couldn't help chuckling. "I wish I were. We don't know what's causing all this, but Doug thinks it's going to last longer than a few days."

"Oh, my. I was supposed to go for chemo today."

Kay's heart sank. Eloise's cancer was aggressive and had already spread to several organs. "What will happen if you miss a treatment?"

"Well, I suppose I can make it up when things get back to normal."

"But it's crucial that you have it, isn't it? We have to figure out a way to get you there."

The woman crossed the room and took Kay's hands. "Honey, don't you give it a thought. The Lord will take care of me. He knows what I need. And frankly, I'm just as glad to have a few extra days before the next treatment. Maybe I'll have time to grow my eyelashes back."

Kay laughed softly. "You look beautiful without them."

Eloise waved her off. "Now you're going too far. I spent the first half of my life trying to have long, silky hair. Now all I want for Christmas is eyebrows."

Thank heaven Eloise still had her sense of humor. "Surely the hospitals are offering critical care," Kay said. "We have bicycles. Maybe we could get you to the hospital on one of those."

Eloise laughed. "Me, on a bike? I could never make it without falling and breaking every bone in my body. It's been thirty years since I've ridden one. And how would I get back, as sick as I am when it's over? No, hon, I'm better off just waiting this out. I'll consider it a blessing from God. A nice reprieve. I'll just enjoy it."

Kay wished she had something more to offer her. "Do you need anything? Do you have plenty of food, water?"

The woman looked around. "Water might be a problem. I have a pitcher of tea, but when that's out, I'll have to make my way to the lake, I s'pose. But I'll manage. Isn't this odd? Wonder what the Lord is doing?"

"You sound like Doug. But maybe God has nothing to do with this. Maybe we should blame terrorists instead of God."

"Well, it's not like a plague swept over the city and struck everyone with illness," Eloise said. "We're all fine. What a gentle way to get our attention."

Kay turned that over in her mind as she studied her friend. "You have a very nice way of looking at things, Eloise."

Eloise's eyes sparkled. "An experienced way. I've seen God do amazing things in my lifetime. Maybe this is one of those things."

ELEVEN

DENI AND BETH TOOK THE LAST OF THE GRILLED CHICKEN
over to the Rowes' house and knocked on the door. Deni
had never met the family. They had moved in just a year ago,
while she'd been away at college.

As Beth knocked on the door, Deni heard a baby crying
inside. Someone called, "Coming!" But no one did.

Finally, when they'd almost given up, the door flew
open.

The woman standing there, with a baby on each hip,
didn't look much older than Deni.

She was pretty, but mascara was smeared under her eyes,
and she wore a wrinkled T-shirt and shorts that looked slept
in. The woman was in serious need of a makeover.

Deni tried to look friendly. "Hi, I'm Deni from next
door. We were cooking our meat and had extra."

"Oh, wow. Come on in."

They followed her into the big house. An older child,
about three years old, sat near the patio door playing with
Legos. The sparse furnishings made it look as if they'd
bought more house than they could afford, so had little left
with which to furnish it.

"You caught me at a bad time ..." The woman set the
babies down on the floor, and Beth plopped down to play
with them. One looked around two, the other about nine
months. "I was losing it. I'm out of diapers, and I don't
know what I'm gonna do."

Deni didn't know what to say. "You want me to put the chicken in the kitchen?"

"Yeah. Hey, thanks for that. We need it. I haven't eaten yet today."

As Amber followed her into the kitchen, Deni set the chicken on the counter and saw a dozen unwashed bottles near the sink. It looked like she was having a hard time.

"I'm sorry for the mess," Amber said, "but without water I can't wash the bottles."

"Everybody's house is a mess. You should see ours. We're getting water down at the lake. You should ask your husband to go get you some."

Amber closed her eyes. "My husband isn't ..." Her voice broke off. "Well, he just isn't home."

"Oh, no. He wasn't stranded somewhere last night, was he?" Deni launched into the story about her journey home from the airport, but Amber didn't seem that engaged.

When Deni stopped talking, Amber said, "He isn't stranded." Tears sprang to her eyes, and she grabbed a paper towel and wiped her nose.

Deni didn't know what had set her off. Frustration at the outage? Three children under three? Marital problems?

Amber stepped into the doorway and made sure Beth was all right with the children. Finally, she turned back. "Do you know anybody in the neighborhood who might have extra diapers? I should have gone to get some yesterday, but then the blackout happened, and I ran out."

"We could ask around," Deni said. "I haven't lived here for a while. I've been away at college, so I don't really know the younger families."

"I know somebody who might have some," Beth called from the living room.

"Who?"

"My teacher, Mrs. Abernathy. She lives two streets over. Before school was out last week, she kept gushing about her grandbaby who was visiting. I'll bet she has some."

"We can go ask her," Deni said.

Amber blew her nose. "That would be great. Thank you."

Deni hesitated. "If your husband's not here, are you going to be able to get to the lake to get water?"

"No, it's kind of hard with the children. I was hoping I could get them to nap later, and I could go then."

As much as Deni hated to help with that particular task, she supposed she'd have to offer. "I'll bring you some. Do you have a way to boil it?"

More tears. "I have a charcoal grill in back, but you can't boil water like that. Oh, I'll figure out something."

Deni couldn't wait to get out of there, but she hated leaving her like this. "Are you all right?"

Amber drew in a deep breath and tried to pull herself together. "Yeah, I'm okay. Frankly, I was a basket case *before* the power went out." She tried to smile. "So are you home for the summer or just visiting?"

"I'm visiting. I have to be in Washington to start my new job on Monday. I came home to do some wedding planning."

The two-year-old called out for his mommy and came running into the kitchen. Amber swept him up. "Married, huh? You sure you wanna do that?"

Deni breathed a laugh. "Yeah, I'm sure. Why?"

Amber got some plates out of the cupboard. "I don't know. You're just awfully young."

Young? Like Amber was any older! "I'm twenty-two. You don't look that much older."

"I'm not," Amber said. "I got married when I was your age. And look at me now."

"Yeah, look at you. You live in a beautiful house in a nice neighborhood, with three beautiful children and a husband—"

"You should have stopped with the three beautiful children."

Deni just looked at her.

"My husband left me two weeks ago."

Deni's heart sank. "Oh, Amber. I'm so sorry."

"And now I'm stuck here in the dark with three babies and I feel totally, absolutely helpless."

"He left you with three children under three?"

"Oh yeah." Her lips quivered as she tried to hold back her tears. "Said it was too stressful at home, that he needed a breather. Like *I'm* not under stress! They're his kids, too, and you don't just run off—"

"What a jerk. No wonder you're losing it."

Amber nodded, as if she appreciated the affirmation. "And when this outage happened yesterday, I was completely unprepared. I planned to go to the grocery store last night. I had a baby-sitter coming so I could do my shopping, but she never showed." She stopped and covered her face, then slid her fingers down. "I need baby food, and I have to wash bottles and dishes ... I don't even have a flashlight or candles. I had to put the kids to bed in the dark. I had so much to do after they went to bed, but I couldn't see to do it. I've never been so glad for morning in my life ... but I *still* feel helpless."

Deni felt pretty helpless, too. "Well, I'm sure we can help. I'll go get you some water, and we'll find diapers, and we have extra candles. That's a start."

The baby started crying, and Amber put the two-year-old down and went to pick up the other one. She turned back to Deni and took a deep breath, pulling herself together. "You're a godsend," she said. "I'm sorry you caught me on a crying jag. But if you could do those things for me, I would be so grateful."

"Consider them done. Come on, Beth."

Amber walked them to the door, and thanked them again on their way out.

When the door closed behind them, Beth looked back. "That's so sad. I want to cry, myself."

"Yeah, it is. But who knows? Maybe she brought it on herself. She's the one who married a loser."

"He doesn't look like a loser. He looks nice. Kind of like Craig."

"Trust me. He's *nothing* like Craig."

"Well, I'm glad you offered to help her."

Deni winced. "Yeah, I guess we're committed. We might as well get it over with."

TWELVE

THERE WAS NO RELIEF FROM THE MAY SUN. IT BEAT DOWN ON them from above, and heat radiated up from the sidewalk as Deni followed Beth to her teacher's house. Deni had taken Amber one of the buckets of water from home, then offered to go with Beth to find diapers. At least that would keep her from being available for any more manual labor her mother might have for her. Sure, they needed to make more trips to the lake, but her brothers could do it.

Beth chattered as they walked. "They seemed like such a cute couple. Amber's husband was really good-looking. And it seemed like he was a good dad. Why would he do a thing like that?"

"Don't tell anybody," Deni said. "Amber didn't tell us so we could blab it all over the neighborhood. We just caught her at a weak time."

"That could be you, you know," Beth said. "You could be just like her in three years, with a bunch of babies and a jerk of a husband who left you for his secretary."

"I told you, Craig isn't like that."

"How do you know?"

Deni grunted. "Because he's better than that, okay? I wouldn't marry some crud who treated me like that."

"Miss Amber probably didn't, either. Or she didn't know she did. So what do you think he's doing now?"

Deni raked her sweat-dampened hair back behind her ears. "What do I think *who's* doing?"

"Craig, your fiancé! Hello! Aren't you listening to me?"

Deni rolled her eyes. "Oh, Craig. I don't know, Beth. What do *you* think he's doing?"

"Depends on whether his power is out or not. Do you think it is?"

"I don't know. If it isn't, he's probably on his way here to get me right now." She sighed at the thought. What a relief it would be to see him driving up in his LaCrosse.

"That would be cool. But if other cities had power, wouldn't we be seeing cars here already?"

"Not necessarily." But even as she said the words, she knew Beth was right. The I-20 corridor would have traffic if any vehicles were moving from east to west, or west to east. Though the interstate was several miles away, she knew that the neighbors who'd been biking around town would have brought word back as soon as it happened. So far, there'd been nothing.

Beth pointed out her teacher's house as they drew near.

"Deni Branning! Is that you?"

Deni turned and caught her breath. Mark Green, a friend from high school, was riding up on his ten-speed. She grinned. The track star who was president of the FCA had clearly grown up. "Hey, Mark! Great to see you!"

He stopped beside her, balancing with a foot on the curb. He reached over to hug her, and she felt his stubble against her face. She remembered when it was peach fuzz.

"I didn't know you were back," he said.

"Just for a few days. How about this power outage?"

He laughed. "Crazy, huh? Unbelievable. It's gonna be one for the history books."

She couldn't help staring. "You look great." He really did. He wore his black hair shorter than he had in high school, and he had a tan that would do a lifeguard proud.

"You don't look so bad yourself," he said. "But then, you never did. Hey, I heard you're getting married."

She thrust out her left hand to show him her ring.

"Sweet. Sure you wanna break all those hearts?"

She laughed and waved him off.

"So are you just out for a walk?"

"In this heat?" Deni said. "No, we're scavenging for diapers for our next-door neighbor. We thought Beth's teacher might have some."

"Mrs. Abernathy? She's my next-door neighbor. Yeah, she might. She had her daughter's baby there last week. Hey, you don't have a saw or an axe, do you?"

"I don't know, why?"

"My mom's freaking because she doesn't have anything to cook with. I have to chop some wood so we can cook over a fire, but I don't have anything to chop with. Our saw is electric."

"We had enough charcoal for today," Deni said, "but when we run out, I guess we'll have to do that, too. You can ride over to my house and ask my parents."

"Okay, I will in a minute. I've got to go in and drink something. It's hot out here." He pushed off from the curve and turned his bike back to his driveway. "Good luck with the diapers."

Deni waved good-bye, then looked down at her little sister. Beth watched, eyes dreamy, as Mark rode up his driveway.

"He's so cute," Beth whispered.

"Yeah, he's changed a lot. College did him good." She turned her sister back to her teacher's house. "Stop staring. He's way too old for you."

Beth's cheeks flushed pink. "I wasn't staring."

They trudged up a steep sidewalk, then up ten steps leading to a massive front door made of leaded glass. Deni drank in the sight of the expensive architecture. "Doesn't look like a teacher's house. What does her husband do?"

"He makes jewelry."

She pictured threaded beads at flea markets. "What kind of jewelry?"

"Diamond rings and necklaces. You should see the rocks on her fingers. They make yours look cheap."

She shoved her sister. "Well, it wasn't cheap, okay? It cost Craig an arm and a leg." She jabbed at the bell.

"Doorbell doesn't work, Einstein." Beth rapped on the door, and it floated open. Deni shoved it open a little wider. "Hello? Hello!"

"Mrs. Abernathy! It's Beth Branning."

No answer, so Deni pushed the door all the way open. She could see through the dark house to the back window. There didn't appear to be anyone out back, either. "Anybody home? Hello!"

Beth peered in past her and took a tentative step inside. Then she gasped, and Deni followed her startled gaze. In the doorway off of the foyer, she saw a bare foot, turned down, as if someone lay there on their stomach.

Deni caught her breath and pulled Beth back, then stepped inside, toward the doorway where she saw the foot.

She screamed.

A woman lay facedown in her own blood. A man lay a few feet away, his dead, white face frozen in horror.

THIRTEEN

BETH STARTED RUNNING, HER SCREAMS ECHOING OVER THE silent neighborhood. Deni ran after her.

Next door, Mark bolted out of his garage. "What is it? Deni, what's wrong?"

"They're dead!" She was trembling, and her legs wouldn't hold her up. "Blood everywhere!"

He grabbed her and looked into her face. "Who?"

"In there!" She pointed to the house, and slowly, he let her go. Beth thrust herself into Deni's arms and clung to her, still wailing.

Mark's mother came outside, following him as he crossed the yard and bolted into his neighbor's house. Deni felt her little sister shivering. She watched the door through her tears, waiting for someone to come back out. Maybe it was a mistake. Maybe the Abernathys were alive. Maybe it was a bad joke they were playing on someone ... a Halloween prank, five months early.

Eventually, Mark and his mother stumbled out, their faces white.

"We've got to get help," he said. "The police ... an ambulance."

Beth's words were half screams. "They can't send an ambulance. You can't even call the police!"

He stood there for a moment, as if trying to think. "Right. I'll take my bike and go to the sheriff."

Deni nodded. "Mark?"

He turned his still-stunned eyes to her. "What?"

"Tell them to hurry."

DOUG HAD JUST GOTTEN HOME WHEN HE HEARD HIS DAUGHTERS'
anguished screams. He threw his bike down and ran around to the
back of the house.

Kay burst out the back door, alarm widening her eyes. "What
in the world? Is that Beth?"

Doug tore across the lawn, out the back gate, and went between
two houses behind them. Kay followed.

He saw them then, Deni and Beth, clutching each other in the
street. Neighbors were coming out of their houses.

"Deni, what's wrong?" he yelled as he ran toward them.

At the sound of his voice, Beth let Deni go and ran into his
arms, hiccuping sobs. "We knocked on the door ... and it was
open ... so we went in—"

"They were dead!" Deni cut in. "Lying on the floor in there.
Dad, they were *murdered*."

Doug looked up toward the house. *"Murdered?"*

Kay pulled Deni into her arms and held her as she stared toward
the house. "Doug, we've got to get the sheriff."

"Mark Green already went for him," Deni said.

Doug eased Beth out of his arms. "I'm going in."

Kay tried to stop him. "Doug, be careful."

"Mark's mom and her husband are in there," Deni said.

He went to the door and stepped inside. Martha stood there
in her husband's arms, weeping. Shock jolted through him as he
saw the two bodies. He closed his eyes. *Get a grip, Branning. Pay
attention.*

"His diamond case is open," Martha said in a horrified whisper. "And all the stones are gone! The house is ransacked."

He looked around, saw that she was right. Drawers were pulled
out, bookcases toppled onto the floor. Wires and cords hung from
the walls where the stereo and TV had been. A door from the

kitchen to the garage was open, and the garage was a mess as well.

Doug turned back to the bodies, and wondered if anyone had checked to see if they were alive. The thought of approaching those blood-soiled corpses made him sick, but slowly, he went into the dining room where they lay. Trying to avoid the blood, he bent over to check for a pulse. Neither of them had one.

The cause of death was clear. They'd been shot. But why hadn't anyone heard the gunshots?

He looked around, wondering how the robbers had gotten inside. And more important, how had they gotten away with the things they'd stolen? How would someone have gotten all this stuff out without a vehicle?

It had to be someone who lived nearby.

"Doug?"

He turned and saw Brad—his next-door neighbor and Jeremy and Drew's dad. "I heard all the commotion. Kay said you were in here."

Doug wiped the sweat from his forehead. "Yeah."

He stood back and tried to make his hands stop shaking, as Brad looked at the bodies. "Have you been upstairs? Is anybody else dead?"

"They lived alone."

Brad and Doug turned at Martha's tear-choked words.

"Still," Brad said. "It's worth a look."

Doug agreed, so he forced himself to go up the stairs. Pictures of the victims' grown children, with a dozen or so grandchildren, lined the hallway. How would they notify their children of their parents' deaths? He went from room to room, and saw more evidence of robbery. Drawers pulled out, an empty jewelry box.

When he'd seen enough, he went back downstairs. "Nobody else. Just the two of them. Brad, whoever did this lives right here in the neighborhood. They took a few big items. Things that would be hard to carry a long distance without a vehicle. They made several trips, apparently. Maybe it was even several people. But why didn't anyone hear the gunshots?"

Brad was shaking now, too. "Maybe they used some kind of silencer. Wouldn't have completely knocked out the sound, like in the movies, but it probably would have muffled it."

Martha's husband shook his head. "Hard to believe we would have missed that. We had our windows open last night."

"We didn't hear anything," Martha said.

Brad stood there for a moment, staring at Doug. His adam's apple bobbed. "Looks like we got more problems than we thought. And we better get outta here, guys. There might be some evidence here that leads police to the killer."

Doug agreed, and as he followed the others out, he wondered what they were going to do with the bodies. How would they transport them out of here? There were no ambulances running, no hearses that could pick them up.

The sheriff and his deputies would be hard-pressed to gather evidence without their usual forensic resources. But they had to get to the bottom of this somehow ... before the killer struck again.

FOURTEEN

SOMETIME LATER, DOUG WALKED HIS FAMILY HOME. BETH had said little since they'd found the bodies, and Deni seemed shell-shocked. Jeff and Logan just seemed excited at the turn of events—another story to tell about this bizarre outage. The gravity of it hadn't slammed them in the faces like it had the girls. They hadn't seen the bodies lying in their own blood.

The few deputies Mark had been able to summon to the scene recorded the information with notes instead of photography, since none of their digital cameras or camcorders worked. They had dusted for fingerprints, hoping that as soon as the power came back on, they'd be able to run them through the AFIS computer system to identify the perpetrators. They'd agreed the killer or killers had to be from close by. The deputies began to canvas the neighborhood, trying to find witnesses who might have seen anyone trekking home with their arms full of stolen goods last night. Word spread like fire around the subdivision, and someone called a meeting down at the lake's gazebo for around sundown that day.

When the Brannings finally got back home, they all collapsed on the couches in the family room, silently looking up at Doug for answers.

Beth leaned against her mother, who stroked her hair, trying to comfort her. Her tears weren't yet spent. "Daddy, why would anybody kill Mrs. Abernathy? She was just a nice lady. Nobody hated her like the other teachers. She was really cool."

Doug wished he had an answer. "It looked like a robbery, sweetheart. Might not have had anything to do with them at all."

"Then it could happen to us." Logan's face glistened with perspiration as he stared up at him. "They could break into our house tonight and kill us in our sleep."

Doug swallowed and sat down on the hearth. "That's not gonna happen. They probably struck them because they were older and weren't likely to fight back. Or they thought they weren't home, and got surprised."

"Weird, huh?" Jeff muttered. "Yesterday we thought terrorists had attacked us. Now we find out we have more to fear from our own neighbors."

Kay kissed the top of Beth's head. Her eyes held a dark, haunted look, and Doug knew he couldn't banish it. "This is sure bringing out the worst in people," Kay whispered.

Deni scowled. "The worst in people? It's turning them into *murderers*, Mom. I want to get out of here. I shouldn't even *be* here. I should be in D.C. with Craig."

"Well, thank heaven you're not." Kay let Beth go and leaned forward as she gaped at Deni. "I'd be worried sick about you if you weren't here. We need to be thankful that we have our comfortable home and that our whole family is together. This is an inconvenience for us, nothing more. We're not as vulnerable as a lot of people."

"Mom, how can you say that?" Deni cried. "There are murderers in our own neighborhood. Maybe our own street. We don't know who they are, and the sheriff can't do anything about it."

Doug knew he had to calm them all down before Deni's mood caused a panic. "Deni, we'll be all right. Jeff and I can protect us. Now everybody go chill for a little while before we go to the meeting."

"We can't chill." Beth wiped her eyes. "Miss Amber still needs diapers."

Kay sighed and looked at Doug. "We'll find her some. You just go lie down, Beth. You need a nap before the meeting."

Doug watched his traumatized young daughter go up to her room. A nap wasn't going to help. The images she'd seen today would stay in her mind for a very long time.

Deni got up and crossed her arms. "I *really* have to get out of here. I'm serious."

Doug shrugged. "Yeah, go for a walk or something if you want."

"Not a *walk*! I have to go home to D.C."

He shot her a disgusted look. "This is your home, Deni."

"Not anymore. And if this outage is gonna last, then I need to get started now in order to be there to start my job on Monday."

Was she crazy? "Deni, I won't allow you to launch out on your own, so you can just stop ranting right now."

"You can't stop me, Dad. I'm over twenty-one. I can do whatever I want." And with that, she turned and ran to her room.

FIFTEEN

DENI'S PARENTS FOLLOWED HER UP THE STAIRS TO HER ROOM, her brothers right behind them. "Honey, I know you're upset about what happened," Doug said. "We all are. But that's no reason to be irrational and—"

Deni got to the top of the stairs and turned on her father. "Irrational? You think it's more rational to stay here with murderers running around? I'll be safer on the road."

"Calm down." Her father's voice was maddeningly even, as if he'd already forgotten the dead people she'd found.

"Where do you think you're going?" Kay asked.

She met her mother's angry gaze. "Anywhere but here."

"So you're gonna do what? Just roll your suitcase behind you and clomp down I-20?"

"No," Deni said. "I'm gonna take my bike. I'll ride up the interstate until I find civilization. Then I'll rent a car or something."

"Honey, there *isn't* any civilization!" Kay shouted. "Not nearby. If there were, someone would have seen cars going by today."

Deni got her suitcase and threw it on the bed. "Fine. Then I'll ride my bike all the way to D.C. But I'm not staying here where it's hopeless. Craig wouldn't want me to do that."

At the thought of Craig, she started to cry. She unzipped her suitcase and flung it open, then realized that she'd never be able to carry it on a bike. Rage mushroomed inside her at her own stupidity. She sank down onto the bed.

Her mother leaned down and put her arm around her. "Honey, I know you're upset. We all are."

"No you're not, Mom. Your life is just put on hold. This is no big deal to you. You have your family and everybody you love around you. You're in your own home."

"And so are you."

"No, I'm not! Craig is my family now. I want to be there with him. I found two people dead today and I can't even tell him."

She knew as she ranted that she wasn't making any sense, but the anger pulsing through her kept her mind from settling back on those bodies. She looked through her bedroom door, and saw Beth across the hall, lying on her own bed. Beth wasn't ranting and raving. She was curled up in fetal position, staring off into space. Deni wished her sister would cry and break something, so there would at least be some sense of normalcy. She couldn't stand the thought that this stupid power outage might traumatize her little sister forever.

She lowered her voice so Beth couldn't hear. "Mom, I'm scared. What if someone tries to kill *us*?"

"They won't." Her dad's voice was calm, confident.

Kay agreed. "There's safety in numbers, and we have three men to defend us."

Deni looked at her brothers standing in the doorway. Logan looked as vulnerable as Beth. And Jeff didn't look like he could defend himself, let alone the whole family.

"But what has it come to that we have to be defended?" she asked. "That people in our own neighborhood are going around killing people? Breaking into cars, looting ... and what if the killer is there tonight at the meeting, enjoying all the gossip about the murders, pretending to be just one of us, trying to get along?"

She saw Beth sit up on the edge of her bed. She'd let her voice rise, and now her sister had heard. She wished she could take it back.

Beth came to the doorway, her face red with her effort not to cry. "Daddy, I'm scared." Her voice was cracked and wobbly. "I don't want to go to the meeting."

"Me either," Logan said.

Her mother's face tightened. "Deni, look what you've done."

She grunted. "What *I've* done? Mom, they don't need me pointing these things out. They're not stupid."

"Deni's right, Dad," Jeff said. "What if the killer is at the meeting?"

Deni saw the struggle on her dad's face, as if he wondered whether to shelter his family with empty, meaningless assurances, or just play it straight.

Doug's answer surprised her. "Maybe we need to assume he will be there." He looked from one person to the other. "The truth is, every one of us will be looking over a shoulder, and rightfully so. We have to be strong, and be careful who we trust. Now, I want everyone to get hold of themselves and take a breath. God is going to protect us, even if He has to use Jeff and me to do it."

It was meant to be funny, but no one laughed.

"So, Deni, I don't want to hear any more talk about you taking off to who knows where. That's not a rational response to this, and you know it. I know you want to be with Craig. And you will. But right now, you're with us, and we have to stick together."

"Write him a letter, honey," her mom said. "It'll do you good."

Deni wiped her eyes. "Can't even mail it."

"That's okay. Write it anyway."

Deni had never written Craig a letter, other than short, matter-of-fact emails. She'd always had a cell phone, and he was usually accessible. But maybe her mother's idea was a good one. At least she could feel like she was communicating with him, even if it was only one-sided.

Jeff's cheeks were mottled with heat and worry. "Dad, you want me to keep the shotgun with me at the meeting tonight?"

"I think we're okay as long as it's still light out. We'll be home before dark." He went to the door, then turned back.

"You know, none of you has to come to the meeting. I could go without you."

"No, I want to go," Deni said. "I want to see what people are saying. Maybe someone has news about the outage."

"Me, too," Kay said. "And I don't want to leave anyone here alone."

Doug looked at his children. "It's going to be all right, guys."

Always before, when her dad said those words, Deni believed them. But today she knew it was completely out of his hands. As everyone left her room, she pulled a notebook off her bookshelf and opened it to a clean page. Slowly, she started to write.

Dear Craig,

I miss you so much. You have no idea how much. I don't think I've gone a day without talking to you in over a year. And now this.

As if you don't know by now, our power is out, our cars don't run, our food is short, people are looting and fighting. But worst of all, there was a murder last night in our neighborhood. Beth's teacher. The two of us found her and her husband dead today.

I'll never get over it. The sight of them lying there like that. A sweet couple who probably never hurt anyone. They have pictures of children and grandchildren on the walls of their house. And no one even knows how to get word to them.

The sheriff's department came, but there's not a lot they can do without computers and labs. I keep thinking of all those episodes I watched of Little House on the Prairie *when I was growing up. They had murders, didn't they? Didn't they have marshals or police of some kind who could solve their crimes and lock up the bad guys? Maybe Michael Landon in all his wisdom was the one who always just knew who had done it. Or Laura would stumble on the criminal and almost get killed, herself.*

But this isn't television. It's real life.

I love you so much. I hope you're all right. You're probably in the Senate Building as we speak, moving and shaking, and figuring out the solution to the problems we're having here.

If you have power and transportation, won't you come get me? I know you will. In fact, even though everyone says you put your job first, that nothing is more important, I just know that you won't let much time pass before you come to get me. We have to be together.

Somehow, we will be, even if I have to walk to you myself. I love you, Craig. I hope I'll see you soon.

Love,
Deni

SIXTEEN

THE NEIGHBORS BEGAN ARRIVING AT THE LAKE EARLY THAT evening, bringing lawn chairs and blankets. Deni dragged a chair into the shade and marked her spot. Some of the neighborhood children splashed and played in the small lake, which had a no-wake, no-swimming rule. But no one seemed concerned, since nothing was normal today. Though she knew it seemed childish, Deni thought of going into the water herself.

The gathering seemed almost festive after the stress of the last twenty-four hours. Two teenagers brought guitars and sat strumming background music in a spontaneous jam session. Brian McMullen, one of Jeff's friends, went home and got his harmonica, and began playing along with them. It seemed like a neighborhood picnic.

But Deni refused to get lulled into a false sense of security. There was a killer among them. He could be one of the dads watching his children splash in the water, or one of the guitar players, or one of the older men in their golf shorts and navy blue socks, who looked so benign and harmless.

She searched the faces for the kind of evil it would have taken to murder the Abernathys. What would that look like in a man's eyes? Or could it be a woman?

"Deni, thank goodness you're home!"

She turned and saw one of her best friends from high school, Chris, whom she'd carpooled with every day since they'd gotten their licenses. They'd been inseparable since seventh grade, then lost touch after parting ways for college.

Deni had simply outgrown Chris.

She got up and tried to look happy to see her. "You, too. I thought you were still at school."

"Nope, graduated last week." She pulled her own chair up next to Deni's. "I'm so glad you're here. I've been dying with nobody to talk to except my parents and my little brother. I wish I'd known you were home. I'm dying of boredom."

Deni didn't much like the idea of hanging out with high school friends. After four years at an eastern college she was beyond that. She'd changed, and didn't want her old friends thinking she hadn't.

She lifted her chin. "I hope I won't be here long. I'm starting a job at an NBC affiliate in Washington as soon as I can get out of here."

Chris looked suitably impressed. "A TV job! Wow. That's perfect for you. I always thought you'd be a star."

Deni laughed in spite of herself. "Well, let's hope that I can get there before they give up on me. My fiancé is there, and he's got to be worried sick about me."

There. She'd gotten in the engagement *and* the television job in one fell swoop. She lifted her left hand to scratch her face, hoping Chris would notice the ring. But she didn't.

"Isn't all this crazy?" Chris's voice lowered to a whisper. "And did you hear about the murders?"

"I'm the one who found them." Deni's gut knotted with the words, but a sense of pride welled up in her, as if that elevated her somehow.

"You did? Oh, my gosh, Deni. Was it as bad as they said?"

"Worse."

"Do they know who did it?"

Deni shook her head. "I don't think so."

"It's so creepy," Chris whispered, looking around. "I don't think many of us are going to sleep tonight."

Deni glanced across the lawn and saw her friend Mark sitting on the pier. He stared down into the water, still clearly shocked at what he'd seen earlier.

"Man, I'd kill for a bath." Chris lifted her hair off of her neck. "I plan to make friends with someone who has a pool tonight. You guys haven't had one put in in the last few years, have you?"

Deni shook her thoughts from the murders. "No. My mom hates cleaning them. All these years I've told her we need a pool. Now she wishes we had one."

"Well, I'll let you know if someone invites me to swim."

The sun was laser sharp and glaring as it made its final blast of heat before setting. "I saw Katie Morris the other day," Chris said. "She's working at Target."

"Did she graduate?"

"No, she said she's got another whole year. She was a partier, you know, and only came out with about nine hours every semester. Her parents stopped paying for it, so now she's having to work to put herself through."

Deni had known many students like that in college, and had even been like that herself for a while. Then it had occurred to her that she had ambitions and goals, and she couldn't meet them if she was up all night drinking and partying. Finally, she'd decided to focus her energies on getting a good job when she got out. That meant getting good grades. It was those grades that had impressed the station that hired her. Her future looked so bright she'd need sunglasses to navigate her way through it.

Someone yelled for their attention, and the milling people began to take their seats.

"If we could go ahead and get started ..."

Her own father called the meeting to attention. That amused her. "What is he doing?"

"Looks like he's taking charge," Chris said. "Why is that funny?"

"Because he's never been to a homeowner's meeting in his life. He was always afraid he'd get elected to something."

As the group settled down, he continued to stand at the front, as if planning to address the crowd. Brad, their next-door neighbor, father to Jeremy and Drew, stood with him. It looked like they were in this together.

Her dad cleared his throat. "Stella Huckabee just told me that her husband, Hank, who's this year's Homeowner's Association president, is in Washington. Needless to say, he hasn't been able to make it home. Randall Abernathy was the vice president ..."

Deni caught her breath. Abernathy—the murdered husband of Beth's teacher.

Her dad cleared his throat again. "Anyway, in the absence of a leader, I offered to open the meeting tonight. I know everybody has a lot of questions about the murders and the outage in general, so maybe we can spend a little while here just exchanging information. My neighbor Brad Caldwell is here to help."

Brad offered a wave. "Before we start talking about the murders, I wanted us to share any hard facts we might have about the outage."

"I don't have any facts," a man said, "but I didn't get home until an hour ago. I was in Atlanta when the power went out, and had to ride home on a bike. I can tell you that things are just as crazy there as they are here."

That was the last thing Deni wanted to hear.

"Atlanta?" Her dad sounded stunned. "The power is out there, too?"

"That's right. Didn't see any sign of anything moving at any of the towns I went through. Cars stalled all along the highways and interstates, people walking around with no information whatsoever about what happened. No communication working at all."

Deni's heart sank, and she looked at her father. Disappointment tugged at his face.

A woman stood. "When that power outage happened in New York a couple of years ago, they started getting power back on by the next day. How come nothing's working? Not the slightest thing?"

"Yeah, and why is our water out?" a man asked. "What's water got to do with electricity?"

Doug tried to answer. "The water gets to us via an electric pump, and the treatment plants work on electricity. But this is clearly a bigger problem than just electricity. A power outage wouldn't affect our cars and watches. I even have a brand-new, never-used generator that won't work. But if everyone will listen, Brad has an idea what might be going on."

Brad raised his hands to quiet the growing chatter. His voice, trained to get the attention of his jurors, boomed over the crowd. "I've been racking my brain all day trying to figure out what our cars, watches, planes, and even our newer model generators all have in common. And the one thing I can come up with is semiconductors."

"What's a semiconductor?" someone shouted from the crowd.

"It's a material that conducts electricity less than a conductor, like metal, and more than an insulator, like rubber. You've heard of chips—silicon chips, computer chips ... Well, they're all made of flakes of silicon, and they're in almost everything. Since this outage isn't just electricity-related but is affecting cars and planes and who-knows-what all else, that must be what's damaged."

Deni couldn't keep quiet any longer. "But why? What happened to them?"

Brad shrugged. "Sounds like an EMP to me. And whatever radiation is causing it is still in the atmosphere. Even brand-new equipment is dying the minute it's turned on."

"Then how long before it passes?"

Brad shook his head and looked at Doug. Finally, her father spoke. "Semiconductors are fragile. If they've been damaged, it's probably irreversible."

There was a collective moan around the group. Amber Rowe, sitting with two of her children in a stroller and the other on her lap, asked, "What does that mean?"

Doug looked as if he hated to spell it out. "It's not like a power outage where the electric company repairs its lines and the lights come back on. This is much more severe."

Deni couldn't breathe. The news couldn't have been worse if he'd told them they were at war! Her eyes widened. Maybe they were. What a way to defeat the country. Knock out their technology and leave them helpless. No one even had to die.

They'd just *wish* they were dead.

Deni glanced back at Amber and saw that she was crying. She wasn't the only one.

"Then we won't make it!" a woman yelled. "We don't have enough food to last indefinitely. Nothing's open, even the banks. What are we going to do?"

"We'll have to share with each other," Doug said. "Help those who need help."

"With what?" someone shouted out.

"With whatever we might have extra."

Ralph Whitson, who'd run for county supervisor last year, stood up. "Why should we provide for families who weren't prepared? I knew something like this might happen one day. I've been stockpiling stuff since Y2K, and I have no intention of sharing it. Not my fault if others were stupid."

Brad fixed the man with a hard look. "No one knew *this* could happen. And it's certainly up to you. You don't have to share. We would just like it if each of you would consider it. We're gonna need to pitch in as a neighborhood to help everyone through this. This outage is going to bring a lot of challenges."

"Yeah, like murder." A retired man from the back of the group came forward to be heard. "Doug, what can you tell us about the killings? Was it a robbery, or does it look like some other motive?"

"Definitely a robbery," Doug said. "They took their television and jewelry and silver and just about everything they could carry out of that house without backing a truck up to it. Looks like the outage was just an opportunity. The sheriff thinks it might be the same thieves responsible for the other two break-ins this month. A lot of people weren't home last night. Maybe the crooks thought the Abernathys weren't home, then killed them when they surprised them."

"What are the cops doing to find the killer?" an old man asked.

"They've been talking to neighbors. Some of you probably got interviewed today. A lot was going on last night, with people trying to get home and all, but if any of you happened to see someone carrying a television or something, you might get in touch with the sheriff's department. We all have to defend ourselves. Maybe it would benefit us to create some kind of neighborhood watch program."

Stella Huckabee got up. "So you think we need to set up guards in the neighborhood?"

Brad nodded. "Wouldn't hurt. We don't know for sure whether we're at war or not. But we do know there's an enemy among us."

"Whoever the enemy is," Doug said, "we could have some kind of neighborhood watch of men willing to patrol our streets during the night, to make sure people aren't roaming around creating mischief. After the meeting, Brad would like to meet with all the men who could help with this. And I urge you to not let your guard down. It's hot in our houses, and we want to sleep with windows and doors open to get the air circulating. But that might not be the best move."

Deni's eyes strayed back to Amber Rowe. She'd never seen a more helpless look on anyone's face. This wasn't going to help her rattled neighbor sleep tonight.

"If the sheriff catches the killer, can he even lock him up?" someone asked.

"Yes. The locks on the jail still work."

Deni's mind reeled as she listened to the rumblings around her about who the killers were. Some suggested it was the reclusive Mr. Miller, who lived in the run-down house that had brought down the value of the neighboring property. Others suggested it was a family rumored to be drug dealers, since a steady stream of seedy characters always came and went from that house. Others named a family of men. The mother had died a few years earlier of cancer, and the boys had run wild ever since, following in their father's immoral footsteps.

Everyone had a theory.

Deni figured she'd just steer clear of all of the suspects.

As her eyes swept over the crowd, she shivered despite the heat. Any one of them could be the killer.

Just as any of them could be the next victim.

SEVENTEEN

DOUG WAS IN OVER HIS HEAD. THE CROWD WAS GROWING hostile, as if he alone were responsible for the outage and the murders.

Merilee Garrison, the golf pro at the local country club, looked downright annoyed. "Doug, how long are we looking at here? Days? Weeks? Months?"

"I wish I knew," Doug said. "I think I can safely say it won't be just days. I could be wrong. Maybe the power companies have some alternative way of getting power to us, without all their computers and electronics, but I doubt it."

An older man raised his hand. Doug had seen him many times before working in his yard, but he didn't know the man's name. "I'm Max Keegan," he said in a phlegmy voice. "Doris and I do a little gardening in our spare time."

Oh, yes, Doug remembered the brouhaha that had occurred sometime last year, when the Keegan's neighbors complained about them turning much of their backyard into a vegetable garden. They'd sued to get them to put up a privacy fence so they wouldn't have to look at it. Unless Doug had missed the resolution, it was still in litigation.

"We have a good bit of food canned and put away. We can share some okra, squash, tomatoes, butter beans, and peas. If we could get some of the ladies to help us, we could get more done and have a good amount to spare."

There now, that was what Doug had hoped for. "I appreciate that very much, Mr. Keegan. Looks like that garden of yours might turn out to be a big asset to the neighborhood." He caught the eye of the Keegans' neighbors who'd sued. They were whispering viciously.

"Wal-Mart has a sign up that it's opening tomorrow," someone shouted. "They don't have much left to sell, but they said they'd stay open until they ran out of stock."

Doug glanced at Kay, knowing she was making note of that. It would be a stampede. He hoped they had some kind of control in the place. "Since it's going to be a madhouse in there, maybe a little organization would be in order. Maybe several families could go in together to get the things they need. There are people who are desperate for diapers and matches and candles—"

"It's every family for itself," Whitson said. "We have to look out for our own families. We can't worry about everybody else."

Doug started to argue, until he realized that he felt the same way. It *was* every family for itself, and if he could get his own family through the Wal-Mart doors tomorrow, the last thing he'd be worrying about was shopping for someone else.

Later, when the group finally broke up, Doug waited for men to approach Brad about the neighborhood watch, but no one did. He supposed everyone wanted to stay at home and look after their own families. He certainly couldn't blame them. It was why he hadn't volunteered. He had hoped the meeting and the exchange of information would make things easier, more hopeful. Instead, he felt the oppressive weight of dread, growing heavier by the minute.

And he wondered if it had only made things worse.

EIGHTEEN

THOUGH THE MEETING WAS OVER, BUSINESS STILL WENT ON among families who stayed after to talk and trade. Darkness began to fall, and mosquitoes had a field day with the pungent neighbors. That was all they needed, Deni thought. West Nile virus on top of everything else.

She caught sight of her little sister sitting on the pier. Beth looked so pale, and she hugged her skinny knees. Her distant gaze flitted from face to face, as if searching for her teacher's killer.

Anger stirred in Deni again. The events of the day seemed so surreal, like a montage of worst-case scenarios. She was ready for it to be over.

She'd just go home and curl up on her bed, and write another letter to Craig.

Help me, Craig. I'm drowning here. Why did I ever come home in the first place? I could be with you.

Even if the outage did stretch from here to the Atlantic, tolerating it would be so much easier if she were with Craig. He and Senator Crawford would know of the resources the country had for such an event. They would fix things, and D.C. would be the first place back up and running again.

"Deni, guess what?"

Chris came toward her after working the crowd. She had that high school look of excitement on her face, the same one she'd had when Carl Stevens asked her to the prom.

Deni was so beyond high school.

Chris leaned over and whispered, "I found somebody who'll let us use his pool if we don't invite anybody else."

"Really?" It would be heaven to dive into the cool water, to wash off some of the sweat. "Who?"

"Mark Green's dad." Chris pointed to the man sitting in his lawn chair, leaned back on two legs. He reminded Deni of Dean Martin in those old movies her grandparents loved—with black hair and a leathery golf tan.

"That's not Mark's dad. I saw his dad today at the Abernathys'."

"That would've been his stepfather. Mark lives with his mom. His dad lives in that big blue Victorian house over on Mercer. He seems really nice."

He looked up and caught their eyes, waved and winked.

"Why doesn't he want us to invite anybody else?"

"He said two of his sons and their families are over using their pool, and he doesn't want a whole crowd. But he heard me asking someone else, and he volunteered."

"Will Mark be there?"

"He didn't say, but it doesn't matter to me. Do you want to come or not?"

Deni found her father in the crowd, then looked for her mother. Chances were, they'd balk at her going to swim in some strange man's pool. But it wasn't like he was a *complete* stranger. She knew his son, after all. Mark was a nice guy, so his dad couldn't be that bad. Besides, she was over twenty-one and almost married. She didn't need her parents' permission.

Chris was waiting. "Come on, Deni. I don't want to go by myself, but I'm dying to swim. He even said we could use a bucket to wash our hair if we wanted."

That did it. "Okay, I'll come. Let me go home and get into my bathing suit, and I'll meet you at your house."

Chris almost danced with delight. "Great!"

Deni's gaze drifted to Mr. Green again as he folded up his chair and gathered his things.

"He's about to head home now," Chris said. "I'll go tell him we're coming."

Deni watched the girl scurry across the grass, weaving between the people. Chris still looked as cute as she had in high school. If she'd put on the Freshman Fifteen, she'd taken it off in the subsequent three years. She wondered if she'd had to work as hard as Deni to do it. Probably not. Chris had always been pretty, with her shoulder-length silky blonde hair that had the slightest wave. The two of them attracted different kinds of guys. Chris, with her delicate build and her innocent-looking features, always attracted the protectors. Athletes and Eagle Scouts vied for her attention. Deni used to call her a serial dater, because she never committed to anyone.

Deni, on the other hand, attracted the thinkers. The more cerebral guys with brighter futures. Men like Craig. Chris's goal in college had been to get her MRS degree. The girl would probably wind up married to some has-been high school football star who worked in his daddy's business, and as long as she had manicure money, she'd be happy as a clam.

Night was just beginning to blacken the sky as Deni walked home. Her suitcase still lay half-packed on her bed, so she riffled through it and found her swimsuit. She put it on, and pulled a pair of shorts and a T-shirt over it. Then she stuffed her twenty-bucks-a-bottle shampoo and conditioner into her purse, and got on her bike to ride over to Chris's house.

The purse dangled over the handlebars as she rode. How absurd that she was relegated to riding a bicycle like some ten-year-old. She felt ridiculous and self-conscious, and that made her angry.

Her friend was sitting on her front lawn, waiting with a towel hanging over her arm. "Just like old times, huh? Remember when we used to have swimming parties at John Frazier's house? Too bad he moved."

Deni sighed. "This isn't a party. I just want to get clean."

"Oh, I know, but it could be fun."

"I'm glad you're enjoying all this." Deni knew she was being a jerk, but she wasn't in the mood to temper her words.

Chris's smile faded. "You're bummed about not being able to talk to your boyfriend, huh?"

"He's not my *boyfriend*. He's my fiancé."

Chris stood there for a moment, looking hurt, as if Deni had just insulted her somehow. It was just like Chris to make this all about her.

"Where can I put my bike?" Deni asked. "I don't want to park it at Mr. Green's, because someone might steal it. As much as I hate riding it, I guess I need the stupid thing."

"Here, put it in my garage." Chris slid the door up, waited for Deni to park it, then closed it again. "Boy, you're really in a mood, aren't you?" Her voice softened. "Guess I can't blame you, after you found the Abernathys. It must have been awful."

"I don't want to talk about it."

"Okay. Then we can talk about your fiancé. Craig, isn't it?"

Deni's mood lifted somewhat as she launched into a description of her beloved. As they walked the few houses down to Vic Green's, she made sure Chris understood what an important man Craig was.

Chris seemed duly impressed. "He sounds like a catch. I dated a medical student for six months last year. I thought he might be the one. But then he got his residency at Johns Hopkins, and had to move away. It just seemed impossible to keep up a long-distance relationship with him under that kind of stress, so we kind of parted ways."

Deni hadn't expected that. Chris dating a doctor at Johns Hopkins? "Do you still talk?"

"Not much. I've kind of moved on. I had a really strong feeling that it wasn't God's will for us to be together. He wasn't a Christian, but he was a really great guy."

"How did you meet him?"

"I worked with him at University Hospital."

She turned to Chris and gave her a puzzled look. "You worked at a hospital?"

Chris laughed. "Of course I did. Didn't you know I graduated from nursing school?"

If Deni had known that, she'd forgotten. "No, I had no idea."

"Yeah. I'm about to start a new job, too, at Children's Hospital next month. I decided to take a month off to find a place to live and get settled."

"So you're staying in the Birmingham area?" Deni asked. "I don't know how you can stand it."

"It's home. I love it here."

"I don't. I can't wait to get out of here."

They were quiet the rest of the way, and Deni wondered if she'd insulted her friend again. She supposed she should be more careful to keep her thoughts to herself.

They reached the blue Victorian down the street. Vic Green was waiting with the front door open, a little brown Yorkie barking at his heels. "Hello there, young ladies." His deep voice would have made for a great radio career. "Welcome to the Copa Cabana."

Deni tried not to roll her eyes.

They stepped into the house, which looked like a decorator's nightmare. The dog kept barking, so Vic bent down and swept it up. "Hush now, Scrappy. These are our friends."

The living room was decorated like a tropical beach resort, with a tiki roof over the wet bar, and red Hawaiian prints covering the sofas and chairs. Bamboo beads hung in the doorways, and beige shag rugs covered the mahogany hardwood floors.

It looked like the brainchild of an actor who played a decorator on TV.

"Looks like a party house," Chris said on a giggle. "Did you decorate it yourself?"

"I got a little help."

From the frat boys at the local college? Deni wondered. She hoped he hadn't actually *paid* anyone for this.

Beneath the bamboo shades, Deni saw through the window into the backyard. Three people sat beside the pool drinking beer, and a couple of others splashed in the water. She felt like she was crashing a party.

"Come on out and meet my sons and their families." He led them out back and, in a bellowing voice, said, "Everybody, meet Deni and Chris. Larry and Jack, remember you're married."

One of the sons pulled out of the water, and greeted them, dripping wet. "So how'd my dad get two babes in bikinis over here? Way to go, Dad."

Deni bristled, and a hint of red tinged Vic's cheeks. "They're nice young ladies who wanted to swim. I'm just trying to be neighborly. Now behave so they don't think you were raised by wolves."

Larry, the other brother, shook their hands. "Nice to meet you. Don't mind my brother. He's a moron."

"A moron with good taste," Jack said.

Deni looked beyond him to the woman in the water who was glaring at them as if they'd come here to break up her family.

The angry woman frowned at Jack. "You didn't tell me Vic was having girls over. I would think you might have told me."

"Nothing to tell. Don't be so rude."

Deni shifted and glanced at Chris. She had that look she used to get when she realized someone didn't like her. Chris couldn't stand not being liked. "We're friends of Mark's," she said, as if to calm the woman's fears. "We're not staying long. We just wanted to get wet, but if it's not a good time—"

The woman flipped her hair back. "No, be my guest. Matter of fact, go get all your friends. The more women the better."

"Don't be so insecure, Grace." The woman sitting at the tiki bar with a child in her lap had a slightly friendlier face.

Vic introduced the two women as his sons' wives, then whispered, "Don't mind Grace. She's a newlywed with jealousy issues, but she's a sweet little gal when you get to know her."

Deni didn't think she wanted to. This was absurd. She didn't want to start trouble between a man and his wife. Then again, it looked like this trouble had started a long time ago.

Jack jumped back into the water, splashing his wife and temporarily distracting her.

"Just make yourselves at home," Vic said. "The water's still cool, even though it's been so hot today."

Chris sat down and slipped off her shoes. "You seem in a good mood. Everybody else is in a blue funk after that meeting."

Vic laughed. "You don't believe that doomsday stuff they were saying, do you? It's pure speculation, and I don't buy any of it. What does that Doug guy know?"

Deni spoke up. "He's my father."

He winced. "Oh, sorry. Seems like a nice enough guy, but really, he's not an electrical engineer, is he?"

"No, he's a stockbroker."

"And that black guy. What does he do?"

"Brad is a lawyer. He's our next-door neighbor."

Vic smiled. "Well, there you go. I choose to believe that this will pass before we know it."

Deni wanted to believe it. "I hope you're right."

"He is right," Chris said. "He has to be. I can't even consider that this is going to last longer than a few days."

A huge splash hit them, soaking their clothes. Jack had done a cannonball in the water, like a ten-year-old kid trying to get their attention.

But the water felt great.

Chris giggled, then turned back to Vic. "So I guess Mark is the baby of the family?"

"That's right." Vic set the little dog down, and it jumped up on the chair next to Deni. The dog had a bad haircut that made it look more like a Koala bear than a Yorkie. She reached out to pet him. "Yes, Mark's the baby. These two sons are mine by my first marriage, Mark's from my second. He's something of a mama's boy, so he lives with her."

"It's nice that you live so close to them," Chris said.

Vic shrugged. "Yeah, but I'm not so sure Mark's always happy I live here."

Deni's heart softened at the vulnerable look that passed across Vic's face. He picked up the dog and put him on his shoulder, petting him like he was his closest friend.

"I don't see Mark much. He's been so busy since he quit college and started working."

"Quit college?" Chris frowned. "Didn't he finish?"

"Nope. Decided he wanted to be a carpenter and didn't need it. He's working in construction now, which is about as different from what I do than anything you can imagine. And here, I always thought he'd follow in my footsteps and work in the family business."

"What is the family business?" Deni asked.

"We own a chain of bookstores. And we have our hands in a number of other ventures. We're businessmen, but Mark didn't want any of it. It's blue collar for him. At least until he comes to his senses."

He handed them some towels. "If you want to wash your hair, just shampoo it over the grass so you won't get soap in the pool, then use that bucket over there to rinse it."

Deni pulled off her shirt, stepped out of her shorts, and dove into the pool, relishing the feel of cool water over her sweat-dampened body. She felt Chris breaking the water behind her, and saw her friend swimming deep with wide, sure strokes. The water was heavenly, and for a while Deni forgot her whirling emotions over all that had happened. She swam underwater, her hair flowing around her, and came up for sweet gasps of air.

Larry and Jack left as they swam, and Vic sat out at the patio table alone, reading an old copy of *Newsweek*. He went inside when they got out and started to wash their hair, and she felt he had retreated to give them privacy.

"He seems nice," Chris said.

"Yeah, nicer than that daughter-in-law of his."

"Yeah, she was kind of scary." Chris began to towel-dry her hair. "I feel like a new person."

"Me, too. This was a good idea."

"So you want to come back tomorrow? He said we could."

"I don't know," Deni said. "We'll see."

"I don't know about you, but I need to wash my hair every day, especially in this heat. And lake water just isn't gonna cut it."

Deni didn't want to commit, but she knew that if the power was still off tomorrow, she probably would be knocking on Vic Green's door again.

NINETEEN

WHEN DENI GOT HOME, NIGHT WAS ALREADY FALLING OVER the neighborhood. The street looked barren, vacant, and she dreaded going into her home and facing more of the silent darkness.

Her family all sat in the kitchen around the table, a kerosene lamp glowing in their midst. "What's everybody in here for?"

"Where else can we go?" Logan sat with a disassembled Game Boy and a small screwdriver in front of him. "There's no light anywhere else. Dad won't let us use the flashlights. And even if there were, there wouldn't be anything to do."

"Logan, you're not going to be able to fix that," Jeff said. "It's hopeless."

"I can, too, fix it." Logan's attention was riveted on the wiring. "If I just had more light."

"Why can't we get the radio to work, at least?" Beth asked. "This is awful. I'm gonna die of boredom."

"A little quiet won't kill us." Her dad sat with his Bible open in front of him. Surely he didn't plan to read to them.

Her mother looked up at her. "How come your hair's wet?"

"I washed it ... at Chris's house."

"What with?"

"We got some water out of her neighbor's pool." She didn't know why she'd felt the need to lie. She was an adult, after all. But explaining about Vic Green might take more

99

energy than she had at the moment. "I'm going upstairs to write to Craig."

"In the dark? Mom gave away your candles."

Deni stopped and stared down at her mother. "What? Why did you do that?"

"I didn't give them all away. But Eloise, across the street, needed one of our kerosene lamps, and you know we took some candles to Amber."

Deni couldn't believe what she was hearing. "You took *my* candle? How many do we have left?"

"Enough," Kay said. "We'll make do."

"But we're already making do. It's not a lot to ask that we keep a little light in our house. It's like a mausoleum in here." She put her hands on her hips. "So you're telling me that if I want to write to Craig, I have to sit in here at this table with my whole stinking family?"

Her mom and dad exchanged looks, like they were offended or something.

Her mother sighed. "It won't kill you."

Logan threw himself back, and banged the table. "Man! I can't fix the stupid thing!"

Jeff jerked the screwdriver away. "Then give up, stupid."

"And do what? Sing campfire songs?"

"That might be fun," Beth said. "We could start a fire in the yard and make s'mores."

"Yeah, if we had marshmallows," Jeff muttered.

"And Hershey bars," Logan added.

Kay laughed. "And graham crackers. Oh, well, it was a good thought."

Deni pulled out a chair and dropped into it. "So we really have to sit here in the same room all night. Unbelievable."

"Either that, or you can go to bed."

Deni grunted. "What is it? Nine o'clock? I'm not ready for bed."

"This is why they went to bed and got up so early in the old days," Beth said. "They had to work around the light."

Deni didn't want to hear it. "Even Laura Ingalls had lamps in every room."

"Deni, can I sleep with you again tonight? I'm scared to sleep alone."

Deni started to tell Beth no, but her heart softened as she remembered her sister's trauma. "Yeah, I guess. But you don't have to be scared. Dad and Jeff have their guns."

"Dad, can I have one?" Logan's question got everyone's attention.

"Maybe later, son. For now, I think Jeff and I need to do the guarding."

Logan sprang up and set his hands on his hips. "No fair. I want to help. I'm one of the men of the house."

"Hey, I don't think it has to be men," Deni said. "Age should matter more than gender. I can shoot a gun. And wouldn't I love to be looking down the barrel at whoever killed the Abernathys."

Doug wasn't impressed with Deni's bravado. "For now, we'll start with Jeff and your mom and me. We have three rifles, and that's all. But it wouldn't hurt for each of us to learn to use them."

"Even me?" Beth asked. "I hate guns. I don't *want* to learn."

"You don't have to carry one. You just need to know how to shoot it. It might be your only protection if you're ever here alone."

Her eyes rounded. "Then don't leave me here alone!"

Kay pulled Beth against her. "We won't, honey. You don't have to worry."

"The Abernathys probably weren't worried, either."

Poor kid. Beth was about to cry again. Deni wished the murdered couple had been strangers, so the trauma didn't have to mix with the grief.

Her dad closed his Bible. "So … anybody up for a game of Monopoly?"

"Monopoly?" Jeff almost spat out the word. "Are you kidding me?"

"No. We're stuck here, basically in the same room. Might as well do something fun."

Jeff shrugged. "I'm not gonna be here long enough. I have plans for tonight."

"Plans?" Doug asked. "What plans?"

"Some of the guys are meeting over at Zach's. He has a pool. It's something to do, Dad. Something to get our minds off of this mess."

"I don't want any of you out after dark, Jeff."

"I'll take my shotgun with me."

"No, you're needed at home. I want one of us on guard all night. I need you to go to sleep so you can get up around two and take over for me."

"But I'm not even tired," Jeff said.

"Fine, then you can take first watch. I'll sleep and you wake *me* up at two."

Jeff leaned back hard in his chair. "Okay, I'll go to bed. I'll take the second watch. But I don't think anybody's gonna attack us. There are too many of us, and everyone in the neighborhood knows we have guns. Come on, why can't I go for an hour or so? There's nothing else to do."

Kay stiffened. "Jeff, I don't want you hanging around at Zach's. I didn't let you spend time over there before the outage, and I'm certainly not going to let you now."

"Fine!" He slapped his hands down on the table. "I'll go sleep." He scraped his chair back, scratching the wood floor with his weight, and stormed off to his room.

Beth smirked. "He's gonna sneak out, you know."

"No, he's not," Kay said. "Jeff wouldn't do that."

"Yeah, right." Deni almost laughed. "Think again, Mom."

Kay looked at Doug. "You don't think ..."

"Of course not."

Deni shrugged. "Okay, then stay deluded. It's just a stupid teenage party, anyway. Girls, booze, maybe a little grass ..."

Doug slid his chair back. "That's enough, Deni. Jeff knows better than that."

"Okay, whatever you say. But remember I told you so."

TWENTY

WHEN JEFF WAS SURE HE'D HEARD EVERYONE GO TO BED, HE got up, grabbed his .12 gauge, and felt his way through the darkness into the hallway outside his room. His brother's and sisters' rooms were next to his on the second floor, so he was careful not to wake anyone. Stepping softly on the plush carpet, he felt for the banister and eased down the stairs.

When he reached the bottom, he saw a faint yellow glow through the door of his dad's study. Careful not to be seen, he peered in. His father sat in the light of the kerosene lamp, his rifle on the desk next to his open Bible.

Satisfied, he made his way in the other direction, through the great room and to the back door that opened onto the patio. Holding his breath, as if that would keep the door from creaking, he opened it and slipped into the backyard. Then he hurried around to the gate, praying it wouldn't squeak as he opened it, alerting his father. He didn't want to get shot by friendly fire.

He walked the three blocks to Zach's house, the muzzle of his shotgun pointed down. He was careful to stay out of sight, since he knew the whole neighborhood was on alert for anyone prowling around at night. He jogged most of the way, and heard the sound of the party before he reached Zach's backyard.

"Jeff, that you?"

He spun around. Brad Caldwell, his next-door neighbor, stood there, a rifle in one hand and a flashlight in the other. Brad shone the light in Jeff's eyes.

He squinted. "Yeah. Hey, Mr. Caldwell."

"What are you doing out this late?"

He might have asked him the same thing. "I'm just going over to my friend's."

"The house where the party is?"

"Yeah. Look, don't tell my dad you saw me, okay?"

The light blinded Jeff, so he couldn't see Brad's expression. But the man's hesitation spoke volumes.

"You shouldn't be out this late, Jeff. It's dangerous."

"All right, I won't stay long," he said. "It's just been a bad day, you know? And I was supposed to have a date last night with this girl I've liked for a long time, but I didn't get to go, and she's gonna be here tonight." Why was he going on and on like this, like Brad would sympathize enough to keep his mouth shut? Fat chance. He might as well go on home now and throw himself on the mercy of his folks.

But Brad surprised him. "I was young once, man. I remember how it is."

"You do?" He breathed out his relief. "Great. Then you won't tell my dad?"

"Not unless he asks. Have fun, Jeff. Don't get into any trouble. I don't want to regret giving you a break."

Jeff couldn't believe his luck. As he walked around Zach's house to the gate, he realized he hadn't asked Brad what *he* was doing prowling around at night with a rifle. Maybe he was doing the neighborhood watch thing.

Jeff opened the creaking gate and saw his friends sitting around the pool in the glow of a fire burning in the barbecue pit.

"Hey, Jeff! Come on in, man. We thought you weren't gonna show!"

"I had some stuff I had to do." He pulled up a chair and took off his shoes. "Man, I can't wait to get into that pool."

Someone tossed him a beer, and he caught it in the air. "Where'd you get these?"

"My old man always has beer around. Don't worry about it."

Jeff looked at the can for a moment, trying to decide if he should open it. It wasn't as if he'd never had a beer before. After baseball games, he and his buddies sometimes went out to the Tower, their favorite place. It was in a cow pasture a few miles away, where a cell phone tower had been built. It was fun to just sit on the trunks of their cars, drinking beer and horsing around, with no worries about parents showing up.

But for some reason, he didn't feel quite that free tonight. So he left his can unopened and stripped off his shirt. "So where's Mandy? I thought you said the girls were coming."

"We thought they were, man, but they haven't shown up yet."

Great. So he'd gone to the trouble of sneaking out for nothing. Biting back his disappointment, he dove into the water. He swam deep, low, washing the sweat from his skin. When he came up, Zach's parents were coming out of the house.

Zach's mother, who had to be at least fifty—and looked every bit of it—was wearing a bikini and walking barefoot, a cigarette dangling from her fingers. He tried not to cringe. He expected her to blow a gasket and snatch the beer cans from Zach and his buddies, but instead she went to the stash and got herself one.

Zach sat on the edge of the pool, the moonlight painting his skin a pale blue. Kyle, Jeff's best friend, kept doing cannonballs off of the diving board, splashing everyone. Chad, the tallest player on the basketball team, sat by the pool, a beer can in his hand. Ali, Jeff's Pakistani friend, had gotten out and dropped into a chair. Jeff watched him for a moment, wondering if he was drinking tonight. His family was Muslim, and Ali usually toed the line to avoid his dad's anger.

Josh and Nat, both college-aged friends of Zach's brother, Gary, looked like they'd had a few too many beers already. They went to the diving board, laughing hysterically, planning to perform a triple cannonball—both of them pounding in at the same time to see how much water they could splash.

Apparently that crossed some line, because Zach's mother stopped them. "Cut it out, guys. Don't waste the water!"

Jeff got out of the water and sat down in the chair where he'd left his beer. He popped the top and took a swig.

Just then, the gate swung open, and he heard a girl's voice. "Can you guys hold it down? I could hear you all the way up the street." Lilty laughter followed.

"Hey, where've you been?" Zach yelled. "We almost gave up on you."

Amy pranced up in her one-piece suit, followed by Stacy and Mandy. Jeff grinned. Mandy was here at last. The risk had been worth it, after all.

"Don't worry about it," Amy shouted back. "We had places to go, people to see."

"Yeah, right," Jeff said as Mandy and Stacy followed her in. "They probably had to wait for their parents to go to bed so they could sneak out."

Stacy laughed and shoved at him. "How did you know?"

Zach handed them each a beer, and as Amy opened hers, she said, "We were all sleeping over at my house. My dad's like a crazy man, scared we'll get murdered."

"I was scared, too." Mandy's voice was softer. "I didn't want to come."

"Well, no one jumped out and got us," Amy said. "We ran all the way."

"Somebody has to walk us home, though." Mandy looked at Jeff. "I mean it. I'm too scared."

Jeff couldn't believe his luck. "I will. Don't worry, I won't let anybody get you."

The guys all laughed, and Josh and Nat came and picked Amy and Stacy up to throw them into the water. The girls squealed and splashed in. Jeff grabbed Mandy, laughing and tugging her to the edge of the water. Finally he pulled her in, falling in with her.

This was perfect. He'd had his eye on Mandy for the last six months, and had wanted to do cartwheels when she agreed to go out with him. The stupid outage had ruined his plans. But now he could see that it wasn't too late.

She splashed him, and he grabbed her arms and dunked her. Giggling, she came up and tried to get even. He loved the way she flirted.

The thought of her college boyfriend flashed through his mind, and he wondered if she gave him the same attention. He'd heard there was trouble in that relationship, and he was happy to step in and heal the wounds.

TWENTY-ONE

Doug rubbed his aching eyes as he tried to focus on the words he read in James 1.

"Consider it pure joy, my brothers, whenever you face trials of many kinds, because you know that the testing of your faith develops perseverance. Perseverance must finish its work so that you may be mature and complete, not lacking anything."

He sat back in his chair, staring beyond the light into darkness. They were all going to need perseverance.

He closed his Bible. His eyes were too tired to read any further. He pulled out the windup watch he'd dug out of his dresser drawer and held it under the light. He'd had to guess at the time to set it today, but if the watch was right, it was only one-thirty in the morning. He'd let Jeff sleep for thirty more minutes.

He got up, stretched, then carried the rifle and the light into the great room. Maybe some night air would invigorate him. He left the lamp on the table and slipped out the back door, his Remington in hand.

The moon was bright, and the stars had never looked more glorious. The absence of streetlights made the heavens seem deeper, more vast, stars upon stars that almost made him catch his breath. He felt so small, so insignificant, just a speck in the universe. Yet he knew he was more than that. He was precious in God's sight.

At that thought, something stirred inside him. He looked up at the skies again, trying to grasp the truth that was running through his mind ... the truth that this outage had to do with exactly that.

How precious he was.

How precious every human on earth was.

His heart began to pound as he got closer to that truth.

What if this was all some kind of divine wake-up call, a loving reminder that there was more to life than hurry and busyness and stress and work? A reminder that God was the only One to be trusted, the only constant in life.

The only sure thing.

He sat down, weighted by a sense of profound loss—and an even more profound gain. It would be all right. God would see to it. This wasn't meant to break those affected. It was only to make them stronger.

That truth seeped into him, settled into his bones, calming and relaxing him. And with that relaxation came a deep fatigue. He could sleep now, knowing that God was in control.

The quiet assurance settled into his bones, making him see the night with new eyes. It seemed less threatening, but he knew better than to let his guard down. The neighborhood *seemed* to sleep soundly, but it had seemed that way last night, too. And all the while a killer had taken over the Abernathys' house.

That peace he'd had for a moment faded, as he remembered those bodies he'd seen on the floor.

He glanced around once more, then went back inside, locked the door, and got a cup of water. Instead of drinking it, he went to the sink and splashed it on his face, trying to stay awake.

It was all he could do to keep his eyes open until two, but finally the hour came. He went upstairs to Jeff's room. The door was closed, so he opened it and stepped into the darkness.

"Jeff, time to get up, buddy."

There was no sound, so Doug felt his way to the bed, reached down to shake Jeff awake.

No one was there.

"Jeff, where are you?" He went to Jeff's bathroom door. It was open, but Jeff wasn't there.

Doug went back to the living room, got the flashlight he'd put on the mantel, and took it back upstairs. He shone it from one room to another, looking to see if Jeff was sleeping with Logan or somewhere else in the house. But Jeff was nowhere to be found.

Anger flashed through him. Racing back down the stairs, Doug headed into his own bedroom and woke Kay. She sat up, squinting at him.

"What is it?"

"It's Jeff. He's gone."

"Gone? What do you mean, *gone*?"

"He must have gone to Zach's after we told him he couldn't. It's two a.m. and he's not home."

"Oh, Doug!" Fully awake, she got out of bed and pulled on her robe. "You've got to go after him."

"I'm going," he said, "but I don't want to leave you alone."

"It'll be all right," she said. "Just give me a gun."

Doug led her into the study, where he pulled out their .22 and loaded it. "I didn't see Jeff's gun. Maybe he at least had sense enough to take it with him."

He helped Kay check all the windows and doors, making sure they were locked. Deni had opened hers, and she protested as he closed them, but he told her to go back to sleep and leave them locked. She was too tired to argue.

When Doug was sure the home was secure, he left Kay sitting alone in the great room and walked to Zach's. What would make Jeff defy his authority this way? Had he forgotten about the murders?

He walked a block in the opaque darkness, his flashlight off to save the batteries, and wished for more moonlight to help him on his way. Then again ... it was probably better for it to be so dark. Less chance someone would see him and suspect him of being the killer. Anger burned inside him that his son had put both of them in such a position.

As he grew closer to Zach's house, he heard the sound of loud laughter, which made him even angrier. He'd forbidden Jeff to hang around with Zach for the last couple of years, ever since Doug and Kay determined that Zach's parents were too "cool" for their own kids' good. Zach was always acting out in school and getting suspended, and his parents blamed the principal and the teachers for his behavior. When Zach and Jeff were in eighth grade, Zach had been caught bringing alcohol to the Valentine's Day dance. That had been the final straw. Kay and Doug forbade the friendship to continue.

So ... had Jeff been defying them all along?

Doug went up the sidewalk to the front door and knocked hard. No one answered. He went around to the side of the house, opened the gate, and stepped into the backyard. He saw his son sitting in the light of the fire blazing in a makeshift pit. Jeff had a girl in his lap and a beer in his hand. The pungent odor of marijuana wafted on the breeze.

Rage launched Doug across the grass. His son didn't see him coming until he was right in front of him.

"Dad!"

"Excuse me, dear"—Doug took the girl's hand and pulled her up—"but Jeff has to come home." He fixed his son with a glare. "Now, Jeff."

"But, Dad!"

"Just tell me one thing," Doug said through his teeth. "Did you bring your shotgun with you or not?"

"Yeah, I did. It's—" Jeff looked around, eyes suddenly wide, as if he'd forgotten where he'd put it.

Doug smelled the alcohol on his son's breath.

"Oh, there it is." Jeff's attempt to walk straight was overdone.

He wondered how many beers the boy'd had. And *where* were Zach's parents?

Jeff retrieved his gun from where he'd left it on the patio, then hung it over his shoulder like a soldier marching off to war. Doug jerked the weapon out of his hand and opened the action to see if it was loaded. It was. Just what he needed. A drunk son with a loaded gun.

"We're going home," Doug said.

Jeff looked back at the girl and shrugged. A few of his so-called friends muttered disappointed good-byes.

Thankfully, Jeff kept his mouth shut as he followed Doug out the gate and into the street.

"Dad, look, I'm sorry. I jus' wanted— "

"Your best bet is to not insult me with your explanations," Doug said through his teeth. "I counted on you to take over for me tonight, but I should have known you weren't mature enough to take that responsibility."

"Dad, you *can* count on me."

"*How?*" he shouted. "How can I count on you when you're drunk?"

"I'm not drunk. I jus' hadda few beers." The assertion would have been far more convincing were it not slurred. "No big deal. I jus' wanted something fun to do. It's been a real drag around that house."

"It's a drag everywhere. You think *I'm* having fun?" Doug asked. "You think your mother's having fun? Do you think *any-body* out here is having fun?"

"Does it have to be that way? What's wrong with having a few hours of fun?" Jeff asked. "It's not like we were drinking and driving. It was no big deal. Just a bunch of guys horsing around."

Doug swung around, putting his face inches from his son's. The smell of alcohol almost knocked him back. "There is a *killer* in this neighborhood, Jeff. Two people were murdered last night. Don't you understand how serious this is? I had to leave our family vulnerable and come looking for you tonight. Your mother is keeping guard. Is that all right with you? Because it's sure not all right with me."

Jeff's face paled. "I'm sorry, Dad."

"Oh, you'll be sorry, all right."

Jeff was quiet as they finished the trek home.

Kay was waiting, and she took one whiff of Jeff and ground her teeth. "How *dare* you?"

"Mom, I'm sorry."

"Don't tell me you're sorry. You're one of the men of this house. You're supposed to help your father. He needs you. He can't do this by himself."

"I'm here now! I'll keep watch for the rest of the night."

"No, you won't." Kay started to cry as she pointed toward the stairs. "You go to your room and go to bed. Sleep it off. We'll deal with you in the morning."

Jeff just stood there. "Mom, please don't cry. I didn't do anything that bad."

"You've been drinking," she said. "You're sixteen years old and you've been drinking. You know that's forbidden in even the best of times. Why in the world would you do it now, when things are so scary? Why would you do that to your father? Why would you do it to yourself?"

"I didn't mean to."

"Didn't *mean* to?" Kay grabbed his chin, forcing him to look at her. "Did someone force you to drink?"

"No."

Doug heard footsteps on the stairs, and he turned to see Deni come into the doorway. "Mom, what's going on? What happened?"

"Your brother snuck out," she said, keeping her eyes on Jeff. "That's what."

Deni looked disgusted. "What is wrong with you?"

"Shut up, Miss Perfect," he said. "I didn't do anything you haven't done a million times before." He stormed past her and marched up the stairs.

"That's not true!" Deni turned back to her parents. "Mom and Dad, he doesn't know what he's talking about."

"I don't want to hear it." Kay sounded as weary as Doug felt. "Just go back to bed."

Deni opened her mouth to argue, but Doug pointed at her.

"Deni, do it!"

She huffed out a breath, but slowly headed for the stairs. He leaned against the wall rubbing his eyes. Doug was exhausted, but he couldn't even consider going to sleep.

Kay eased one of the guns out of his hand. "Honey, you go to bed. I'll stay up and keep watch."

Doug straightened. "No, that's my job."

"Don't be macho, Doug. You're not doing anybody any good by depriving yourself of sleep. The fact that I'm a woman does not make me helpless."

"Yeah, Dad."

He turned and saw that Deni stood in the darkness at the bottom of the stairs. "I told you to go to bed!"

"But I can help, Dad! I can stay up with her."

He didn't know how much more he could take. He turned back to Kay. "I didn't say you were helpless, Kay. I just feel that it's my responsibility."

"It's all our responsibility. I'm going to be fine. I'm wide awake now, anyway. Now go to bed."

Deni stepped back into the light. "I'll keep her company, Dad. It'll be fine."

"No," Kay said. "I don't want to talk to anybody right now, and you need your sleep, too, Deni. Just go to bed. I'm going to need you more than ever tomorrow. We have to get up early and get in line at Wal-Mart. Everyone needs to be at their best."

"But, Mom—"

"Deni, enough!"

Deni blew out a heavy breath, then muttered as she headed up the stairs.

Kay looked at Doug. "So, are you going to go to bed?"

He slumped down on the couch and slowly lay down. "I'm just gonna lie here for a minute and close my eyes. You can keep watch while I do that, but I'll be close by if you need me."

She sighed. "All right, if you'll sleep." She left the room, then came back a few minutes later with a pillow. She slipped it under his head. Doug put his arm over his eyes and tried to do as she had said, but he couldn't escape that feeling of failure. He wondered what he had done wrong to make his son rebel this way. And was it true that Deni had a history of sneaking out when she lived at home? Why would Jeff have said that?

Despite his whirling questions, fatigue swept over him, fogging his thoughts until he finally surrendered and fell into a shallow sleep.

JEFF WENT TO HIS ROOM, CHANGED INTO SOME DRY SHORTS, THEN climbed into his rumpled bed. His head was beginning to hurt, and nausea lurked at a distance, threatening to take him down.

He'd disappointed his father and made his mother cry. But what was the big deal? It wasn't like he'd gone out and looted someone's house. All he'd done was drink a few lousy beers.

And if he got right down to it, his father had disappointed him, too. He squeezed his eyes shut, mortified that his dad had pulled Mandy off of his lap and dismissed her, like she was some kind of tramp.

He hated to think what she was thinking about him now. Would she even give him the time of day tomorrow? Somebody else was probably walking her home as he lay here in his bed, punished like a four-year-old.

He thought of his mom downstairs, sitting with the gun in her lap, guarding the house that he should be protecting. Yeah, well ... it was her own fault. He could have taken over. Just because he'd had a few stupid drinks didn't mean he wasn't able to guard their house.

Fatigue pulled over him, and he turned on his side, giving in. Sleep. He needed sleep.

He'd deal with his parents' wrath tomorrow.

TWENTY-TWO

Kay kept herself awake by making a list of things they could get at Wal-Mart when it opened in the morning. As she did, thoughts of Jeff's defiance raced through her mind. Where had they gone wrong? What could have sent him into such rebellion?

She thought back on exact moments in her son's history, when key choices had been made about punishments and consequences. That time he was in fifth grade and got caught smoking in the bathroom at school ... She should have handled it differently. She should have come down harder on him, taking away his television and video games. But no, she'd just confined him to his room, where he had all his entertainment at his disposal.

Last year he'd flunked a midterm. She should have grounded him through the Christmas holidays, instead of putting it off and giving him a chance to pull up his grade.

Incident after incident ran through her mind, opportunities she'd had to discipline her son. Opportunities she'd let pass out of ... what? Fatigue? Apathy?

If she'd handled things better, maybe he would have thought twice before sneaking out tonight.

The sound of a distant scream startled her, and she jumped up with the shotgun, and ran to the back door. She peered out the window, but couldn't see where the sound was coming from.

Another scream cut through the night. Trembling, she backed away from the door.

A popping sound followed, like a gunshot or a firecracker, followed by more screams. *"Doug!"* she shouted.

He sat upright on the couch. "What?"

"I think I heard a gunshot, and a woman screaming!"

He launched off the couch and took the gun from her hands, and opened the door to listen. The screams were escalating, and there was another shot.

"Get the other gun and wait here," he said. "I'm going to see what happened."

"Doug, be careful. Please!"

Her trembling hands closed and locked the door behind him, and she watched out the window until he was out of sight. Then she ran for the other gun, and keeping it aimed at the door, she sat like a sentinel, waiting for her husband to come back.

DOUG FOLLOWED THE SCREAMS TO A HOUSE ON THE NEIGHBORING street. People were coming out of their homes, racing toward the sound. He got to the yard and ran to the open front door. The soft glow of a lantern inside allowed him to see the other neighbors who had rushed over to help. A woman he'd never met sat inside, crying hysterically.

He stepped inside. "What happened?"

Brad, Doug's neighbor, turned back to him. "She had an intruder."

"I heard gunshots," Doug said.

The woman was trembling as she tried to control her sobs. "I shot at him! But I couldn't see him well in the dark, and I must have missed. He got away."

Doug stooped down in front of her. "Did you get a look at him at all?"

"No. I just heard him breaking in. We've been out of town and only managed to get home today. He probably thought the house was still empty. When I heard someone down here, I came down and called out, thinking it might be someone in my family. But I frightened him, and he knocked over that sculpture over there."

Doug saw the toppled bust lying on the carpet.

"When I fired my gun, he took off. He couldn't have gotten far."

Doug left the others to calm her and stepped back outside, looking up and down the street. Whoever it was had to be long gone by now.

Brad came out of the house and joined him on the street. "So it goes on." Brad's voice was deep, sullen. Doug looked at his neighbor. Brad was wearing a black T-shirt and a pair of black shorts. With his black skin, he blended into the darkness.

"Maybe he left fingerprints, footprints," Doug said. "Somebody needs to go get the sheriff."

"Can't be me," Brad said. "I've got to guard my family. No way I'm leaving them alone after this."

"Yeah, me either." He looked back over his shoulder, into the house. "At least no one was hurt this time."

"Who knows what might have happened if she hadn't had a gun?"

Doug didn't want to think about that.

When someone went for the sheriff, and it seemed that enough people were at the house calming down the woman, Doug went back home.

Kay was waiting at the door. "What happened? Was there another murder?"

"Not this time. The woman who lives there—Brenda Grant—had an intruder, but he got away."

"The gunshots?"

"They were hers."

Kay caught her breath. "Did she hit whoever it was? Can she identify him?"

"No, she thinks she missed him. And she didn't see a thing. It was too dark."

Kay started to cry and sank down onto the couch. "Oh, what are we going to do?"

He sat down next to her. Rubbing a weary hand across his face, he tried to think of something to say, something to give her some peace. But he wasn't sure there was any to offer.

TWENTY-THREE

NEITHER DOUG NOR KAY SLEPT FOR THE REST OF THAT NIGHT. While Doug paced from window to window, Kay tried to refocus her thoughts to the Wal-Mart list. She may not be able to do anything about a killer lurking in their neighborhood, but she could at least plan a strategy for getting what they needed at the store.

It wasn't likely many of the things they needed most would even be on the store shelves, so Kay figured she'd shoot for things others might not think of, things that would make their lives easier if the outage continued. She prioritized her list, then divided it into five small lists—one for each member of the family ... except Jeff. She had other plans for him.

By the time dawn began to break, Kay's shoulder muscles ached with fatigue, and she longed to take a nap. As light filtered in through the window, Doug finally seemed to relax.

"Why don't you go to bed?" she asked him. "We can go to Wal-Mart without you."

"No, we all need to go. It's too important."

She was glad he felt that way. "I've made a list of things we can try to get, but we all need to put our heads together and make sure we've thought of everything."

"What time does the store open?"

"Nine o'clock, they said last night."

He yawned. "You know they're going to be out of everything."

"Food and perishables, of course," she said. "But if we're smart, we might get some other things we need."

"Such as?"

She looked down at her lists. "Plastic bins, garbage cans, anything with wheels for carrying lake water. Wagons, dollies, garbage bags, bleach, camping equipment, lanterns, ammunition, candles, matches, axes, saws"—she shrugged—"and a lot of stuff we may not think of until we get there. But we should tell the kids the kind of things we're looking for, then they can grab them and meet us at the registers."

"You're sure the store is taking checks?"

"That's what they said last night."

He seemed to consider that for a moment. "I guess they figure they can cash them as soon as the banks open. But that could be awhile, and even when they do, the checks will probably be worthless."

"Why? We're good for it. We have plenty of money in our account."

"Kay, if this lasts as long as I think it might, the whole banking system could collapse. We're talking economic catastrophe."

Her mouth fell open. "But they have to give us our money!"

"Not if they don't have it."

Kay just stared at him for a moment, realizing he was right. Finally, she swallowed the panic trying to rise inside her. "I can't think about that right now. I have to focus on Wal-Mart."

He pulled her close and kissed her forehead. "Good idea. One thing at a time."

DOUG WELCOMED THE FRESH FEEL OF CLEAN CLOTHES WHEN HE changed a little while later. He went back downstairs to help Kay flesh out the lists the best he could. Then, when time was growing short, he woke the kids, briefing them one at a time on what needed to be done.

"I don't want to go," Beth said. "Can't I stay home? We're not gonna be able to get anything. It's just gonna be crowded and hot."

"I'm going." Deni slid out of bed. "I need a million things. Mascara, deodorant, fingernail polish—"

Doug groaned. "Deni, we're going for necessities. Come on, Beth. Get up."

He went to Logan's room, got him out of bed, then headed to Jeff's.

His son lay facedown on his bed, his sheets tangled around his legs. His mouth was mashed against the pillow, and a wet spot had formed where he'd drooled.

The dull ache of disappointment knotted Doug's stomach. He touched Jeff's leg. "Get up, Jeff. Come on. Time to wake up."

Jeff slowly turned over and squinted up at him. Wincing, he clutched his head.

"It's called a hangover," Doug said. "Now get up and get dressed. We have to go to Wal-Mart."

Jeff turned back over. "I don't need anything."

"Get up! I'm not telling you again. Be downstairs in ten minutes, dressed and ready to go."

Doug went downstairs and ate dry cereal for breakfast, wishing for coffee. But there wasn't time to get the fire going on the pit.

A few minutes later, the kids had gathered, and Kay doled out their breakfast as she went over the lists she'd made.

"We can't get all that stuff!" Deni said. "There's no way."

"We'll do the best we can," Doug told her. "And you can each make substitutions if you see something that would work just as well. Or if you see something we don't have on the list, and you know it would help us, grab it. Just remember, don't waste time looking for the obvious stuff. You'll never get it. Food items are probably already gone. Anything to drink is probably going to be cleared out. So each of you head for the department your mother gives you, and find the things we need."

"*I* need mascara," Deni said. "And deodorant."

Doug didn't have the patience for her. "We don't have time for cosmetics."

"She's right, Doug." Kay leaned over the table and made a notation on her list. "Deni, go ahead and go to the hair and makeup aisle. You'll need to grab some hair dye. I use Fountain of Youth brand, number 43 — Soft Brunette."

"Hair dye?" Doug gaped at his wife. "Shouldn't we go for the higher priority items first?"

She lifted her eyebrows. "Hey, in about three weeks that *is* going to be a high priority item. Deni, get the other things first, since I doubt there'll be a run on cosmetics. After you've finished the rest of your list, go and grab as many boxes of that color as they have. We don't know how long this outage will last, and I don't intend to go gray. And we should get toiletries. Anyone who sees toilet paper should grab as much of it as they can. Also paper towels, plates, cups."

Jeff scanned the lists. "There's not a list for me. What do you want me to get?"

"You're going to stay outside the store and watch our bikes."

"*What?*" He looked at his mother like she was crazy. "Why?"

"Because. We don't want our bikes stolen, and you can fend off the thieves. You'll take your shotgun with you and wait until we come back out."

Jeff groaned. "So how will we get all our loot home?"

"We'll cross that bridge when we come to it," Doug said.

When they'd finished breakfast, they all mounted their bicycles and headed to Wal-Mart. It was only five miles away, and as they pulled onto the main road leading there, they saw the other bike traffic heading that way. It was going to be a madhouse.

Jeff pulled up beside Doug as they pedaled, zigzagging through the stalled cars. "Dad, I know you're mad about last night. I was just trying to have a little fun. It's been really depressing around here. I just went over to Zach's to swim and be with my friends."

"After I told you not to."

"But you were being unreasonable."

Doug breathed a bitter laugh. "So you bucked my authority and took matters into your own hands, went over there, and got drunk."

"It's not that big of a deal, Dad. There's not all that much else to drink."

Doug gaped at him. "Oh, that's rich! You drank beer because you were *thirsty* and there was nothing else to drink. Beautiful." The kid was clueless. "Bottom line, Son, that's not going to happen again. We're in a crisis, and I need your help and support. I'm not going to tolerate your disobedience when lives are at stake."

They reached the parking lot, full of stalled cars. A mob had already formed in front of the doors, waiting for them to open. "So what are you gonna do, ground me?" Jeff asked. "There's hardly anything you can take away. I can't use a television, a phone, a computer, video games ..."

"I'm not going to ground you, Son. I'm going to work you."

Jeff moaned. "Well, that's just great."

"Your mother and I are tired, so you're going to take up the slack today."

Jeff muttered something Doug couldn't hear as they got to the edge of the crowd.

Almost everyone had a bike. Doug wondered if they planned to take them inside. He led his family to the side of the crowd, and ordered the kids off their bikes. Then he took the chain he'd brought with him, laced it through the wheels, and locked it with a padlock he'd found in his tool box. The key was in his pocket. Hopefully that would keep anyone from grabbing one and flying.

The morning grew hotter as the crowd pressed in, waiting for nine a.m. Though the mood was somewhat lighthearted, everyone wore an expression of stark determination. Doug studied those around them. Were they as organized as his family?

A couple of employees showed up at eight-thirty and slipped in the door to the optical department. He hadn't noticed that door before. As he watched them close and lock it behind them, it occurred to him that the front doors were electric. Would they even be able to get them open?

He nudged Kay. "I think we're at the wrong door."

She glanced back at the other door at the center of the building. "Why?"

"This door's electric," he whispered. "You think we ought to wait by that one instead?"

She eyed the front doors again. "You're right. Those may not open. Let's go."

Quietly, they motioned for the kids to follow, and went to stand in front of the optical department's door. Several others noticed and immediately followed. Within a few minutes, much of the crowd had moved.

But the Brannings were at the front. That meant they'd have the best shot at getting the items they needed.

He peered in through the glass. The small optometrist's waiting room on the other side of that door was dark. He hoped it wasn't like that inside the store itself. He wished he'd brought his flashlight. The Wal-Mart he and Deni'd stopped at on the way home from the airport had skylights that made it possible to see. Maybe this one did, as well.

At eight forty-five, the crowd pressed closer, threatening to stampede the moment the door was thrown open. Doug looked down at Logan, who was almost crushed in the crowd. The boy was sweating profusely. His face was red, but he stood like a track star waiting for the starter's gun.

"You okay, Son?"

Logan didn't take his eyes off the door. "I'm ready, Dad."

Doug glanced back at Jeff, who stood away from the crowd. He'd leaned the bikes against the brick wall and sat down on the sidewalk, sulking with the .12 gauge in his lap.

Some of the people around them still clutched their own bikes, clearly planning to roll them in with them. He hoped they'd stop them. Hundreds of bicycles in the store would only add to the chaos.

Finally, they saw someone emerging from the darkness, and the manager began to unlock the door. Carefully, he opened it and stepped out of the way.

The Brannings burst inside, grabbed shopping carts, and took off in five different directions. Behind him, he heard the manager yelling that bikes weren't allowed inside. Perfect. They'd have an even greater head start as people scrambled to take care of their bikes. Thankfully, there were skylights, so the building wasn't dark.

Doug headed to the firearms section for more ammo. He was the first one at the counter, but there wasn't an employee there to help him. The ammunition was locked in a glass case. There was no time to wait. He'd have to come back when he'd gotten everything else.

He hurried to the camping supplies instead, trying not to run anyone over as he pushed his cart to the back corner of the store. He passed rows of televisions and stereos lined up on the back wall. There was no one in those sections, but dozens of others rushed to sporting goods. He hoped he wouldn't have to fight anyone for the lanterns he was going after.

When he got there, the lanterns were already gone, but he managed to find two axes in the next section over. He tossed them into his cart, then scanned the aisles to see if there was anything else they could use. The area was getting too crowded, and people grew more agitated as the shelves emptied. Disheartened, he decided to head for the batteries.

He saw Kay rushing across the floor, rolling a two-wheeled garbage can behind her. It was one of their priority items, since they could transport water from the lake in it. He congratulated her as he ran past.

The checkout lines at the front were already beginning to form. The manager looked frazzled as he stood at one of the two open registers, yelling out, "Cash or checks only, please! We can't take credit cards! Cash or checks only! And have all your information on the checks, including social security numbers."

Doug pressed through the crowd to the paper towel section. With all the people filling the store, it felt as though the air was being sucked from the room.

He caught a glimpse of Kay making her way through the aisles again, rolling that garbage can beside her and dodging runners with their kamikaze carts.

It was absolute chaos, and Doug knew his own family contributed to it. But what else could they do?

KAY HAD MANAGED TO GET SEVERAL OF THE ITEMS ON HER LIST. The rolling garbage can was a major win, and she'd filled it up with waste baskets and stacking bins, two bottles of bleach, and several packs of diapers and powdered formula for Amber Rowe. She spotted some kerosene lamps on a top shelf, and letting go of her can, climbed the lower shelves to reach them.

"Score!" A teenage girl grabbed Kay's garbage can and started away with it.

Kay leaped down. "Wait! That's mine!"

"Ain't yours yet, lady!" The girl tried to get around a cluster of people blocking the aisle. Kay caught up to her and grabbed the can back, but the girl had no intention of surrendering it.

"You're not taking this!" Kay said through her teeth. "Give it back."

The girl swung and hit Kay in the stomach. Kay let go, doubling over, the breath knocked out of her. The girl started running, dragging the can away. Kay launched out after her, but the girl pushed through the crowd, disappearing out of her sight.

She tried to go after her, but there were dozens of people between them. And what would she do if she caught her? Attack a teenager? She couldn't have her children see her fighting, or have Doug stumble upon her in a catfight on the floor.

She had to face it. She'd lost it all.

There wasn't time to wallow in defeat, so she hurried back to the plastics aisle and grabbed the only two remaining Rubbermaid bins. They didn't have wheels, and they weren't very big, but she knew she could use them. She stacked one inside the other, then tried to run back through the store again, retracing her steps, hoping to find the items she'd just lost.

All but a package of diapers were gone.

Tears welled in her eyes as she hurried from one place to another, finding nothing on their list. The only things left were clothing, greeting cards, electronics, and DVDs.

She saw Beth and Logan coming toward her with a red wagon. Beth was crying.

She hurried over and grabbed the wagon's handle, determined not to let anyone snatch it. "What's the matter, honey?"

"We had some butane tanks in the wagon. And this man came along and just grabbed them out."

"I tried to stop him," Logan said.

"He went after him and kicked him, but the man pushed him down and got away."

"Logan! Never kick a man!" The thought of what might have happened made her shiver. "Are you all right?"

"Yes. But I'm gonna find that man and tell Dad. He won't let him get away with it."

"There's no time," she said. "Let's just stay together and make sure no one takes anything else. Come on, let's find the others."

While they were looking, they made their way past the untouched racks of clothing and headed back to the toy section.

"Look, Mom! Skateboards! There are two left." Logan ran ahead and climbed up three shelves until he could reach them.

"Logan, you don't have time to look at the toys!"

He grabbed the two boxes and jumped back to the floor. "Mom, look," he said on a whisper. "We can use the wheels. Make another wagon or something. It'll be good for hauling things."

Kay hesitated, then realized her son was wiser than she thought. "You're right. Let's look for more wheels. Skates. Riding toys. Anything that's left."

Kay's spirits rose as they found several wheeled toys—apparently no one else had thought of them. She grabbed them and piled them into the wagon.

The wagon piled high, they ran to the hardware section and grabbed several rolls of duct tape, then made their way back to the front of the store. They took their place in the long line of people waiting to check out. Fights were breaking out all over the store, and people were shrieking and yelling. There was no one there to help keep order.

A young employee stood at the doors, trying to make sure no one escaped without paying for their merchandise, but as Kay stood there, she watched several people push out past him. There was nothing he could do. Things were getting dangerous. She couldn't wait to get home.

She hoped Doug and Deni would make their way to the front before either of them was injured.

DENI DRAGGED THE WHEELLESS GARBAGE CAN BEHIND HER AS SHE ran through the aisles. She saw her dad in the housewares section, putting two windup clocks into his cart.

"Dad!"

He looked up and grinned when he saw the garbage can. "Great, you got one."

"It doesn't have wheels. Are you sure it's worth the trouble?"

"Yes, it's worth it." They could find a use for it. He looked into the can and saw the other items Deni had collected. She'd scored several packs of batteries before the crowd had cleaned them out. That must have been her first conquest.

"Mom's already in line," she said. "I saw her at the front."

"Okay, let's go. I think we've got about all we're going to find."

He dumped most of the things he'd accumulated in his cart into the garbage can, then carried it to the line where Kay waited.

"No breaking in line, buddy," the man behind her shouted.

"We're together," he said. "We're writing one check."

"No way. I've been waiting here for twenty minutes."

"We're all gonna get waited on," Doug said. "You got your items."

"You're not pushing in front!"

Doug sighed. "Fine. We'll get at the back of the line."

"Not fair!" Logan cried. "We were here first!"

Doug shot the man a bitter look. "Just do it, Logan."

The kids looked as if they'd just been disqualified from the big race, but they convoyed back to the end of the line, and Doug brought up the rear.

Kay's face glistened with sweat as she scanned the items they'd found. "Deni, thank heaven you got a garbage can."

Doug looked for hers. "I saw you with one that had wheels. Where is it?"

"Stolen," she said. "Right out of my hands. I almost got beaten up trying to get it back."

Doug groaned, and pulled all their things together. "Let's get in a circle around them," he said. "That way no one can grab anything."

The family encircled their plunder, dragging everything up as the line moved forward.

"I hope Jeff's all right." Kay looked toward the entrance of the store. "It's a madhouse here. People are going absolutely nuts."

"He's fine," Deni said. "He's got it easy, the wimp."

Doug hoped she was right.

TWENTY-FOUR

JEFF COULDN'T BELIEVE HE'D BEEN RELEGATED TO SITTING outside like some kid who couldn't be trusted with anything really important. Yes, he'd messed up big-time last night, and he knew there would be repercussions. But his parents were cutting off their noses to spite their faces. He could have been helpful inside, but instead he had to sit here wasting time.

He could have slept later.

An hour went by, the sun rising ever higher in the sky, its heat beating down on him with relentless oppression. His head still pounded from last night's events, and he wished he'd eaten more breakfast. He felt a little sick, and dreaded the thought of throwing up on the pavement. He didn't think he would, though. No, this was the kind of nausea that hung with you all day long, like a stalker waiting to strike.

The first shoppers started coming out of the store, their arms loaded with purchases. A group of guys gathered outside the door, talking quietly and looking his way. He recognized them from school, though they weren't in his circle of friends. They were a year or so behind him, probably freshmen.

They'd each cultivated that "tough dude" look, the one that dared anyone to cross them. He tensed up as they came toward him, then decided to stand to look a little more intimidating, just in case they planned to start trouble.

The tallest one, whose sleeves were cut off at the seams, wore a tattoo of a snake that wound around his biceps. The ringleader, Jeff thought. The others followed him like little dogs.

The ringleader grinned as he came nearer. "How's it goin'?"

Jeff nodded. "Fine. You guys get anything good?"

"Not yet. You're Jeff Branning, right? The pitcher?"

He grinned and stuck out his chest. "Yeah. You guys play?"

"Not us. No way."

The kid eyed the bikes behind him, and Jeff's muscles went rigid.

"What you doing with all these bikes?"

"They belong to my family. They're in the store, so I'm watching them. There are a lot of freaks around, you know. Taking stuff that doesn't belong to them."

The barb amused the kid, and the other four guys slipped behind Jeff, admiring the ten-speeds.

"Nice," the tattooed one said. "Ain't they nice, guys?"

"Yeah, real nice."

"What's this one?" one of them asked. "A BMX? Looks brand-new."

Jeff glanced over his shoulder. "It's about a year old."

"Let me get a better look at it." The kid took it by the seat and handlebars and tried to lift it free.

Jeff lifted his shotgun. "Sorry, man. Hands off."

The kid raised his hands. "Hey, I wasn't doing nothing wrong. I just wanted to see it."

Jeff didn't let his gaze waver. "Look without touching."

The ringleader started to laugh then, and the others seemed amused, as well. Jeff braced himself for a fight. He took a deep breath and stood with his legs slightly apart, ready for whatever they pulled.

Whack!

Pain smashed through the back of his head, knocking him to the ground. The bikes crashed beneath him. The tall one grabbed his gun, but Jeff didn't let it go. He got to his feet and chambered a round. "Back off!"

His assailant backed away. The other guys were rattling the bikes, trying to get them apart. No way, he thought. Not on *his* watch.

He fired into the sky, startling them all.

"Get out of here, or I'll kill you!"

The thugs hesitated, as if waiting for the ringleader to act.

Jeff chambered another round. "You guys have a death wish?"

They all backed off then, and scattered like billiard balls. Jeff waited until they were out of sight, then touched the back of his head.

He was bleeding, big-time. Shaking, he pulled his T-shirt off over his head, wadded it up, and pressed it against his gash.

At least the bikes were intact.

He stood there, trying to catch his breath as reality hit him. This wasn't just a frivolous day in the life of a shopping family. And this was no ordinary power outage. There might not be terrorists overthrowing the government, but one thing was painfully clear.

They were at war.

And like it or not, he was a soldier on the front lines.

TWENTY-FIVE

KAY BREATHED RELIEF AS SHE CAME OUT OF THE STORE. They had taken her check with no problems, but she knew the fight wasn't over. Their purchases were fair game to anyone bigger than Doug.

She looked for Jeff through the people in the parking lot, and saw that the bikes were all toppled over. Jeff sat on the ground.

Deni gasped. "Mom, he's bleeding!"

Kay started running. As she grew closer, panic exploded through her. Blood was smeared under Jeff's nose and across his cheek. He had taken off his shirt and pressed it to the back of his head, where blood had soaked through.

"Jeff!" Doug passed her, bolting toward his son. "What happened?"

"Got hit from behind," he said. "I don't even know what with."

Kay fell to his side and took the shirt from his hand, carefully peeled the wad away. At the sight of the gash, she started to cry. "You could have been killed! Who did this?"

"Stupid jerks trying to get the bikes. But they didn't get any, Dad. I ran them off."

Deni and Beth stood over him, horrified, but Logan was revved up and ready to go after them. "Which way did they go?"

"Every way. They scattered."

Deni stooped down in front of him. "Do you know who it was?"

"Some freshman freaks from school. I'd know them if I saw them again. You bet I'm gonna look them up in the yearbook and report them to the sheriff, whatever that's worth." He got up as his mother kept the bloody shirt pressed to his head. "Let's just go. I want to get out of here. I'm sick of this."

"But you're still bleeding! We'll just sit here a minute until it stops. Doug, we have to get him to a doctor. He needs stitches."

Doug nodded. "That Morton couple that moved in behind us ... isn't he a doctor?"

"I think so."

"Then let's get Jeff home, and I'll go get him."

Jeff took the bloody shirt from his mother, and he got on his bike. Deni touched his arm. "Jeff, I'm sorry for what I said about watching the bikes being an easy job, calling you a wimp and everything."

Jeff breathed a bitter laugh. "Yeah, next time we'll leave *you* out here. This whole thing stinks, you know! It's like the end of the world. The power's been out for less than thirty-six hours, and everybody's gone crazy."

Doug looked around as if to see if anyone else threatened them. "Come on, guys. Let's get the bikes up, and I'll unlock the chain. We'll go home the back way, so we won't have so much trouble. Jeff, can you ride?"

"Yeah, no problem."

"The bleeding is letting up," Kay said. "Doug, I'm not sure he can handle the gun, so I'll take it."

Jeff shook his head. "No way, Mom. I'm doing it. Dad, I'll lead us home, and you can bring up the rear with your rifle. If we all stay together, we should be all right."

Kay started to protest, but she knew it would do no good. Besides, Jeff needed to get his dignity back.

Deni mounted her bike, her eyes darting back and forth, waiting for another attack. "But how are we gonna get all this stuff home?"

Kay had been wondering that herself. In answer, Doug pulled some backpacks out of his bike's carrying pouch and passed them around.

"Stuff whatever you can into the backpack, even if it's sticking out the top. Deni and Kay, you'll need to ride side by side carrying the garbage can between you. Logan and Beth, see if you can balance any of the containers on your handlebars, but only if you can handle it."

Everyone got on a bicycle. Doug looked at Jeff again. "You sure you're up to this, Son?"

"Oh yeah," he said. "Just let somebody try to mess with us."

"Don't get cocky," Kay said. "Just stay alert."

"I will, Mom. Don't you worry about that."

Kay didn't like the Rambo attitude, but she couldn't blame him for his bravado. His pride was wounded, and he had the gash on his head to remind him of his humiliation. And it didn't help that the attackers were younger than he.

They took off through the parking lot, dodging people and trying to stay together, and Jeff led them down the back streets where there weren't as many stalled cars or bikers trying to get through town. Kay and Deni struggled to keep the heavy garbage can between them as they rode.

"I'm dropping it, Mom! Move closer to me."

Kay tried to ride at the same speed as Deni without pulling her own bike over, but it was difficult with the heavy backpack on her back. Logan and Beth each balanced Rubbermaid containers full of stuff on their handlebars as they rode.

The family was quiet as they sailed through the streets, past people walking down the center of the roads. Some of those walking called to them, trying to make them slow down and stop, but Jeff slowed down for nothing.

Kay wondered if this was how soldiers felt in a time of war, driving through a hostile town in a Humvee convoy, waiting for a rocket launcher to shoot out of nowhere. *Was* this hostile country? Had it gone from being America the free, where people helped each other for the common good, to America the terrorized, where death could come from any quarter? Whatever caused this power outage sure had brought terror on the people.

When they finally made it to their own street, they rolled up their driveway and into the open garage. Everyone was exhausted, sweating, and red-faced. They let their bikes fall, and Doug quickly pulled the garage shut behind them.

Finally, they were safe.

Kay dashed into the house and headed for the bathroom. She grabbed the alcohol and a towel, and hurried to doctor Jeff's wound. Doug headed out the back door. "I'll go see if I can get the doctor to come."

"Good. Tell him to hurry."

Jeff winced as she began to clean the gash.

TWENTY-SIX

THE MORTONS LIVED TWO HOUSES DOWN FROM DOUG'S backyard neighbors. They'd met the young couple a few months ago when the mailman delivered a piece of their mail to the Brannings. Doug and Kay had returned it together and welcomed them to the neighborhood. He hadn't seen either of them again until Cathy came to the meeting last night.

Cathy, who looked about five months pregnant, let him in and told him Derek was sleeping after being at the hospital all night, then doing the twenty-mile bicycle commute back from the city. When Doug told her about Jeff, she woke her husband, and he agreed to come.

Back at the Branning house, Derek donned his rubber gloves and checked Jeff's pupils and his coordination. "I think you're okay. No sign of a concussion. I'll stitch it up and you'll be good as new."

Jeff's face twisted. "That's gonna hurt worse than being knocked in the head."

Derek chuckled. "No, it won't. I'm going to deaden your scalp with a shot of xylocaine first."

Doug watched as the doctor got a vial out of his bag and stuck a syringe in it. When the needle was ready, he turned to Jeff.

"Ready?"

Jeff squeezed his eyes shut as Derek stuck the needle into the skin around the wound. When he was satisfied it was numb, Derek began sewing up the wound.

"So did you hear all the commotion last night?" Doug asked as the doctor worked. "It was just down the street from you."

Derek tied off the first suture. "No, I wasn't home. Cathy heard it, though. She was scared to death for the rest of the night. She didn't find out what happened 'til this morning."

"I don't think many of us got much sleep last night," Doug said.

"So have they found the intruder?"

"No, not yet. He didn't leave any clues behind. The sheriff dusted for prints, but that's not going to do any good unless they catch a suspect and compare his fingerprints. Without a suspect or the computer system that searches for matching prints, fingerprints aren't much help."

Derek finished the second stitch and closed it off. "He probably wore gloves, anyway."

"May have."

Derek finished the third and fourth stitches, then cleaned them up with alcohol. "Now, that wasn't so bad was it?"

Jeff shook his head. "I guess not."

Derek took off his gloves and returned his supplies to his bag, then looked up at Doug. "I did want to ask you about the meeting last night, since I couldn't come. Cathy said you thought the outage was going to go on for a long time."

Doug told him Brad's theory about the semiconductors being damaged.

"Unbelievable," Derek said. "I was thinking it couldn't possibly go more than another few days. But I should have realized that was wishful thinking when we tried to start up our generator at the hospital and it failed. Even this morning, one of our administrators brought his own little generator from home. The minute he started it up, it conked out, too."

"I guess that's a real problem for a hospital," Doug said.

"You have no idea. I don't know what we'll do with all our patients. And I thought malpractice was going to be my major problem as a doctor. Who would have ever thought?"

"So you have to ride twenty miles back and forth to work?" Jeff asked.

"Yeah. Every muscle in my body hurts from this morning's ride, after a tough night of work. I'm not in shape for this kind of thing." He rubbed his stubbled face. "The thought of going back just wears me out. And if this is going to go on for a while, then we need to make some long-term plans. We're running out of food at the hospital. There's no place to cook. Our monitors and equipment don't work. If the power doesn't come back on, people are going to start dying."

The words shuddered through Doug. The minor inconveniences they'd suffered were minimal compared to the tragedy this outage was to others.

When Derek went home, Doug sat down with Jeff at the table. "You okay, Son?"

Jeff's face glowed with sunburn. "Yeah. Just mad. Those guys were like animals. They might have killed me. And I would have killed them. All to defend a bunch of bikes."

"Been there, done that," Doug said. "And yes, it seems pretty silly in retrospect. But at the time, it feels like life or death."

Jeff's weary eyes met Doug's. "A ten-speed bike is *not* life or death. Or it shouldn't be. This is bringing out the absolute worst in people."

"Yeah, I know. It's likely to get worse before it gets better."

Jeff looked down at his hands. "Dad, about last night ... I'm really sorry for sneaking out. It was immature and irresponsible and deceitful. I don't even know why I did it."

Doug leaned on the table. "Tell me how often you smoke pot, Jeff. I smelled it when I came through the gate."

Jeff looked surprised. "I didn't think you knew what it smelled like."

"Hey, I was your age once. I had friends tugging me that direction, too."

"Well, I didn't smoke it. It was Zach's brothers. They weren't even near me when they did it."

"You didn't answer my question."

Jeff grunted. "Never, okay? I don't smoke pot. I was a little hacked when they lit up."

"But not hacked enough to leave, huh?"

Jeff sighed.

"What about alcohol? How often do you drink? And don't tell me that was your first time."

Jeff seemed to consider how to answer. He folded his arms in front of him, and stared down at the grain on the table. "No, it wasn't. But I don't drink a lot, Dad. Just a beer every now and then, when I'm hanging out with the guys."

"You know how your mother and I feel about that."

"Yeah, I do. You think a person can't be Christian if they drink. But Jesus drank."

Doug had been all through this when Deni went to college. He was ready. "Son, let's just cut to the chase. When you drank that beer last night, did it make you more careful, more intelligent, more mature, more trustworthy?"

Jeff closed his eyes. "No. But it didn't make me *less* those things, either."

"Well, let's see. You snuck out to go over there, probably fully intending to come back before I knew you were gone. What happened to that plan?"

He waited, knowing Jeff didn't want to admit that, with his inhibitions lowered from intoxication, he had forgotten his intentions. "Time got away from me. It's hard when you don't have a watch."

"I see. And what about the bikini-clad girl in your lap? Was that part of your plan? How much farther might *that* have gone if I hadn't shown up when I did?"

"No farther."

"Oh, really? Jeff, I raised you to be a gentleman, with moral values. I taught you Christian principles about how to conduct yourself with girls. Would you have had that girl sitting in your lap if you'd been sober?"

Jeff didn't answer.

"So what makes you think drinking didn't change your behavior, lower your inhibitions, and cause you to do things you would never have done before?"

"I have my values," he said. "I told you, I'm not gonna have sex before marriage. None of that has changed."

"Can you be sure of that? With a few more beers, and a willing girl? Privacy didn't even seem to be an issue for you. You were making out right in front of everyone."

"It was dark, Dad. Nobody was paying attention."

"That's supposed to make me feel better?"

Jeff set his cheek on his palm. "I won't do it again, okay? You don't have to worry."

Doug looked into his eyes. He'd grown up so fast. It seemed like only yesterday he'd been learning to play T-ball. Man, he'd been cute running those bases, his little cap flopping on his head.

Doug's voice softened. "Jeff, every day of your life you'll have to make decisions about what kind of man you want to be. It's not going to start when you're older. It starts right now. And every time you make a decision to be less than what God wants for you, you're denying yourself some of God's blessings. It's up to you. You can live a life with God's blessings, or just exist with all the consequences of choosing wrong."

Jeff held Doug's gaze, and he knew he was listening.

"When you put it that way, it sounds easy."

"It's *not* easy. I'm not saying it is. But once you make up your mind whose side you're on—God's or your drinking buddies' or a pretty girl's—it's up to you to make sure you don't compromise those decisions through drinking or anything else. One wrong choice can change your whole life, Jeff. Just one. And one right one can turn you away from a world of trouble. So next time someone offers you a beer, I hope you'll make the right decision."

Jeff only nodded.

Doug rubbed his sweating face, raked his fingers through his hair. "Jeff, why do you think this outage is bringing out the worst in people?"

"I really don't know."

"Because without transportation and communication, there's not all that much accountability. People think they can get away with things. And they all have some overblown sense of entitlement. If things are hard, then they think they have a right to act like animals—to loot and rob and attack."

"I'm not like that, Dad."

"No, you're not. But it's not that big a step to cross the line into immorality. We have to agree that we're not going to cross it."

"Okay, Dad. I'll do my best."

Doug believed he meant it.

"So what's my punishment?"

Doug sighed. Jeff had had a really bad day. He'd been punished enough. Maybe it was time to move on. "Let's call it even," he said. He slid his chair back and got up. "Well, I have work to do. I need to go to the lake and get water."

"I'll help."

"You sure you're up to it? You have a good excuse—"

"I don't need an excuse, Dad. I can pull my weight."

Doug rubbed his son's neck. Jeff was going to be all right. Doug had no doubt about it.

Together, they'd be ready for whatever came next.

TWENTY-SEVEN

THE MORNING'S EVENTS WEIGHED ON DOUG LIKE A LEAD blanket, as mounting fatigue slowed him down. Each muscle group in his body had convened to register its protest. If only the Jacuzzi were working. A good hot soak would relax the lactic acid right out of his thighs, his calves, his feet, his toes, his shoulders, his arms.

Dream on.

He'd gone through the motions of the day regardless, bringing water from the lake and trying to think hours ahead to what they would need to have done before dark. When Sam Ellington approached him about coming to a meeting for some of the men in the neighborhood, he'd hesitated. But Sam convinced him it was for the safety of Oak Hollow.

He wondered why Brad hadn't told him about the meeting. When Doug saw Brad earlier that day, he'd complained that there had been no takers on his idea. Well, maybe they had surprised him in the last few hours.

Doug reached Sam's house on River Oak Drive, and saw the man's mud-covered pickup sitting in the driveway. The front door was open, so he knocked and stepped inside. Six men, sitting in the living room, looked up at him. Brad was not among them.

Sam welcomed him in. "Come on in, Doug. You know these guys? Alan Newman, John Henderson, Mike Hinton, Lou Grantham, and Paul Burlin." Each man stood to shake

Doug's hand. "We're all members of the same hunting group, but we wanted to bring you in since you're kind of taking the lead in the neighborhood."

Doug recognized some of them from the meeting the other night. The men sat back down, and Doug took the empty place on the couch.

"Doug, we're glad you came," Sam said. "Me and the guys were just doing a little strategizing about how we're gonna protect these streets since the sheriff is failing to do his job."

"Good," Doug said. "That's what I was hoping we'd do when Brad brought it up at the meeting last night."

He noticed the looks pass among the men. Sam went on. "We decided the way to go about this is to set up nightly patrols for a while until we catch the killer. If we see somebody suspicious, we'll search their property."

"Search their property?" Doug sat straighter. "We don't have the right to do that, do we? I mean, that's the sheriff's job."

"We ain't got time to worry about the law right now," Lou Grantham said. Doug regarded the man, taking in his western-style shirt and the big belt buckle that sported a mustang. Grantham looked like he belonged on a Texas ranch rather than in an Alabama suburb. "We got to root out the problem before anybody else winds up dead."

"And we don't plan to wait for the justice system to act when we catch the guy."

Doug looked at John Henderson, who spoke in a low, modulated voice. "What do you mean?"

"When we catch the guy, he won't make it 'til trial."

"Nope," Sam agreed. "We won't bother the sheriff with it. We'll take care of it ourselves."

Doug shot to his feet and looked down at the men. "We can't do that! We're three days into a power outage, and you guys are acting like the only solution is anarchy. Yes, there's a killer somewhere, but we can't prowl around the neighborhood with our guns drawn, kicking in doors and searching homes."

Sam's friendly look turned hard. "Who's gonna stop us?"

Doug recognized the threat in his tone. "Look, before we start taking the law into our own hands, let's get Brad Caldwell involved. He's an attorney. He can advise us on what rights we have and which ones will get us locked up. Besides, I thought he was heading up the neighborhood watch. Does he know about this meeting?"

Again, looks passed among the men.

"We don't need some black ambulance chaser telling us how to protect our families," Sam muttered.

Now Doug understood. They were forging ahead with Brad's idea, but leaving him out. "Are you seriously telling me that you'd deny the help of a very capable and willing man because he's *black?*"

"He don't even belong in this neighborhood in the first place." Lou crossed his cowboy boots as if that settled the matter.

"Why not? He's a good man with a great family. Why shouldn't they live here?"

Sam stood up, looking eye to eye with Doug. "We don't trust Brad Caldwell. Now, either you're with us or you're against us."

Doug wasn't going to back down. "I just want an explanation. Why don't you trust him? And you've got to have a reason better than the color of his skin."

"You want a reason?" John Henderson's low, calm voice belied the hatred in his eyes. "His kind thrive on criminal activity. It's natural to make him the first suspect when things start happening."

"No, it's not!" Doug stared at the men for a moment. Didn't they realize this was the twenty-first century, and not 1960? "You're out of your mind. Brad Caldwell is *not* the killer."

"How do you know?"

"Because, he wouldn't do that. I'd suspect any one of *you* before I'd suspect him." The second the words were out of his mouth, he knew they were a mistake.

Two more of the men got to their feet, staring him down. What would they do? Jump him right here in Sam's living room? Clearly, it was time to leave.

"Look, I don't want any part of what you're doing here." He started to the door, then turned back at the threshold. "And I'm giving you a warning. If I see any of you breaking the law, I'm going to the sheriff. The last thing this neighborhood needs is six more gun-wielding yahoos with bad intentions."

He almost expected them to come after him as he marched down the sidewalk toward home, but none of them did. They were probably already marking his address as the first door they would kick in. Either that, or they'd burn a cross in his yard. Let them try. He'd be ready for them.

TWENTY-EIGHT

Jeff's headache got worse as the numbness around his stitches wore off, and his mouth felt full of cotton as the temperature and humidity rose. His dad had put him to work in the garage, fastening wheels on the containers they'd bought. Thanks to duct tape and a dolly, he managed to convert the new garbage can into something that rolled.

Deni sat on the floor, duct taping skateboards to the bottom of some of the larger Rubbermaid tubs.

"Hey, Jeff."

Jeff looked up and saw Mandy standing just outside the garage. "Hey, Mandy." He got to his feet, grinning like an idiot. After his embarrassing exit last night, he figured she'd never again give him the time of day.

"Whatcha doing?"

"Working." He glanced at Deni, wishing she weren't here. "Mandy, this is my sister Deni."

The girls exchanged greetings, then Mandy turned back to Jeff and lowered her voice. "Is everything okay after last night? Your dad looked really mad."

"He was. I was supposed to take second watch and I forgot and let the time get away from me."

"It was my fault, wasn't it?" she asked.

Deni looked up at them, a smirk on her face.

Jeff shot her a look. "Don't you have a zit to pop or something?"

"Hey, I'm just sitting here minding my own business."

Jeff left his garbage can and walked out of the garage to where Mandy stood on the driveway. Lowering his voice, he said, "I admit, you distracted me a little."

Her grin said she was flattered by that.

"Hey, check this out." He turned his head and showed her his wound.

She caught her breath. "What happened to you? Did your dad do that?"

Deni laughed. "Our dad? He might have *wanted* to beat him, but that's not his style. He's more into psychological torture."

Jeff's look warned her to shut up. "No, it wasn't my dad. I kind of got mugged at Wal-Mart this morning."

"Really? I heard it was a madhouse there."

"Yeah, I got whacked in the back of my head. Doctor had to give me stitches."

She winced. "Ouch. What were they trying to get?"

"Our bikes."

"Did they get them?"

"No way. I fought them off."

Admiration sparkled in her eyes. "Good for you."

"Is it?" He set his hands on his hips. "I don't know. I was ready to shoot their heads off, but for what? A few stupid bikes."

"They're not stupid bikes," Deni said. "They're our family's only transportation. What else would you do? Let them have them?"

He wished she'd go into the house. "I wasn't talking to you, but since you insist on listening ... I'm saying that I fought for the bikes this morning because something inside me reacted, and in the heat of that moment, I would have killed to protect our property."

Mandy seemed moved by his honesty. "We fight for what's important, Jeff. You did the right thing."

"Yeah, but if we're going to fight to the death for something, shouldn't it be something worth dying ... or killing for? Would you kill someone for a bike, Deni?"

Deni winked at Mandy. "Depends. Is it a ten-speed or one of those no-frills kind?"

"So you'd kill for the frills?" he asked.

Mandy laughed, which only encouraged Deni. "Yeah, maybe." Deni rolled her eyes and headed for the door into the house. "Right now I'd kill for a glass of water, so don't get in my way."

Mandy giggled as Deni went in. Jeff didn't find it funny. "She is so clueless."

"I like her. She's cool."

Her giggle was good medicine. It was the best he'd felt all day. "I'm glad you came by."

"Hey, why don't you come back to Zach's tonight? We're going to be over there swimming again."

Jeff saw his dad coming up the driveway, and his smile faded. "No, I can't. I'm in enough trouble already, and my family needs me."

"All night? Can't you come for part of it?"

"No, I'd better not."

His father had an angry look on his face as he came into the garage. Jeff hoped he hadn't reconsidered grounding him.

"Dad, this is Mandy."

His dad wore a guarded look as he reached out to shake her hand. "Hi, Mandy. Nice to meet you."

Jeff braced himself, expecting him to comment on meeting her in Jeff's lap last night. But he didn't, and his silence was almost as awkward.

A hint of red crept into Mandy's cheeks. "Uh, well, I guess I should go."

"Yeah," Jeff said. "I'll see you around, okay?"

She smiled. "I'd tell you to call me, but ..."

It was enough that she wanted him to.

"See ya." He watched her walk away. When he turned back to his father, he saw the disapproval in his eyes. His joy faded.

"Dad, she's the best-looking girl at school. I've tried to get her attention forever, and now I think she likes me."

"I'd say she does, judging from the way she was acting last night." He looked at the wheels on the garbage can and rolled it to see how it worked.

"Dad, she's a nice girl. I know you might not have thought so last night, but she is. It's not like she just plopped down into my lap. I pulled her there. It was my fault."

"I agree. I blame you completely."

Jeff sighed. He couldn't win.

"Nice job here." His dad's face softened. "Let's try it out and head down to the lake. We need more water."

Jeff felt his father's anger still radiating between them, even though his words suggested he'd forgiven him. But why else could he be in such a sour mood? He hated it, but all he could do was earn back his respect. And he was starting to realize that might take longer than he'd hoped.

TWENTY-NINE

Doug kept what had happened at Sam's house to himself, since it wouldn't make the family feel any more secure to know that a bunch of angry, racist rednecks with guns were "protecting" their streets at night. But the conversation ate at him. That afternoon, as he got the family busy taking inventory of their food, he found his mind sinking back into that maddening conversation. He couldn't believe what jerks some of his neighbors were.

Trying to keep his mind focused, he went over the list the family had come up with. The provisions looked grim.

"We need to make up some very rigid menus, guys," he said. "No snacking. We have to make this food last as long as we can."

"Yeah, Jeff," Deni said. "He broke into the potato chips earlier."

"Hey, I'm not the only one who ate them," Jeff said.

"You opened the bag."

"And I forced them into your mouth and moved your jaw to make you chew?"

Doug sighed. "That's enough, you two. I'm serious. No more chips, unless they're on the menu."

"Then you'd better tell Mom to stop giving stuff away."

At Deni's remark, Doug looked up at Kay. "Giving what away?"

She sighed. "I gave some of our canned vegetables to Amber. I'm worried about her, Doug. She has to feed those kids somehow."

"Well, you have to feed *us*," Deni said.

As much as he understood Kay's helping the woman next door, he found himself more on Deni's side. She was right. They didn't need to be giving away their food. He studied the list. "We need to be realistic. This thing hit us unprepared. We don't have enough."

Deni pulled up and sat on the counter. "Dad, you have to be wrong about how bad things are. The power will be back on before we know it. It has to."

Beth started spinning a quarter on the table. "Hopefully before the next episode of *Thunder Down Under*."

"That's Thursday night," Doug said. "I can almost promise you nothing will be resolved before then."

Deni didn't want to hear it. "I'm leaving Friday, and that's all there is to it."

"In what?" Jeff asked.

"I don't know, but I'm going. And before I leave, I have a million wedding details to settle. I have to pick out the cake, order invitations, shop for my tiara."

Jeff moaned. "Give me a break! A crown? You're letting her wear a crown?"

Kay chuckled. "It's her wedding, Jeff."

"Shows what you know about weddings," Beth piped in. "That's what brides wear now."

"I thought they wore those stupid veil things."

Deni looked disgusted. "They wear the tiara *with* the veil, moron."

He grinned. "Tell the truth. You're really just marrying the guy for the crown. It's not him you love, it's the power."

She threw a pot holder at him. "Why don't you shut up?"

Jeff laughed. "Well, you gotta admit the guy isn't even your type. He's a workaholic and treats you like you ought to feel privileged he gives you any time at all."

Doug started to stop him, but these were things that he'd wanted to say for some time. He met Kay's eyes, but she didn't intervene, either.

"He's a mover and a shaker, okay?" Deni threw back. "That's what attracts me to him."

"Attraction is one thing, but marriage is another."

Doug stared at Jeff. When did his son get so wise?

"And you're a mover and a shaker, too, but you always have time for him whenever he can fit you into his busy schedule."

Deni threw her chin up. "You clearly have no concept of what an important person he is. And I'm not going to be some whining housewife who needs her husband's undivided attention twenty-four/seven!"

Doug braced himself as Kay flinched at that comment.

"Excuse me, young lady?" Kay said. "Are you insinuating that there's something wrong with being a housewife?"

Deni backed down then. "No, Mom. I didn't mean *you're* whiny and attention-starved. Just that I want to do more with my life. I want to make a difference."

Kay's jaw dropped. "And I haven't done anything with my life? I haven't made a difference?"

Doug tried to suppress his grin at the hole Deni had dug for herself. How in the world would she get out of it now?

"I didn't say that. Did I say that?"

"Sounded like you said that," Beth muttered.

Jeff crossed his arms and grinned. "That's what I heard."

Her siblings leaned back in their chairs, enjoying her predicament.

She took a deep breath and started over. "I'm glad you were a stay-at-home mom. It did make a difference. I wasn't making a comment on what *you* do. I was just saying that I'm strong enough to handle a powerful man who puts his work first."

Her words punctured something in Doug's hopes for her, and the air spilled out in a long sigh.

Kay just got up and grabbed the broom, and started to sweep the kitchen.

"Don't you believe me, Mom? That I didn't mean to insult you or any other housewives?"

"I worry about your attitude, Deni," she said. "I worry about your expectations. I worry about your arrogance."

"Me? Arrogant?" She grunted. "You've *got* to be kidding."

Finally, Doug entered the fray. "Deni, if you really want to suc-ceed in life—in the important ways, I mean—you need to put others first. That means you don't look down on people for any reason. A plumber can be much more important than a senator. A farmer could be a thousand times more important than an astro-naut. And the job of a mother is more important than any other job a woman can have. It requires strength, character, discipline, patience, organization, intuition, and a strong work ethic. And when you can't see those things, when your eyes are dimmed by your own ambitions and dreams, then sometimes God has to teach you how wrong you are. I don't want Him to have to do that. I'd rather you just loved people and saw them as worthwhile."

Deni's hands went to her hips, in that posture of arrogance again. "So you're saying I shouldn't have dreams? That I'm wrong to be ambitious? Then why did you send me to Georgetown in the first place?"

"We sent you there because of your grades, Deni. We felt you'd earned the right to go to the college of your choice. And yes, it's fine to have dreams, and I'm glad you're ambitious. But you shouldn't put yourself above others who choose differently."

Deni looked as if she'd been desperately misunderstood. "I *told* you, I'm not doing that. I know other things are important. So sue me for getting excited about my future. Maybe you'd rather I moped around all the time."

Kay sighed and got the dustpan, swept up the dirt, and dumped it into the ever-growing trash bag. "We want you to be happy, Deni. We really do. Let's just start over, okay? We have work to do, and we don't need to drag this conversation out anymore. We have more important things to talk about, like how we're going to man-age this crisis. We could be in the dark for weeks. Months, even."

Logan's face mottled red, and his mouth fell open. "There's no way I can sit in this house for months, in the dark, with no TV, no radio, no computer, no air conditioner, and no video games!"

From one fight to the next. Doug was too tired for this. "Logan, you may not have a choice." Doug got up, feeling the pull of those aching muscles again. And the oppressive heat didn't help matters. He wiped his forehead on his sleeve. "Now, Deni and Beth, I want you to help your mother make up menus for the next three weeks. Jeff and Logan, we're going to rig up something in the barbecue pit so we can boil water over the fire. We're also out of charcoal, so we'll need to chop wood."

"Dad, that's impossible. We can't get all that done today."

"We're all going to help. When the girls get finished with the menus, they can help us with the wood."

"I'd rather chop wood now than sit in this hot house making menus," Beth said.

Deni agreed. "Me, too. I can swing an axe."

Doug shot Kay a look, and she gave him a smirk. *Let them go,* it seemed to say. *Give them what they ask for.*

"Fine. Mom will stay here and work on menus, and the rest of us will go. But I don't want to hear any complaining. I expect hard work."

A LITTLE WHILE LATER, DOUG HAD RIGGED UP SOME SLOTS ON THE sides of the barbecue pit, so that they could raise and lower the grate depending on the kind of heat they'd need. That way, they'd be able to do more stove-top type cooking, rather than just grilling everything.

He'd led the kids to a forest area near the subdivision and instructed them to cut up fallen limbs. With the two axes they'd bought at Wal-Mart, they managed to make pretty good progress, tag-teaming as each got tired.

They had a good-sized pile and were loading it onto their wagon, when Doug saw Amber pushing her stroller through the woods, her three-year-old running ahead of her to pick up sticks.

"Hey, what are you guys up to?" Doug called.

Amber swung around, startled. "Oh, you scared me!"

"Sorry. It's just us."

She relaxed a little. "We're trying to gather some wood so I can cook. I don't have any charcoal, so I can't use my grill."

She took the sticks from her three-year-old and shoved them into the rack at the bottom of the stroller. Her nine-month-old slept, and her two-year-old whined and tried to undo the strap that held him in.

"We can give you some wood," Doug said. "We've got a good bit here. We'll bring some over when we get back to the house."

"Really?" Her eyes shone with relief. "Thank you so much. But I can't keep relying on other people. I've got to start doing some of this myself. I just ... don't have anything to cut the wood with. My husband took all his tools with him when he left. We were trying to collect the smaller pieces that we could break."

Doug glanced at the two axes his boys held. They needed both of them so that more than one person could work on these things at a time. No, instead of giving one to her, he'd rather just cut her some wood when he cut his own.

Then again ... with all the stuff he'd have to do over the next days and weeks, he hardly had time to take care of another whole family. But Amber needed help. What if that was Deni, abandoned by her husband and left with three kids? Wouldn't he pray that someone who lived near her would take her under his wing?

He set his hands on his hips. "Don't worry about it. We'll take care of it. How are you doing besides that? Is everything all right?"

"Yes. The diapers were a godsend. Thank you for grabbing them at Wal-Mart. I've been cleaning out my closet and trying to make some cloth diapers out of my old clothes, for when I run out."

"Good idea."

"The only thing pressing on my mind right now is safety. I can't sleep at night because I'm so busy listening for every little noise. I'm scared to death someone's going to break in ..."

She needed a gun. That would give her some measure of security, and provide a defense if the killer learned she was alone and vulnerable.

He looked at the shotgun Jeff had carried with him. It lay on a stump, close by in case they needed it. He had two others. He could certainly spare one.

As quickly as the possibility flitted into his mind, his reason replaced it. *Don't even think about it, Branning. You can't give her the gun. Your family needs it.*

But what would she do without it? If the killer knew her husband wasn't there, she'd be a perfect target.

His mind drifted back to Deni. She wasn't much younger than Amber, and he'd want her to have a weapon if put in the same situation. Somewhere, Amber's family was probably praying for someone to help her.

"I'll tell you what, Amber. I'll go home and get you one of our rifles. We'll be all right with just two."

"No, I can't take that from you! Your family needs it. Besides, I don't even know how to shoot it."

"I'll teach you." Even as he said it, he knew that was just one more thing he'd have to squeeze into this day. Teaching her the proper respect for the weapon would take more time than he could spare.

"Are you sure?"

He glanced at his kids, saw Deni's mouth open, and Jeff's eyes shooting spears into him. *Don't you dare, Dad*, they both seemed to say.

He looked back at her. "Yes, of course I'm sure. For the sake of your kids, you *have* to take it from me. You have to protect your family."

Her eyes glistened with unshed tears, and she thanked him profusely as she pushed the stroller back out of the woods.

Deni waited until Amber was gone, then spun on Doug. "How could you do that? We can't do without one of our guns!"

"And we have to cut twice as much wood from now on?" Jeff whacked his axe into a log. "Come on, Dad, what were you thinking?"

"What would you suggest? The woman is there alone with three babies. She needs help."

"Mom's gonna freak," Beth said.

He hoped that wasn't true. In fact, he was sure it wasn't. Kay was as giving and loving as anyone he knew. She would have done the same thing, had she been in his shoes. Hadn't she given Amber some of their food earlier today?

No, she would insist that he'd done the right thing.

"You're not giving her *my* gun," Jeff bit out.

"I'll give her the .22."

"No way!" Logan cried. "That one's mine!"

"It'll be okay. It's just a loan."

"Man!" Logan stomped his foot. "Not fair!"

"Nothing's fair, these days," Deni muttered. "So you might as well get used to it."

"YOU DID *WHAT*?" KAY'S FRUSTRATED QUESTION CLEARLY INDICATED he'd made a mistake.

"What would you want me to do, Kay? Amber's all alone and she has to defend her family."

"Doug, it's fine to give her some of our wood. And it's nice to help her when we can. I don't intend to pretend she's not in trouble. But our guns?"

"Just one of them."

"We'll need them when we split up. Say Jeff goes to a friend's house, and you're here, and I'm somewhere else. We'll each need to have one with us. It's dangerous to be unarmed with a killer running around. I wish we had five of them, but we *cannot* get down to just two."

"I understand how you feel. But I already told her we'd give her one."

"Well, you shouldn't have!"

Doug slammed his hand on the counter. "Okay, do you want to go over there and override me? Tell her that you're sorry, but you can't agree to giving her one of our guns? Kay, she's not much older than Deni. I keep thinking how I would want people to respond if it was our daughter in this situation."

Kay wilted. "No, I don't want to tell her that. I can't believe you put us in this position. Just give her the stupid gun. In fact, give her some of everything we have. Give her half of our food. Our toilet paper. Give her our water. Then she'll think we're really nice people, and that's what it's all about with you, isn't it, Doug?"

He couldn't believe her attitude. "Why are you acting like it's some mortal sin to care for people?"

Kay looked as if he'd slapped her. "How dare you suggest that I don't care for people? I gave her food today. I bought her diapers."

"And I want to help her protect her family. What's wrong with that?"

"Your first priority should be taking care of your family!"

Doug wanted to kick something. "My family is fine."

"She's right, Dad."

Doug shot Deni a warning look, then turned back to Kay. "I have to do this, Kay. Amber's husband is a jerk, and he's left her to endure this alone."

"So you have to be completely responsible for her now?"

"Kay, it's not like that."

"Isn't it? You'll take something important from your own family to give to some needy woman, and I'm supposed to just accept it?"

"Yes, just like I accepted it when you gave her food, even though I don't know how we're going to feed our family much longer!"

Kay's eyes filled with livid tears. "You didn't say you were upset about the food I gave her. You didn't say anything at all!"

"I was biting my tongue, okay? But I know why you did it. It's the same reason I'm doing this." What was left of his energy seemed to pool in his feet, and he pulled a chair out from the table and dropped down. Would this day never end? "Look, if it means this much to you, I won't give her the gun. I'll tell her the family talked about it, and decided we couldn't. Maybe someone else can give her one."

Kay leaned on the chair, gritting her teeth as she thought that through. "No one else is going to want to part with theirs, either."

"Then this is a lose-lose situation. Kay, what do you want me to do?"

She blew out a long breath and raked her fingers through her hair. "Just give it to her. With all the other stress, I don't need guilt hanging over my head, too." With that, she stormed out of the room.

Doug sat there a moment, looking up at Deni. "I really don't know what to do."

Deni grinned. "If you ask me, I think we should go find her husband and kick his rear. You haven't been in a good fight today."

"Not funny."

"And while we're on the subject, you can quit picturing me in her situation. That would never happen to me."

Doug didn't respond. Instead, he forced himself up, got a box of .22 caliber cartridges and the .22 Winchester, and he and Beth took them over to Amber. After a lesson in how to use the gun safely, she thanked him again. "I don't have any money to pay you. I didn't get to the bank before the power went out, but I'd like to give you this." She went to her refrigerator and pulled out a watermelon sitting on the bottom shelf. "It's not cold anymore, but it's ripe and probably really good. It might refresh your family."

"Sweet!" Beth said.

But Doug pushed it away. "No, Amber, I can't take that."

"Please, do. I had it for my parents, who were supposed to come from Tuscaloosa this weekend. They won't be coming now. And I don't like to have watermelon just for us because it's such a mess. I don't have enough water to clean us up. I'd feel so much better knowing you all could enjoy it."

"Come on, Dad!" Beth started jumping up and down. "Watermelon! It would be so good to eat watermelon."

He grinned. "All right. Thanks, Amber."

They crossed the yard, and as soon as he walked in the door, Logan and Jeff attacked him.

"Watermelon. Cool!"

"Can we eat it now, Dad," Jeff asked, "or do we have to save it?"

"We'll eat it now," he said. "Take it outside and cut it on the patio table."

He found Kay sulking in their bedroom, looking out the window at the kids and the watermelon.

"She gave us a watermelon as thanks for the gun."

"That was nice."

"Yes, it was."

She turned back to him, and tears came to her eyes. "You know, I don't like what this is doing to me. I'm not like this. I feel this desperate need to hoard what we have. Whenever I think about our neighbors, I start realizing we might have something they need. Maybe that's why we were so detached from them before. I thought it was because we were so busy, we only had time for an occasional wave across the yard. But maybe it was really because I'm selfish and didn't want to get in a position of having to give."

"That's not true," Doug said. "If you knew they had a need, you'd have given them the shirt off your back."

"That's just it. I *didn't* know, and I wasn't all that interested in finding out. I'm scared, Doug, and I don't want to give anything else up."

He sat down next to her and pulled her against him. "I feel exactly the same way. It's gonna be okay."

"Is it? I keep waiting for the other shoe to drop. Are there Muslim militants waiting to invade our neighborhoods? Maybe they've already invaded the big cities. Are we sitting ducks?"

He wished he could reassure her, but the same questions had been spinning through his mind. "Whatever happens, we'll be all right. God will protect us and provide for us."

Kay nodded. "I know He will. I keep telling myself that. The thing is, I've never had to really believe it before. All these years,

I've been so arrogant, thinking that whatever happened, you and I could provide. I haven't really known what it's like to be in need. But here we are, three days in, and I'm already losing it."

"You're not losing it. It's just been a bad day all around. And hey, maybe this is a good thing. Maybe it's time we find out what it's like to need, so we can see how big God is."

But even as he said the words, that fear in his mind seemed to grow a few inches.

THIRTY

FRIDAY—THE DAY DENI WAS SCHEDULED TO RETURN TO Washington—came without any change in their situation. She woke angry, feeling sticky and filthy, her hair plastered to her head. She had dirt under her fingernails from chopping wood and working like a slave. What if Craig somehow showed up and saw her like this?

Even worse, what if he didn't?

She'd gone days without talking to him before, when he'd been so busy with work that he didn't have time to pick up the phone. But mostly she talked to him every day. She missed him, and wanted to hear his deep, rumbling, hurried voice. She wanted to see the smile in his eyes when he came to her door. Wanted to feel his arms around her—those arms that made her so proud that he would want her when he could have almost anyone.

She wondered what he was doing today. Was he in the dark, too? Was he upset, realizing that he wasn't going to see her soon? Was he making plans to come and get her? Maybe he was already on his way.

After a grueling day of work, she put on makeup and pulled her greasy hair up into a ponytail at the top of her head. With bobby pins, she secured it in a bun, then used hair spray to hold it in place.

The spray was a bad idea, its scent adding to the smell of sweat and smoke from the barbecue pit. But at least she didn't look as much like a hag as she had for the last few days.

When she went down for their pitiful supper, Beth looked up at her. "We're going fishing tomorrow at Lake Bishop! All of us, even Mom."

Great. Another family field trip. "I don't want to go," Deni said.

Her mother frowned. "Why not?"

"Because, I don't feel like it, okay? I was supposed to go back to Washington today. It stinks that I'm still here, and I don't want to go fishing."

"If you don't fish, you don't eat."

This was ridiculous! "Then how come Amber Rowe always gets to eat? I'll bet *she's* not going fishing, but you'll surely bring something back for her."

Her mother's face tightened. "If there's extra, we will. But our first priority is to feed *our* family."

"Yeah, right." Deni looked at her father, who had that tight look on his face. "Can't you give me a break? Don't you realize what I'm going through? I haven't talked to Craig in five days! I'm going nuts. All I want to do is go back to Washington, but it's like the universe has conspired against me." She slammed her hands on the table and got up, went to the kitchen sink to get some water from the pitcher. She poured a glass, took one drink, then spat it out. "It tastes like mud flavored with bleach. I'm *sick* of this!"

"Deni, we're all sick of it," Kay said. "This has curtailed all our plans. And Craig will be all right. If you love each other, then you can handle being apart for a while. He'll still be there."

She spun to face her mother. "*If?* That's it, isn't it? You don't think he loves me! You think I'm just some starry-eyed girl who's in love with the wrong guy. You've never liked him, either of you!"

Doug's jaw dropped. "What? Why would you say that?"

"I see that look on your face whenever you're around him, like you've bitten on a lemon. And everything you say to him is sarcastic. You're happy we're not together, aren't you? You've probably been praying for divine intervention to stop our marriage from happening."

Her dad just stared at her. "Right. The outage is all about you. Somehow your mother and I rigged up an EMP to keep you away from Craig."

"Stop putting words in my mouth!"

"Deni, I know you're upset." Her father's tone was sharp, and his eyes told her he wasn't going to put up with much more. "But you are not going to talk to me or your mother that way."

She chewed on her bottom lip, expletives flying through her mind—but she knew better than to utter them. "I'm still not going fishing."

"Fine." Her mother showed no sympathy at all. "Then you won't eat fish. Be satisfied with a helping of peas for supper tomorrow."

"Maybe I'll go to *Amber's* for dinner."

Kay was fed up. "Go to your room, Deni."

She breathed a laugh and looked up at her mother. "I am twenty-two years old, not some kid who can be grounded."

"You're a guest in my home," her mother bit out, "but if you insist on acting like a child, you will be treated like one. Go to your room. I've had enough."

Deni wanted to upend the table, with all the dishes on it. She wanted to kick a hole in the wall. She wanted to get on her bike and ride until she couldn't ride anymore.

Instead, she stormed up the stairs, and sat like a kid in Supernanny's "naughty room." Defiance spiraled through her, and finally, she got up and donned her swimsuit, and put her clothes back on over it. She needed a swim, and she'd promised to go with Chris to Vic's tonight. She packed a towel in her tote bag, then headed downstairs.

Her family was out on the back patio, so she slipped out the front, knowing they'd stop her if they knew what she was doing. It was after eight, and dusk colored the street in gray tones As she headed to Chris's, she feared the swarming mosquitoes more than the killer, since there was still some light. Didn't killers only strike after midnight?

Out of habit, she glanced to the right and left before crossing the street. As she did, she caught a glimpse of someone several houses back stepping behind a house as if hiding from her. She looked harder, trying to see who it was. They were gone.

She crossed the street, then turned back. She saw the shadow of a man coming out from behind the house, but quickly he stepped behind a tree.

Was that Brad Caldwell?

She turned from him and walked faster, wondering if he was watching her. If so, what for? It wasn't like she needed a babysitter.

No, his hiding seemed more sinister than that. Like he was stalking her or something.

She glanced back, and didn't see him. Maybe he was gone. Maybe he was playing hide-and-seek with his children. This was, after all, Brad Caldwell, Birmingham attorney, Jeremy and Drew's dad.

But until the outage, they'd hardly interacted with him at all. How did they know what kind of man he really was? People had secrets. Some deadly.

She was out of breath by the time she reached Chris's. Her friend had been waiting for her. Deni told her about Brad as they walked to Vic's. As they turned up his driveway, she saw Brad again. He was closer now, but still trying not to be seen. Thankfully, Vic answered the door quickly. The dog yapped up at her.

"Deni! Chris! What a surprise!"

Deni looked over her shoulder and bolted inside without being asked. "Close the door!" she said. "We're being followed."

He picked up Scrappy. "By who?"

"My next-door neighbor." She went to the window, looked out. "Never mind. I don't see him now."

"That black man? He was following you?"

She turned back to him, surprised that he knew where she lived. "I think so. I'm not sure. Maybe I'm just on edge. But I saw him and it made me nervous."

Vic and Chris looked past her out the window. "Well, you're welcome to stay here until you feel more comfortable," Vic said. "I can walk you home if you want."

Chris gave a nervous laugh. "Actually, we intended to come here. We were hoping you'd let us swim."

"Of course you can. It's all yours."

He stayed inside while they went out, and Deni swam laps. His little dog sat on the side of the pool, seemingly fascinated with both of them. After they both washed their hair over the grass, Vic came out with two glasses of lemonade. Sitting down on the lawn chair next to her, he handed her one. "Here, maybe this'll cheer you up. That guy really shook you up, didn't he?"

Deni took the glass and drank it gratefully. Chris was still in the water, floating on her back. "It's not just that. I've been in a blue funk all day. I'm furious at my family. They don't understand how much I want to get to my fiancé. I'm going crazy, and they think I should be happy as a clam to be here in Crockett with them."

"Crockett's not a bad place to be."

"No, if you don't mind living in the neighborhood with a killer."

He nodded. "Yeah, there is that. Have they gotten any closer to finding out who did that?"

"No, but there are a lot of rumors going around. I have a few ideas of my own."

"Don't tell me, let me guess. Are any of them saying Brad Caldwell was involved?"

She looked at him, startled. "No. Look, just because he was following me doesn't mean I think he's the killer."

Vic set Chris's glass down. "There are rumblings that he was out the night the Grant house was broken into, prowling around the neighborhood with a gun. When he first moved in, lots of people were suspicious of him, anyway."

"Why? Because he's black?"

"That probably has something to do with it."

"Well, I don't think his race should make him more of a suspect than anyone else. My dad and brother were out that night, too, and my brother's friends were getting drunk and partying. I'm sure they're all being looked at."

"Yeah, but we can't ignore the obvious. Especially if he was following you."

She didn't know what to think. "That's just it. This is not a safe place. That's only one of the reasons I don't want to be here."

"Then leave."

"How will I do that? Got any ideas?"

"A few. If this outage lasts much longer, I'm going to have to hit the road myself. I've been trying to think of what I could rig up to carry my stock in so I can visit my stores and make sure they're back up and running. I've got a few ideas for a wagon pulled by horses. I won't be ready for a few days yet, but when I go, you're welcome to come along."

She looked at him, struck by the simplicity in his tone. "You'd take me all the way to D.C.?"

"Sure. I have to go that far, anyway. My stores are all across the south. I'd have to stop at each one along the way, so if you don't mind that, I'd be perfectly willing to take you all the way to Washington."

She imagined telling her parents that she was leaving town with Mark's father. What would they say?

You can't go off with a perfect stranger. You don't know any-thing about this man.

But she knew his son, and he was a nice guy.

She regarded Vic as he fluffed his Yorkie's coat, pampering and kissing him. A man who loved his dog so much couldn't be bad, could he?

Of course, her parents would forbid her to leave, but that would carry little weight. She had to follow her heart and couldn't let them make decisions for her anymore.

Still ...

She didn't know Vic that well, and it would be awkward being on the road with a stranger for days, maybe even weeks. There must be some other way.

"I don't know," she said. "It's a possibility. I'll think about it."

"Do. You have a little time. It'll take me awhile to get things ready. And of course, I'm hoping that it won't come to that. If the power comes back on soon, then we'll both have our problems solved."

When they left Vic's, she hurried home, constantly looking over her shoulder. She didn't see Brad as she went by his house and slipped into her own.

Evading her parents again, she hurried upstairs and plopped onto her bed, as that seed of hope took root in her heart.

If things continued the way they were, at least she had one option. She could leave Crockett with Vic. It was something to hang on to.

THIRTY-ONE

FOR THE NEXT SEVERAL DAYS, DOUG AND KAY DIDN'T TALK again about the gun he'd loaned to Amber. But the tension was still there, rippling on the air like deadly fumes. There was never a time to air their marriage out. No date night to talk things over, no stolen trips in the car for a moment to work things out. At night, when they fell into bed, they were both too exhausted to tackle the subject.

Doug watched his wife flit around the house taking care of menial things that kept them going. While they were at the lake, Kay stayed home boiling water. While they dug a garden, Kay scrubbed dishes out on the back patio. While they met neighbors in the streets, Kay put together feasts from a can of green beans and a pack of dried noodles.

Recognizing her weariness one evening after supper, he told her he and the children would wash the dishes so she could go visit down at the lake. It had become the hub of the neighborhood, a place of fellowship and swapped information, where many gathered at the end of each day.

Kay stayed out until dark, then came back with new life in her eyes. She'd met several women she'd never seen before and reacquainted herself with others. She couldn't stop talking about a family who'd just moved in two weeks before the outage.

"They're about our age and have children the same ages as Deni and Jeff. Before they moved, they sold their children's bikes in a garage sale, so they're stranded. I think we should give them one of ours."

Doug thought he'd heard her wrong. "What?"

"Doug, imagine what this outage would be like if we didn't have bikes. They might have an emergency or something. They need a way to get around."

Doug couldn't believe he was hearing this. "I understand loaning it when they have to go somewhere, Kay, but not *giving* it to them. We need our bikes. It's the only thing making this whole thing bearable."

"They need them, too. We have six, Doug. We can do without one."

"So how come you're so charitable to them, but you were so upset when I gave Amber a gun?"

"I was upset because you told her she could have it without even asking me. But I'm asking you now. I haven't promised it to them yet."

"Then don't give it. Tell them they can borrow it when they need it, but I want it back."

Kay didn't like it, but she finally agreed.

Doug lay in bed that night, his rifle on the bed table next to him. Jeff was taking first watch. As exhausted as Doug was, he couldn't sleep.

Desperation was starting to sink in as he thought about the dwindling food supply in the pantry. What would they do when they ran out?

Each time he drifted off, he dreamed of himself and his family sitting in a basement room with shelves and shelves of things. Diapers, baby food, bags of flour, rice, water jugs, cans of beans and vegetables and soups, candles and kerosene lamps, toilet paper and napkins, plastic utensils, paper plates. People banged on the door, crying for him to open it and share, but he and his family sat there among their provisions, trying to ignore the cries of need outside.

He woke in a cold sweat, got out of bed, and went into the kitchen. Jeff sat at the kitchen table, nodding over last month's

Time. It had been a slow news month, so they'd focused on fad diets.

"Must be a great article." His voice startled Jeff awake.

"Sorry, Dad. I was trying to stay awake."

Doug smiled and pulled the magazine toward him. "They left one diet out. The running-out-of-food diet. Guaranteed to work."

Jeff stretched. "Yeah. Or the giving-it-all-away diet."

Doug looked at him in the lamplight. Had his son been worrying about the food they'd shared with Amber? Was that hoarding mentality plaguing him at night, too?

"Son, go on to bed. I couldn't sleep. I'll take the watch."

"You sure?"

Doug nodded, yawning. Jeff got up and quietly padded up the stairs.

Carrying the kerosene lamp into his study, Doug sat down at his desk. His Bible lay on the corner, so he pulled it to him and stared down at the cover. He needed to read it ... but where should he look for the answers to all the questions plaguing him?

He needed to know how to act in a time of crisis, when they didn't know if they had enough food or provisions, when people around them were desperate and in trouble. He needed to know what the line was between caring for your family and caring for your neighbors. He needed to understand what God wanted from him during this outage.

Teach me, Lord. Show me what You want me to see.

As he prayed, the Lord's Prayer came to his mind. *Our Father who art in heaven ...*

No, he didn't need to pray that. He needed to spill his guts to God, cry out to him for real answers. He needed to hear God's voice, not recite some rote prayer that didn't cover his needs.

Give us this day our daily bread...

Something told him to find that passage in the Bible. Where had Jesus said it? He filed through his memory bank. The Sermon on the Mount. Quickly, he turned to that passage — Matthew 5, 6, and 7.

And as he began to read, he realized why God had led him there.

KAY WOKE HALFWAY THROUGH THE NIGHT AND FELT THE BED next to her. It was empty. Doug still hadn't surrendered to sleep.

She lay there a moment, staring up at the opaque darkness, wishing for the light on her clock that she used to complain about. She had a washcloth that she threw over the red digital readout, and another that covered the cable box next to the television. The slightest light used to keep her awake—now the utter darkness disturbed her. It was like a living thing, its tentacles reaching around and into her, changing her in ways she didn't expect.

She sat up in the blackness, hating what this outage had done to her. It had caused tension in her marriage, made her angry and brooding. She and Doug were moving through their days like business partners rather than lovers. Loneliness enveloped her.

She got out of bed, slipped into her bedroom slippers, and felt her way through the house. She saw a yellow glow coming from the study, and stepped into the doorway.

Doug sat at his desk, studying the Bible that lay open before him, under the glow of the kerosene lamp.

"Couldn't sleep?"

He looked up at her, and she saw the dark circles under his eyes. "No. You either?"

She shook her head. "It's too dark, if you can believe that."

He smiled and reached for her, pulling her onto his lap. She melted like butter when he did that. Sliding her arms around his neck, she kissed him.

It had been a long time since it was just the two of them.

Keeping her head against his, she looked down at his Bible. "Find any answers there?"

"Yeah. Even some I didn't want to see."

"Oh yeah?"

He rubbed his stubbled jaw. "We're doing this all wrong, Kay. All the hoarding, all the clinging. I was just flipping through, trying to find relevant passages. Trying to understand what God might be doing, and what He might want from us."

"And?"

"And Matthew 5 and 6 kind of hit me between the eyes."

She looked at the page. "The Sermon on the Mount?"

"That's right. It's full of stuff we need right now. Like in chapter 5, verse 42. 'Give to the one who asks you, and do not turn away from the one who wants to borrow from you.' "

"But, Doug, that's for a time of normalcy. We're in survival mode. If we gave to everyone who asked for something, we might not have what our family needs. I understand why you didn't want me to give the bike away."

"And I understand why you didn't want me to give the gun. But look at chapter 6, verses 25 through 34."

Kay almost didn't want to know what it said. Grudgingly, she looked down at the passage, and began to read: " 'Therefore I tell you, do not worry about your life, what you will eat or drink; or about your body, what you will wear. Is not life more important than food, and the body more important than clothes?' " She paused and looked up.

"Go on," Doug said.

" 'Look at the birds of the air; they do not sow or reap or store away in barns, and yet your heavenly Father feeds them. Are you not much more valuable than they?' "

She stopped reading and got off of Doug's lap, moved across the room to a chair in the shadows.

"What's wrong?" he asked.

She sighed. "It's not that simple. People all over the world go hungry. They starve to death. I know God *can* feed them, but sometimes He doesn't."

"Sometimes He sends us to do it." Doug's eyes held hers.

"So what do you want us to do? Give away all our food? Put our family in jeopardy?"

"I don't know." He looked back down at the passage. "Look what Jesus said here: 'Who of you by worrying can add a single hour to his life? And why do you worry about clothes? See how the lilies of the field grow. They do not labor or spin. Yet I tell you that not even Solomon in all his splendor was dressed like one of these. If that is how God clothes the grass of the field, which is here today and tomorrow is thrown into the fire, will he not much more clothe you, O you of little faith? So do not worry, saying, "What shall we eat?" or "What shall we drink?" or "What shall we wear?" For the pagans run after all these things, and your heavenly Father knows that you need them. But seek first his kingdom and his righteousness, and all these things will be given to you as well. Therefore do not worry about tomorrow, for tomorrow will worry about itself. Each day has enough trouble of its own.' "

Kay pulled her feet up beneath her. "Boy, that's for sure."

Doug rubbed his tired eyes. "Kay, I know you hate uncertainty. I do, too. I hate not knowing what's going on, why this happened. I hate wondering how I'm going to provide for the family, when I've always been able to do a good job of that before. But I think God is telling us something tonight. He's saying that we don't need to worry. We need to have faith. And we need to give to the people around us who have needs. Instead of worrying, we need to be seeking His kingdom and His righteousness."

Kay came back out of the shadows and sat on the desk, just inside the circle of light. "I want to be a Christian in this, Doug. If there's some kind of test He's putting us through, I want to pass it. But how? What does it mean to seek Him first? I've always thought it meant starting your day reading the Bible and praying, going to church, thinking about Him. But what does it mean in *this* context? When people are out there looting and killing, and all the things we've relied on aren't working? When our minds are so full of all the stuff that has to get done, how do we seek Him first?"

Doug studied the passage again. "It says to seek His kingdom and His righteousness. Maybe that means that we look at this as an opportunity. Maybe we see it as a way to do His kingdom work. What would Jesus do if He were here? He wouldn't be hoarding, I'll tell you that. He'd be out going door-to-door to see who needed what. He'd help people. He'd show them love. And because He loved them, they'd want to follow Him."

She sighed. "Is that why God let this happen? To see if we had it in us to be like Christ?"

"Why *wouldn't* He let it happen? There are countries where most of the population functions without electricity. Why are we so special? He knows we can get by without it. He might just want to see what we're made of."

"I think He might be disappointed."

"We might be disappointed in ourselves. But we need to think about what He wants to teach us in all this. And we need to be ready to learn it."

Kay started to cry, and Doug reached up and wiped the tear from her cheek. She caught his hand and pressed it against her face.

"What if we used this as an opportunity for God's kingdom, Kay? What if we didn't see it as being about us, but about them? In Matthew 5, He talks about being salt and light. What if we really were salt and light, Kay? What would we do?"

Kay laced her fingers through Doug's and wiped her tears. They were tears of purpose, like the tears she cried in church, when the preacher talked of their kingdom work, and reminded them that they were to continue the work that Jesus started.

"I've always thought I trusted Jesus," she whispered. "But it was kind of easy, living in a four-thousand-square-foot house, parking my Expedition next to your Mercedes, cooking in a state-of-the-art kitchen and relaxing in the air-conditioning, in front of twenty-four-hour television that entertained us and informed us about everything going on in the world."

"Now's your chance to show that you trust Him without all that stuff, too."

Her face twisted as she met his eyes. "I hope it's true. I hope I do."

His smile warmed her. "There's one way to find out. It's time to start storing up our treasures in heaven, instead of hoarding them on earth." He got up and pulled her into his arms, and held her while she cried. Then, sweeping her hair back from her face, he whispered, "I think we need to pray. If we have willing hearts, we need a plan. And I don't have a clue how to start."

She pressed her forehead against his, and slid her arms around his neck. "You're right. Let's ask God how."

Clinging to each other, they began to pray.

THIRTY-TWO

THE WINDUP WATCH THAT DOUG HAD FOUND IN THE BACK of his dresser drawer said it was seven a.m. From his children's reaction when he tried to wake them, one would have thought it was still dark.

They assembled at the kitchen table in the light of the bay window, looking bleary-eyed and disheveled as they munched on the last of the Pop-Tarts.

"Dad, why can't we sleep late every now and then?" Deni muttered. "Everybody else in their right mind is sleeping."

"Yeah—" Beth yawned—"why can't we just sleep?"

"Because we have work to do," Doug said. "We need to get an early start."

"Work?" Jeff spoke with his mouth full. "Dad, if I had more sleep I could work *harder*. I don't even get a whole night's sleep. Shouldn't I get to sleep in?"

Doug almost felt guilty. It was true that Jeff had it worse than the rest of them. But he needed his help more than the others.

He looked from one child to the other. How would he ever motivate them? Deni looked hungover, as if she'd just come in from a wild party the night before. Jeff looked almost as bad. He hunched over his Pop-Tart, his hair stringing into his eyes. He needed to shave as badly as Doug did.

They could all stand a bath. All except Deni, whose hair looked cleaner than the rest of theirs. The sweat from the last few days had left a sour smell on their skin and in their

179

clothes. Their sponge baths with lake water had left a lot to be desired. Doug was glad when Kay opened the door to let some air circulate.

Beth looked bored, as if she had little interest in whatever her parents were going to say, and Logan, the one who seemed the most awake, flipped through a comic book he'd brought from his room.

Doug reached over and took it away from him. "I need to talk to you, and I want you to pay attention."

All eyes settled on him, annoyed.

"Guys, I've been thinking about our situation. It's been ten days and the power hasn't come back on. I'm guessing it's not likely to any time soon. Some people are getting desperate by now, and others are hoarding."

"People like us?" Beth said.

"Yes, exactly," he said, proud that she'd seen it. "People like us. But God dealt with your mom and me during the night, and we've realized that, as Christians, we're supposed to act differently."

"Uh-oh." Deni wiped her fingers on her paper towel. "Here it comes." Sighing, she tipped her head. "Different how?"

"I'm going to tell you. But first, is it all right for me to assume that everyone at this table is a Christian?"

They looked at each other as if they were insulted.

"Deni?" he asked.

"Well, yeah. You were there when I went down the aisle and got baptized."

"Was it real? In your heart, real?"

She huffed. "Yes, Dad. I'm a Christian, all right? You raised me that way. I've been indoctrinated."

Doug didn't know how to interpret that. "Wow. That sounds really sincere."

She looked away. "I'm sorry. It's just that you can't really be raised in this family without being a Christian, you know? That's all I meant."

"Being from a Christian family doesn't make you a Christian any more than sitting in a garage—"

"Makes you a car," Jeff finished. They'd heard it a million times.

Doug looked at Jeff now, since he'd jumped into the conversation. "And since you understand that principle, where do you stand?"

"I'm a Christian, Dad." He sounded as defensive as his sister. "It's not like we're drug addicts. We haven't given you reason to doubt us."

"I'm not doubting. I just want to hear it."

Beth spoke up. "*I'm* a Christian, Dad."

"Good, Beth."

"See?" She made a face at her brother. "He didn't even have to question me."

Doug met Kay's eyes. She shook her head.

"What about you, Logan?"

Logan got on his knees in his chair and leaned his elbows on the table. "Hello–o. Weren't you there when I got baptized at Easter?"

"Yes, I was there."

Deni gave him that sour look she reserved for those she loved most. "Hey, punk, you can come out of that water just as dirty as you went in."

"Well, I didn't, moron!" he shouted across the table. "I came up clean. Didn't I, Mom?"

Kay didn't answer. She looked almost amused, but struggled not to show it. "You were saying, honey?"

Doug took back the baton. "Okay, so it's established, pretty much, that we're all Christians."

"You didn't ask Mom," Jeff pointed out.

"I'm confident in your mother's sincerity, since she puts up with me. That's the greatest act of charity I've ever seen."

The kids moaned, and Beth pretended to gag.

"So if we're all Christians, then we'll all be interested in what the Bible says about our situation."

"The Bible talks about this?" Deni asked. "Where?"

"In the Sermon on the Mount." He turned his Bible to the passage he and Kay had been reading, and read to them about being salt and light, trusting God to provide for them, giving away what people asked for. When he finished, he looked up at the four of them.

"What are you gonna make us do?" Jeff asked.

Doug left the Bible open, but he crossed his hands over it. "In light of what we've just read, our family is going to approach this thing differently today. We're going to be proactive. We're going to think of this as an opportunity instead of a crisis."

Deni propped her chin on her hand and narrowed her eyes. "An opportunity for what?"

"An opportunity to shine for Christ. We're going to realize that God put us here for a purpose, in this exact time, in this exact neighborhood, and we're going to fulfill that purpose."

"Like Esther," Kay said. "Maybe we're here for such a time as this."

"Esther who?" Deni asked.

"*Queen* Esther from the Bible, genius," Jeff said.

Doug sighed, but pressed on. "It's going to take all of us, working together. Today, we're going around to every house in the neighborhood. We're going to ask everyone to write down what they need and what they can share. Then we're going to tell them to come to the lake after dinner for another neighborhood meeting. We'll work out the exchanges, talk about what's happening, maybe get the sheriff to come for an update."

Deni folded her arms. "What if they need what we have?"

"Then we'll give it to them. Or maybe someone else can. We'll try to work it out so that no one has to do without, but everyone has what they need."

"There are a lot of houses out here, Dad," Logan said. "We're gonna do all of them?"

"That's right. I looked in my files where I keep all the Homeowners' Association newsletters. We have sixty-three homes here. We'll go in groups of two. Deni, you and Jeff go together. I'll take Beth, and Mom will take Logan."

"I want to go with Jeff!" Logan said. "I'm not some little kid who needs to be with his mommy."

"And please don't make me go with Jeff!" Deni cried. "Come on, Dad, he'll embarrass me. Let me take Beth."

"Yeah, I want to go with Deni!"

Kay looked at Doug. "What does it really matter?"

Doug shrugged. "All right. Jeff and Logan, Beth and Deni, and Mom and me. But I don't want any of you alone at any time. Don't split up. Got it? And don't go into anyone's house."

They all agreed.

"Each of you take a legal pad for writing down things that people tell you. Needs they have, things they can share. But don't try to carry the stuff yourself. Tell them to bring what they can share to the lake tonight if they can. If they can't, we'll try to work it out where they can make the exchanges themselves. That way we get everybody involved."

"This is a good plan," Logan said, catching the vision.

"It could work," Deni conceded.

Doug felt encouraged by that. They sat down with the map of the neighborhood and divided up the streets. Then they armed each pair with legal pads and pens.

Before he sent them out, they stood in a circle, holding hands and praying that God would protect them and use them for his purposes today.

THIRTY-THREE

DENI WAS ONE OF THE FIRST TO ARRIVE AT THE LAKE THAT
afternoon, despite her exhaustion from the grueling day of
getting the word out. She'd planned to stay home while the
neighbors had their swap meet, but then her father came
home with news that Sheriff Scarbrough had agreed to
come to answer questions about the murder investigation.
Almost as important, Hank Huckabee, the Homeowners'
Association president, had just gotten back into town. He'd
been in Washington, D.C., when the power went out, and
was full of news about the state of the country. He planned
to share it all tonight.

Did that mean the power was out there, too? That Craig
was as helpless as she? And if Hank had made it here from
there, could Craig be on his way?

It seemed to take an eternity for everyone to convene
and set up their families on their lawn chairs and blankets.
Since most had heard about the two speakers, the turnout
was greater than it had been at the last meeting. Even with
the breeze blowing across the small lake, the crowd packing onto that community lot seemed to make the heat more
sweltering.

Finally, the meeting was brought to order, and Sheriff
Scarbrough stepped up on the truck bed of an F150 that
someone had pushed onto the grass. The big man with the
tired, no-nonsense face wore a soiled, wrinkled uniform

with sweat rings under the armpits. He yelled through an old-fashioned megaphone to make his voice heard.

"Thanks for inviting me here. I know you're all interested in knowing what we're doing to find the Abernathys' killer or killers, and whoever it is that broke into Mrs. Grant's home the other night. While we haven't yet solved these crimes, we are actively working, given our limited resources, to find this person and bring him to justice. Right now, we're asking for leads. If you know of anyone who was out that night and looked suspicious, we need to know about it."

He stopped and mopped his forehead, then took a drink of bottled water. "I've asked Hank to put up a message board down here at the lake. You can use that to post leads, and we'll check it each day and follow up with visits to interview you. If you don't want to post it publicly, you can come to my office on West Street and tell us in private. We're interested in anything you have to offer. Suspicions, anything you might have seen that night, or any other evidence you'd like to bring us. We'll follow up on everything that has substance."

"Sheriff—" Brenda Grant waved her hand in the air— "are you doing anything to protect our neighborhood?"

"I'm sending bicycle patrols through here at night, but as you know, we're shorthanded, and this isn't the only neighborhood in our jurisdiction that's had a rise in crime. We're doing the best we can. Meanwhile, I urge all of you to diligently guard your own property and tell us if you see anything suspicious."

The crowd erupted with dozens of questions, and Sheriff Scarbrough tried to answer them all. Deni looked around at the rapt faces, looking for a sign of guilt or evil. Her eyes rested on Brad Caldwell, and she remembered how he'd been watching her a few days ago.

But her dad sat next to him as if they were big buddies.

Brad seemed so concerned as the sheriff droned on about the investigation, and with his boys sitting at his feet next to Logan, he even seemed innocent. That's why she hadn't brought it up to her parents. She was probably overreacting.

When the sheriff stepped off the truck, Hank took his place.

Thoughts of the murders faded into the back of her mind as she sat on the edge of her seat, waiting for news from D.C.

Deni recognized Hank as one of the joggers who ran every morning. For years, he'd jogged past and waved as she'd gotten in her car to go to school. The fifty-something corporate attorney had always had a lean, athletic build, but now he was skin and bones, and his face was as tanned and wrinkled as used grocery sacks.

"Thanks, everybody," he said. "I can tell you I've never been so glad to see home in my life. It's been a long couple of weeks. I think I'll start off by telling you about my trip and the things I saw, and then I'll open it to questions and answers."

Deni leaned in to hear every word. Hank slid his hands into the pockets of his baggy shorts and cleared his throat. "I was in our nation's capital on business when the power went out. Just like here, nothing worked."

So it was true. Craig was in the dark, too.

"Cars are stalled in the roads there, too. Everywhere I went, it's the same. Everybody's in the same boat, and nobody knows what happened. I hung around there for a few days, trying to find out what was going on. And then someone posted signs out in front of each of the government buildings, with a message from the White House. I wrote down the notice."

He pulled a piece of paper out of his pocket and unfolded it. "Here's what it said."

Everyone seemed to lean in, holding their breath. "Use the megaphone, Hank!" someone shouted.

He brought the megaphone to his lips and yelled through it. " 'Dear Citizens, the government of the United States of America has been diligently working to determine the cause of the failure in technology across our continent. Though we haven't determined the exact cause, we do not believe it was the result of any terrorist activity, and in fact, it is our informed belief that this outage extends to the far reaches of the globe. It is not unique to the United States.' "

A rumble went over the crowd. Deni stared up at him. The whole world? How could that be? She wanted to stand up and scream, "NO!" But she sat speechless, waiting for more.

" 'The scientific community agrees that this was caused by an atmospheric event, never seen before. Though it is similar to the effect produced by an Electromagnetic Pulse, nonlethal radiation continues to damage new equipment, meaning that it lingers in the atmosphere. The damage to electronics is likely irreversible. For this reason, we see no resolution to this event in the near future.

" 'To avert economic collapse in our country, we are ordering our financial institutions to remain closed until solutions are found to the inevitable problems generated by a run on US banks. We realize this creates extreme hardship for our citizens, but it cannot be avoided.

" 'For now, we ask that all our citizens do their best to help themselves and those who are in need. God bless you, and God bless America.' And it's signed by the president of the United States."

An angry roar swept over the crowd as they took in the horrible news. It hit Deni like a death in the family. It was one thing to hear her father say it, but to hear it from the government... Tears came to her eyes as she gaped at the man on the stage.

The rest of the neighbors seemed caught in the same reaction. She heard a lady sob behind her. Others yelled at the messenger.

Deni sought out her family, and saw Logan and Beth sitting with her parents next to the Caldwells. Beth was crying, and Logan's face had turned blotchy red. Her dad didn't seem that surprised, but she could see her mother struggling with her own emotions. Worry narrowed Kay's eyes, and she rubbed Beth's back, as if to comfort her.

"Why can't they open the banks?" someone shouted. "It's our money in there! They can't keep it from us!"

"They're trying to protect it," Hank said. "Think about it. With computers down, they're hard-pressed to even know what customers have in the banks. And banks don't keep all the money we deposit in a vault somewhere. They use it. They loan it out, invest it. But now, who can pay their loans back? We won't even be able to pay our mortgage payments. We're talking massive loan defaults. There's no way banks can give everyone the money they've deposited. The banks would fail, and everything we've put in would be lost. The only way to protect that is to keep the banks closed."

"But we have to have cash!" a woman cried. "We can't survive without it!"

"We can survive." Hank's firm tone gave Deni some comfort. "I came most of the way here without any cash and I made it. I used the last of my money to buy a bicycle, and I went up through Pennsylvania to check on our son who's in college in Philadelphia. He had a bike and joined me on my trip home. We tried to get a horse and carriage from an Amish family, but I didn't have enough cash and had nothing to trade. It's bad for them up there. People are ripping them off left and right, taking advantage of them. It's even gotten violent. Though they're not that impacted by the outage, since they aren't dependent on technology, anyway, they're becoming the victims of lots of burglaries.

"Anyway, my son and I made it home on our bikes. We slept in stalled cars, hunted for water, and ate whatever we could find or convince someone to give us. I thought we'd never make it home, but finally we did. Boy, was Stella glad to see us."

Deni bit her lip, trying not to cry. If this was true, then this could go on for months, even years.

She stood up and waved her arm. "Mr. Huckabee, besides the president's message, did you see any sign that the government is up and running?"

"I went to the Capitol Building one day and saw some activity. But anything they do now is largely ineffective with no communication. Some of the senators and congressmen were there, though. I didn't get to talk to any of them."

She sat down, hoping she could ask him later if he'd seen Senator Crawford or any of his aids.

"Hank," someone else asked, "can we believe what the government says about it not being an attack? Are you sure they're not just hiding some kind of nuclear explosion in the atmosphere?"

"I did go over to the Pentagon the day after it happened, to see what I could find out. I didn't get the feeling they were hiding anything, or that they were on high alert. I talked to several reporters who were there, and they had found no reason to suspect any kind of attack. The most common refrain was that it was some kind of astronomic event, such as radiation from a nearby star, with catastrophic effects on our atmosphere. Even the military's hardened equipment didn't survive. And without power and computers, they can't use their high-powered telescopes and they can't measure the radiation. They're pretty sure it's not damaging to humans, but that's about *all* they're sure of."

If this was true, their technology, finances, communication, entertainment, transportation—everything that made their lives easy and rich—were gone. And there seemed no hope of getting any of them back. Now they had to wonder if the scientists were right about this thing not damaging their health. How would they know? Would it take an epidemic of cancer sweeping across the land?

No, this couldn't be true. It was too absurd. It was the twenty-first century, not the Dark Ages. That sign had to be a hoax that someone put up for kicks. Either that, or Hank Huckabee was just trying to look important. Maybe he hadn't come from Washington at all. Anger flushed her cheeks, and she thought of springing back up and accusing him in front of everyone.

Uncertainty paralyzed her.

"I wish I had some answers," Hank said. "But all I can suggest is that you settle in and do what's necessary to cope long-term. Be glad you're home with your families. They made it for hundreds and thousands of years before Edison revolutionized our lives, and we can make it, too. It's just going to be a challenge. And it's going to take all the strength and ingenuity we've got. Personally, I like a challenge. And compared to what I've been through the last two weeks, anything that happens here is going to be a piece of cake."

"But we're running out of food!"

Deni turned and saw a weeping woman standing there, her hands on her little boy's shoulders. "We have no money. What are we going to feed our families?"

"We'll have to fish and hunt for our food," Hank said. "We'll have to learn to grow it."

"On what?" a young man asked. "We live on half-acre lots. Where are we going to farm? Our backyards aren't that big."

"Then we'll need to plow up our front yards. And once everyone gets the message and starts settling in, the better part of our nature will kick in. We'll figure out a way to get commerce up and running again. Steamboats and steam locomotives will still be able to run. I'm thinking antique cars—the ones built before they started using computer chips in the seventies—might run, if you could get gas and clear the stalled cars from the roads. We'll make a way to get merchandise in, get the banks open, revive the postal system. Little by little, we'll make it work. But it's not going to happen that way until we all accept that we're in for a long ride."

When Hank finished and left the truck bed, Doug took the stage and faced the angry crowd. "Well, given that news ... I guess our need to share is even more grave. It looks like our list of needs is a lot longer than our list of things to share. We're all going to have to chip in. Help our neighbors who are in trouble. Trust me, if you sacrifice to help someone else, they'll be more willing to sacrifice to help you."

After her dad dismissed the meeting, Deni sat there a moment as those around her folded up their chairs, speaking to each other in soft exchanges. Some of them cried, others looked frantic.

They believed what Hank said, but Deni wouldn't. Technology didn't just come to a screeching halt. The world didn't just shut down, with no real explanation.

She saw Chris walking toward her through the people, tears rolling down her face. "You believe that?" she said, plopping down on the grass at Deni's feet.

"No," Deni bit out. "I don't."

"I can't take this. It's too much."

"You don't *have* to take it, because it's not true." The words came out through Deni's tight lips. "This is America. We'll get the power back on. The government has safeguards, crisis plans. They're not going to let this go on that long."

Chris smeared her tears across her face. "What can they do? Not even the government really knows what happened. Even the smartest people in the country."

"They're not smart. They're idiots. And here we sit just listening to it all like a bunch of hypnotized fools." Deni got up, and snapped her chair shut. "That Hank probably made the whole thing up. He's probably been with his mistress on the other side of town for the last two weeks."

"Deni, I don't think so."

She swung around to her friend. "Then you're a fool, too." She didn't wait for Chris's response. She just started home, hatred and rage pounding in her heart.

THIRTY-FOUR

DENI WAS THE FIRST ONE HOME. WHILE THE REST OF THE
family were gluttons for punishment and stayed at the lake
to rehash Hank's news, Deni refused to listen to another
word. Hank Huckabee may have hoped to hammer the last
nail into the coffin, but she saw through his story.

If Hank had really come all the way here from
Washington, D.C., then Craig could have made it by now,
too. Since he hadn't, she could only assume that Hank was
full of hot air. And if he'd lied about that, then he'd probably
lied about everything.

She despised the darkness as she made her way to her
room, but she let it swallow her as she slammed the door
and sat down in the overstuffed chair facing the useless
television. Pulling her knees up to her chest, she started to
cry—angry, hot, helpless tears that only made her madder.

What if he was right?

No, she couldn't face that. The idea that they'd be living
in this primitive limbo for weeks ... months ... even years,
was more than she could take.

Would she ever see Craig again?

Smearing her tears across her face, she jerked back the
curtain, letting in what was left of the light. She grabbed a
legal pad and pen off of her bed table and, in the twilight,
started a new letter to Craig. Tears dropped onto the page
as she wrote.

Dear Craig,

Tell me it isn't true. Tell me that this whole outage is just some fluke that's going to be fixed in a few days.

Hank Huckabee came from Washington, so you could have come, too. If you loved me, and worried about me, or even missed me at all, you could have been here by now.

It seems to me that when two people are about to get married, they should be home to each other. Am I your home? You feel like mine. I want to be with you, riding this nightmare out with the man I love most in the world. I want to feel your assurances and hear your ideas on how to cope. I'll bet you and Senator Crawford already have answers. But where are you? Are you shadowing him, reassuring him, seeing to his every need? Is that your priority now?

She threw her head back on the chair, and sat there crying like an abandoned child. Maybe she was being hard on Craig. Maybe he was trying to get to her. Maybe he hadn't had as good luck on his journey as Hank had. Maybe he was sick.

She closed her eyes and imagined him doing everything he could to reach her, starving and scrounging for food, having to stop somewhere each day and work for a meal. With his determined spirit, she knew he would stop at nothing to get to her—if he was inclined to come.

But that was just it. She wasn't sure he was.

That was silly. Of *course* he was. He was going to marry her, wasn't he? Covenant to spend the rest of his life with her?

Then why had she had no word from him?

Had it even crossed his mind that she was in a plane about the time the power went out? Was he content to wait and see if she was dead?

Biting her lip, she flung the legal pad across the room, watched it land facedown. It didn't matter, since she couldn't send the letter anyway. The good old US postal service couldn't get its act together enough to get the mail up and running. So much for *neither snow, nor rain, nor heat, nor gloom ...*

As the candle flickered, sending shadows dancing on the walls around her room, she looked around at the Laura Ashley wallpaper, the satin comforter, and all the silk and satin pillows decorating her bed. They all seemed so useless, so ridiculous now.

She was stuck here, in a place she hated, uncertain if she was loved or forgotten by the man who'd promised to marry her for better or for worse. Had he rethought the worse? Had he decided she was okay as a trophy wife when things were going great, but not when times were tough?

She threw herself on her bed, and wept into the pillow, cursing her plight, and wishing she knew who to blame.

THIRTY-FIVE

IT WAS DARK BY THE TIME DOUG MADE IT HOME FROM THE lake. A lamp burned on the coffee table in the great room, but the rest of the house was dark. Man, he was sick of the darkness. Until now, the prospect of this outage being long-term had been a challenge that he'd embraced. But now that they had word from the government about how massive and catastrophic it really was, reality settled like arthritis into his bones.

Some of the neighbors were hysterical after Hank's announcement, and he'd spent the last two hours helping Hank try to calm them down. The ones who'd blown this off as a temporary outage had taken it the hardest. It was a huge jump from denial to stark-raving truth.

The swap meet they'd hoped for never quite happened the way he imagined. Though there were hundreds of needs, very few were willing to share what they had. He'd heard Kay making deals as he put out the fires of panic. She'd offered one of their bikes to the Keegans. In return, they'd given her several jars of vegetables from their garden. The new family had traded some assorted items for another bike. A few people had been out of batteries, so Doug shared what he'd gotten from Wal-Mart. Several young mothers were out of diapers, so a few of the older ladies had stepped in to help them make cloth ones.

Those with medical needs had flocked to Derek Morton like children to the Pied Piper. The young doctor had commented that he probably had enough business here to set up a clinic in his home. Doug figured he was looking for a reason not to make that long commute into the city each shift. Judith Caldwell, Brad's wife, and some of the other nurses had offered their help.

But that was the extent of the generosity tonight.

He found Kay in the bathroom, supervising Logan's sponge bath by the light of several of the candles. Their son stood in a pair of shorts that hadn't been that baggy two weeks ago, and dribbled water all over the ceramic tiles as he scrubbed off the sweat and dirt.

Doug leaned in the doorway. "Hey. Where is everybody?"

Kay almost couldn't look at him. "In their rooms. Grieving."

"It's not like somebody died."

The shadows cast by the candlelight made Kay look exhausted. "Yes, it is. To the kids it's a lot like that. It's the death of the world as we know it." She left Logan to finish bathing and went with Doug into the family room. Sinking onto the couch, she looked up at him. "So it's official."

He sat down next to her and kicked off his shoes. "But it wasn't a surprise. We'd already figured out this was long-term."

Kay's sigh spoke volumes. "We didn't know it was worldwide. That no one can explain it. That no one knows what to do to end it."

He laid his head back on the cushions, staring at the shadows dancing on the ceiling. "I know. That letter Hank read kind of declared the end of life as we know it."

"It did." Kay pulled her feet up on the couch and set her chin on her knees. "And when the kids and I got home, I went into the bedroom and had a good cry. I started thinking about what a catastrophe this is. Feeling real sorry for myself. Then an image popped into my mind, of a huge mushroom cloud chasing people covered by ashes and blood through the streets of Manhattan ... buildings falling, people jumping ... dying."

"September eleventh?"

"That's right. *That* was a catastrophe. This is an inconvenience."

Relief flooded through him. He'd fully expected to have to calm her down, too. "I'm proud of you for taking it like that."

She sighed. "I'm not saying I'm looking forward to any of it. I hate not having electricity. I hate feeling dirty all the time. I hate the desperation of trying to feed the family. But I think we were onto something this morning. God *has* given this to us for a reason. And our question shouldn't be 'why?' but 'what now?'"

Doug had never loved her more. He leaned over to kiss her.

A banging on the front door startled them apart, and Doug grabbed his Remington. The banging didn't let up.

He ran to open it. Judith Caldwell stumbled in. "Doug, you've got to help us! They're gonna kill him!"

She pulled him outside. In the moonlight, he saw the fight that had broken out in the Caldwells' front yard. Surrounded by men armed with guns and baseball bats, Brad seemed to be fighting for his life.

Doug winced as one of the bats swung. He heard a *thwack*, and Brad hit the ground.

Judith screamed.

Some of the men descended on Brad, and Doug heard his grunts as the beating grew worse. Bolting toward them, Doug chambered a round in his rifle and fired into the sky. That got their attention, and the men backed away. "Get back or I'll shoot! All of you!"

Panting like dogs, the men backed away. Doug wasn't at all surprised to see Sam Ellington and the others who had tried to enlist him the other day.

"You gonna defend a murderer?" Sam spat out.

Brad scrambled to his feet, blood running into his eye. "Tell them, Doug," he said through his teeth. "I'm not a killer."

"I did tell them. They wouldn't listen." He chambered another round.

"We won't listen because he's the one everybody saw out on both nights the killer struck," Lou Grantham said. "We're gonna protect this neighborhood if we have to kill him to do it."

Breathing hard, Brad spat the blood out of his mouth. "Who's gonna protect the neighborhood from *you*?"

Doug aimed the gun, ready to use it. He heard Judith crying in Kay's arms on his front porch, and saw Kay coaxing her into the house. This was his fault. He had planned to report their vigilante plans to the sheriff. But he hadn't wanted Scarbrough to start blaming Brad, too. Despite the supposed advances in overcoming prejudice, the lone black man in the neighborhood was an all-too-convenient scapegoat.

"Pop?"

He turned and saw Jeremy and Drew standing barefoot in their pajamas, gaping at their wounded father. Brad forced himself to stand straighter. "Hey, guys." He was still out of breath, but kept his voice calm. "Everything's all right."

Jeremy started to cry. "No, it's not. You're bleeding."

Brad leaned over to comfort him. "Pop's okay. I just bumped my head, and these folks are trying to help me."

"Tell him the truth, Caldwell." It was Paul Burlin who spoke.

Doug had never wanted to shoot a person before, but his finger itched on the trigger. "If you value your lives, you'll get off this man's property before I lose my temper."

Slowly, the group gave up. As they left the Caldwells' yard, Doug heard them muttering about coming back later and finishing the job.

When they'd gone, Judith came running over. She threw her arms around Brad. "Did they hurt you, baby?"

Still aware of his children, he pretended to be fine. "You know I don't break easy. Why don't you go put the boys back to bed?"

Judith followed his lead. "See there?" she told her crying children. "Pop's fine. Come on, now."

Doug followed him in, and as Judith herded them upstairs, Brad seemed to wilt. "Man, are you all right?"

There was a lamp burning in the kitchen, and as Brad limped into the light, he saw the damage they'd done. His lip was busted and swollen, and his teeth were bloody. A big gash bled on his head, and one eye was almost swollen shut. He clutched his ribs as if they, too, were injured. Leaning over the sink, he spat out blood.

A pitcher of water sat next to the sink. Doug poured him a glass and watched him wash out his mouth. "You want me to get Derek? He can stitch up that wound."

Brad shook his head. "I'll be fine."

"But you need stitches, man. I can have him over here in a few minutes."

"I said no." He turned to Doug, his face hard. "You knew they suspected me, and you didn't tell me?"

Doug leaned back against the counter. "I didn't think it would go this far. They tried to enlist me in their little vigilante gang, but I told them no thank you. I defended you—"

"Why did I need defending? All I've done is try to watch out for this neighborhood." He got a towel and pressed it against his gash. "Yeah, I've been out at night. But that's because I was trying to start a neighborhood watch, and nobody signed up. I felt like I had the responsibility. *Somebody* had to do it."

"I know that."

"And this is the thanks I get?" He kicked a chair, almost knocking it over. "It's because I'm black, isn't it? Because I had the unmitigated gall to move into this neighborhood."

Doug couldn't look him in the eye. "They don't represent the whole neighborhood, Brad."

"But while they're scheming about how to take me out, the real killer's getting away with it."

That was true—and that, added with his concern for Brad, made up Doug's mind. "We'll go to the sheriff first thing tomorrow. He needs to know Sam and his goons are as much of a threat to the neighborhood as the killer himself. But right now, I'm worried about you. You need a doctor. Derek would come—"

"I don't want Derek Morton in my house!"

His outburst made no sense. "Why not?"

"Because I don't trust him. There's something not right about him. I've seen him out at night, sneaking through the streets like some kind of prowler."

"*What?*" Doug gaped at him. "Are we talking about the same person? Why haven't you told me this before?"

"Because I wasn't sure. I'm still not. But I don't have a good feeling about him. Don't worry about it. Judith can nurse my wounds."

So now they couldn't even trust the one doctor in Oak Hollow? Doug stared at Brad. Was he just jumping to conclusions, the same way that group of rednecks had done?

Suddenly, he was out of reassurances. The bright side had lost its shine. Everything looked tarnished, hopeless.

He was tired, so very tired. He hadn't slept at all last night, and today had been jam-packed. His head throbbed with information overload, and he hadn't had time to process any of what had been thrown at him tonight. Yet he knew he couldn't let his guard down.

If anything, life had just gotten a little more dangerous.

THIRTY-SIX

KAY WENT OVER TO CHECK ON THE CALDWELLS THE NEXT
morning. Judith had all the windows closed and locked.
She told Kay she feared opening the doors to let any air
circulate. Their home had become a ninety-degree fortress.
The children sat coloring at the kitchen table, forbidden to
go outside for fear that the neighborhood men might lynch
them to prove a point. Judith kept Brad's rifle within reach
at all times, certain she would need to use it.

"Brad's sleeping, finally." Judith stood at the kitchen
window, eyes sweeping what she could see of the street. "I
think he has a couple of broken ribs. I stitched up his head
with dental floss. He has some loose teeth, but at least none
were knocked out."

Kay could only imagine what Judith was going through.
"I hope you plan to press charges. Doug's going to find the
sheriff today and bring him here."

"It won't do any good. It'll only make him suspicious
of Brad, too." She led Kay into the living room and busied
herself cleaning up the evidence of the nursing she'd done
last night. A bottle of alcohol, a hand towel with blood on
it, a pack of needles ...

After she'd gathered them up, she sank onto the couch.
"Kay, there's a reason Brad was so dead-set on guarding the
neighborhood. There's something you should know about
him."

Kay sat down next to her. "What?"

Judith glanced toward the kitchen, making sure her sons weren't in earshot. "When Brad was growing up, his little eight-year-old brother was murdered."

Kay sucked in a breath. "I didn't know that."

"You wouldn't. He never talks about it. But the killer was never caught. And when the Abernathys were found dead, it was like those old feelings of injustice and fear crept back up in him again. I think in his mind, the Abernathys' killer was the same guy who killed his brother. Not in a real sense, of course, but he feels like there's some kind of connection. Even though he couldn't stop what happened to his brother, he feels like he's the one who has to stop this. He's been bound and determined to figure out who this guy is."

"I can't say I blame him. Maybe if he explained that to those men, they'd stop suspecting him."

"Are you kidding?" Judith's laughter was bitter. "You can't explain things to a lynch mob with baseball bats and guns."

Kay knew she was right.

Later when she went back home, Kay found Doug with Deni and Jeff on the back porch. They'd gotten water from the lake already and were trying to filter the dirt out of it by pouring it through a towel before they boiled it. The process wasn't perfect, but it helped some.

Doug set a pot of water on the grate over the fire in the barbecue pit. "Where've you been?"

"I went to check on Brad and Judith. You won't believe what she told me."

Deni stopped pouring and looked up at her. "That he's really the killer after all?"

Kay shot her a look. "That's not funny, Deni. She told me that Brad had a little brother who was murdered when he was growing up." She related what Judith said about the connections Brad had made.

Doug took it all in. "Well, that does explain his walking the neighborhood every night. Why he was single-handedly trying to protect us all."

Deni wiped her hands on her shorts. "If he really was trying to protect us."

Kay turned back to her daughter. "What do you mean?"

"I mean, I'm not sure you should be so quick to defend him." She straightened the towel over the bowl and started pouring again. "Maybe the truth is that his brother's murder pushed him off the deep end. Maybe it turned him into a killer."

"What?" Kay couldn't believe Deni had said that.

Doug grabbed the bowl out of Deni's hands, sloshing the water all over both of them. "So help me, young lady, I better not ever hear you say those words again!"

Deni's eyes flashed. "Why, if it's true? Admit it, Dad, you hardly know him. We barely waved at each other before the outage. Now you're willing to risk your life to defend him? Maybe you'd feel differently if I told you that I've seen Brad following *me*! Stepping behind houses and peering out, watching in that creepy way he has—"

"You're exaggerating," Kay ground out.

"No, I'm not."

"She's right, Mom."

Kay hadn't expected Jeff to take Deni's side, but now he took off his baseball cap and raked his hair back. "That night I snuck out to Zach's? Brad was out that night, too. He just walked up out of nowhere. I didn't think about it then, but I can see how someone might think he was up to no good."

"He probably thought *you* were," Doug said. "You weren't exactly where you belonged, either."

"The point is that he *has* been acting kind of weird," Jeff said. "You just need to consider that. Don't just rush to his defense because you think he's a nice guy."

Doug set the bowl on the patio table. "I don't *think* it, I know it. He *is* a nice guy. What motive could he possibly have for killing that couple?"

Deni had clearly given this a lot of thought. "Maybe he's an opportunist, Dad. Just took advantage of the darkness to rob them blind. You know, he wasn't home the night they were killed."

"Neither were we, until very late!" Doug pointed out. "That was the first night of the outage. Brad was walking home like everybody else."

"But how do we know he went straight home?" Deni pressed. "How do we know he didn't take a detour by the Abernathys?"

"Because he didn't!" Doug brought his livid gaze to Kay. "You believe this?"

Kay swallowed. Had he really followed Deni? Why would he do such a thing? "Deni, are you sure about him watching you?"

"Yes, Mom. I'm almost positive."

Kay met Doug's eyes, silently telling him they might need to listen. Yes, Deni could be a drama queen. But she knew when someone was following her.

Doug just shook his head. " 'Almost' and 'positive' don't go together, Deni. If he was watching you, it was because he was worried about you. The color of his skin is the primary reason he's a suspect, and you know it."

"Fine, Dad. Think what you want. But if you're refusing to consider him because of political correctness, and he strikes again, then you're no better than the racists who've accused him."

"Yeah, Dad." Jeff's tone was level, careful. "Guilt is guilt, no matter what color your skin is."

Kay let her gaze float to the backyard next door. Had they failed to consider the things that were right under their noses? Could it be that Brad *was* the killer?

THIRTY-SEVEN

KAY STRUGGLED WITH HER DOUBTS ABOUT BRAD OVER THE next few days. Doug was firm in his defense of him, and when she saw Brad or Judith, Jeremy or Drew, she was, too. But then she'd think of the things Deni and Jeff had said, and she'd wonder.

But there were other things weighing on her mind, things that also threatened their survival.

Like what they were going to eat.

Kay sat on the floor in the pantry a week after Hank's announcement, staring up at the empty shelves. How on earth was she going to feed her family? Though they'd all worked hard to plan their meals and ration their food, they were still running out.

She rubbed her face hard, then let her fingers slide down it as she took a mental inventory. There were a couple packages of dried beans, several bags of rice, and a few jars of canned tomatoes and squash the Keegans had traded for a bicycle. There wasn't enough to last more than a few days. Then they would be desperate.

She wanted to believe things would be all right. God had provided so far, hadn't He? They'd had something to eat every day, and no one had gotten sick from the water. But things were getting scarier. The banks still hadn't opened and no one had access to their cash. People were scrounging for things to trade or barter.

If she were the only one losing weight, she wouldn't mind it at all. She'd needed to lose ten pounds, anyway. But Beth was getting too thin, and Logan could hardly keep his shorts up. The nine-year-old's ribs were starting to show through his tanned skin, and the athletic bulk Jeff had worked so hard to build was slowly shrinking. A few more weeks, and Deni, who used to count every calorie that went into her mouth, would begin to look anorexic.

Doug stepped into the doorway. "Honey, are you all right?"

She set her elbows on her knees, and looked up at him. "I don't know what we're gonna do, Doug. The shelves are almost empty."

"We'll just have to start hunting more, bringing home meat."

"It'll spoil. I don't know how to preserve it."

He stared at her for a moment, as if he hadn't thought of that. "We'll ask Eloise. I'm sure she knows. If not, we'll find some others who are old enough to remember how it's done. Or we'll talk the librarian into opening the library, so we can look it up. And Hank's right about us starting a garden, plowing up the front and back yards. I think we should start on that this week."

Her face twisted. "Doug, we spent thousands of dollars on landscaping. Now we're going to dig it all up?"

"A beautiful lawn is worthless, Kay. We can't even mow. We need the land, and that's all we've got. Maybe it's not too late to plant. By fall we'll have some of our own produce. We can learn how to can and put up enough to get us through the winter. And we'll figure out some way to get some chickens so we can have eggs."

She breathed a laugh. "Chickens. They'll be worth a fortune. The farmers are going to be the richest people on the planet. Whoever would have thought?"

She wished she could be strong, stoic. A good wife and mother would know how to cook from scratch and keep her family healthy. She would even know how to make the drab, repetitive, day-to-day meals taste good.

"I'm tired of this, Doug. I'm tired of feeling inadequate. I keep begging God to help me be a better wife and mother."

He stooped down beside her. "You're a perfect wife and mother. Why would you think you're not?"

"Because I don't know how to do any of the hard stuff. A month ago the main things on my mind were the wedding, the soccer and baseball schedules, and keeping my manicure appointments."

"We've all done a little growing up. We're figuring out what's important."

Tears burned her eyes. "I feel like one of those families on some stupid reality show. Take everything away from them and see how they react. I keep looking around for the camera!"

Doug laughed. "Me, too. Like some network would have enough money to stage a prank at this scale. No, this is definitely a God thing."

Kay looked up at him. "What if God doesn't provide, Doug? What if making us go hungry is part of His plan? I never dreamed the day would come when I couldn't feed my family. I'm the college-educated mother, who could get a job and do what was necessary if money ever got tight. But none of the rules apply anymore. It's worse than the Depression. At least then they had places they could shop if they got two coins to rub together."

Doug slid down to sit opposite her on the floor. "Don't forget what Psalm 37:25 says. 'I was young and now I am old, yet I have never seen the righteous forsaken or their children begging bread.'"

"I know what it says."

"Don't you believe it?"

She sighed. "I want to."

"Then do. Just make up your mind to take God at His word."

She closed her eyes. "I'm just tired, Doug."

He crossed the floor and slid his arms around her. "So am I."

She laid her head against his shoulder, and tried to stop crying. It was silly, blubbering on the floor like this, when there was so much work to do.

A door slammed, and they jerked apart.

"Dad! Dad, hurry!" Logan's panicked cry shook the house. "Dad!"

They launched out of the pantry. "In here!"

Logan skidded into the kitchen, his wide eyes wet with tears. "Dad, they're dead. Murdered, like the Abernathys!"

Deni? Jeff? Beth? Kay's heart felt like lead. *"Who?"*

"The Whitsons."

Relief sighed out of her, and her heart began beating again. It was someone else.

But Logan was losing it. "They have a kid who's only six years old, and he's dead, too."

Kay grabbed her son and held him while he cried. "The Whitsons? The ones who said they'd been stockpiling since Y2K?"

Doug nodded. "That's them. Who found them?"

Logan almost couldn't talk. "Their neighbors hadn't seen them in a couple of days, so they went to check on them. They've been dead for a while. Whoever it was took all their food and supplies."

Doug's face was white. "They were survivalists, so they were better set than any of us. I heard they had oil lamps in every room, lanterns, a ton of food that they wouldn't share ..."

"Mom, what is it?" Deni and Beth came into the house. "Did something happen?"

Logan sniffed. "More murders."

Kay let Logan go, and grabbed Doug. "Go see what you can find out, Doug. Maybe the killer left clues this time. Maybe someone knows who did it."

"Dad?"

Doug turned to Deni. "What?"

Her face was white. "Find out where Brad was when it happened," she said.

Kay looked down at Logan. He hadn't been privy to the conversations about Brad. She'd insisted that Deni and Jeff keep their suspicions to themselves, because she didn't want it getting back to Jeremy and Drew.

Logan pulled away from her. "What are you talking about?"

"Nothing." Doug silenced Deni with a look.

Doug went to get his rifle and told everyone to stay in until he got back.

As Kay watched him head out across the back lawn, between the houses on the other street, her own despair choked her. She didn't want to cry in front of her children, but she couldn't seem to help herself.

They all needed a good cry. And now was as good a time as any.

THIRTY-EIGHT

THE WHITSON MURDERS PROVED TO BE MUCH LIKE THE Abernathys', as far as Doug could tell. Ralph Whitson must have heard the intruder and gone to confront him. A fatal mistake. According to the sheriff, Ralph lay on the living room floor, a .22 caliber bullet through his head, and his wife was dead just outside the bedroom door. Their six-year-old had been shot in his bed. Again, none of the neighbors had heard the gunshots, so the killer must have used a silencer. The assailant had taken all the Whitsons' survival supplies and food.

One man couldn't have done that on his own. Even with two or three people, it would have taken several trips.

Deputies dusted for prints, but it was difficult to know whether the prints belonged to the victims or the killer.

Doug hung around outside the Whitson house, listening to the rumors being swapped like baseball cards. Everyone had something to tell the sheriff. There were so many leads it was hard to take any of them seriously. One blamed Zach and his brothers, who were heard partying every night. Another blamed a family of teenage boys who lived with their father.

But most of them blamed Brad.

Doug knew it couldn't have been him. He hadn't been out at night since the beating days ago. But how could anyone prove it?

After the family went to bed that night, Doug kept watch, but he doubted anyone in the house slept very well. He listened all night for sounds of approaching enemies. Every chirp of a bird or cricket, every creak from wind blowing against the house, set him on edge. When Jeff got up to take over, Doug napped like a grunt in a foxhole.

But deep sleep was impossible. There would be no end to the fatigue—or the fear—until the killer was found.

THIRTY-NINE

After breakfast the next morning, Deni went down to the lake for her first water run of the day. Chris was there, sitting on the grass in front of the message boards that someone had put up in the last few days, reading the myriad messages that already covered the plywood. Deni hadn't seen her since the night Hank popped all their bubbles a week ago. She didn't even know if her friend was speaking to her after she'd called her a fool.

Deni offered a tentative smile as she approached her. "Whatcha doing?"

"Reading." Chris glanced up at her without returning her smile. "Did you know the Broadwaters are interested in trading three chickens for a .12 gauge shotgun? And the Stedmans are looking for a cow to buy. He'll barter with the use of his tiller."

Deni lifted her eyebrows. "We could sure use that tiller, if we only had a cow."

That solemn look on Chris's face cracked, and a grin tugged at her lips. "I never dreamed I'd hear you say those words."

"I never dreamed I'd really mean them."

They gave in to the laughter overtaking them, erasing their angry exchange days ago. Deni dropped down on the grass next to her friend. When their laughter faded into sighs, Deni looked at her. "Hey, I'm sorry about calling you a fool and everything."

Chris shrugged. "It's okay. You were upset. We all were. What a night that was. The night of our rude awakening. Thought it couldn't get worse, and then ... the Whitsons."

Deni nodded. "Yeah, it got worse, all right."

Chris sighed. "I don't know who to trust anymore. And all the rumors going around ... that your next-door neighbor is the guy."

"Yeah, I've heard. My dad had to keep people from killing him the other night."

"Did you tell them about him following you?" Chris asked.

"Yeah, but they think I'm just paranoid."

"Everybody's paranoid. There's another rumor going around that Dr. Morton is the murderer. Apparently, he was seen out the night before last, when the Whitsons must have been killed. And he wasn't just out, he was kind of sneaking between houses and across backyards."

Deni frowned. "Really? That's weird."

"Yeah. My neighbors, the Abrams, said their dog started barking. They went out, and there he was. He said he was walking to the Gradys on Arbor Drive to help their little boy with asthma. Only guess what? There aren't any Gradys on Arbor Drive. In fact, there aren't any Gradys anywhere in the neighborhood."

Deni's mouth fell open. "Has anyone told the sheriff?"

"Yeah, the Abrams did. Nothing's come of it yet, though."

Deni heard someone behind them, and glanced back. Cathy Morton, Derek's pregnant wife, stood there with an empty pail. Deni's heart sank. Had she heard every word?

The woman, who usually looked so vibrant and put-together, had a gray cast to her skin and dark circles under her eyes. Her lips trembled. "My husband is not the killer."

Deni got up, reaching out for her. "I know. Of course he's not. They're just ... rumors. I'm sure he has a perfectly good explanation."

Tears came to Cathy's eyes, and muttering something under her breath, she went to the water and dipped her bucket in, her hand on her belly.

Feeling like a jerk, Deni sat back down on the grass. "Well, that stank."

"Yeah, it did," Chris whispered. "When will I learn to keep my mouth shut?"

"Well, if she didn't hear it from us, she'd hear it from someone else."

Chris's sad gaze followed Cathy back to the street. "She seems so nice. It's hard to believe he could be involved. Why would a guy who'd vowed to save lives go around taking them? And your neighbor seems nice, too. I don't think he did it, either. I'm leaning toward some of the troublemakers in the neighborhood. Like the Emorys."

Zach's family, Deni thought. Yes, Zach and his brothers were known to cause trouble. But could Jeff's friend really be a killer?

"Whoever did this did it out of greed," Chris said. "Taking the Abernathys' diamonds and the Whitsons' food and survival supplies. There's money to be made in those things, both during and after the outage."

"Which makes it more unlikely that someone who makes plenty of money, like Dr. Morton, would need to do that."

"Everybody's poor right now," Chris said.

Deni knew that was true. Even the most affluent among them was desperate for money now. "The thing is, it could be anybody. Somebody we least expect. The person we trust the most. Let's face it. Oak Hollow just isn't a safe place right now. That's why I'm thinking about leaving."

Chris caught her breath. "Leaving? Where would you go?"

"I might take Vic Green up on his offer and let him take me to D.C. I have to be with Craig."

"What? Are you crazy?"

"Not crazy," Deni said. "Desperate."

"Not *that* desperate." Chris got up, gaping at her. "Deni, you haven't thought this through. You don't even know him! You're gonna take off with him, be totally dependent on him, for the time it would take to get across the country?"

"I don't have any choice."

Chris's face twisted. "Of *course* you have a choice. What's gotten into you? You don't even have any money."

"He's one of those misers who keeps his money under a mattress or something, instead of the bank. So he has plenty, and he doesn't want anything from me."

Chris let out a bitter laugh. "Think again! You think he just has wholesome feelings about a pretty twenty-two-year-old woman who wants to travel with him?"

"He's Mark's dad," Deni said. "He's been nothing but nice. He's going anyway, and he offered to take me along as a favor. It's not like he's pressuring me or anything. I don't think he cares whether I go with him one way or another." She rose and got the garbage can she'd rolled here, then pulled her shoes off. Stepping into the lake, she filled it up.

Chris stood on the edge of the bank. "What are your folks going to say? Surely your dad won't stand for this."

"I'm twenty-two, Chris. I have every right to live where I want to. I'm getting married, and I'm going to be with my future husband."

"They'll stop you. You'll leave over your dad's dead body."

She shot Chris a look. "Don't be such a drama queen. If I decide to do it, I won't tell them. I'll just go."

"Deni, you're making a terrible mistake. I really wish you'd reconsider."

She finished filling the garbage can, then dragged it out. "I'll die if I stay here. If we're going to be stuck in the dark ages, I at least want to be with the person I love. I have to get there before he ..." Her voice trailed off.

"Before he what?" Chris asked. "Before he forgets about you?"

"Of course not. He's not going to forget about me. He loves me."

"Then let *him* come to *you*. It's his job to come for his bride, especially when he doesn't know if she's dead or alive!"

Deni's face burned. "I'm sure he would if he could. The fact that he hasn't tells me something's wrong. All the more reason I have to go."

Disappointment glistened in Chris's eyes. "Now who's being the fool?"

Deni was getting tired of this. What did Chris know about love and commitment? What did she know about moving on? "Chris, if you had a fiancé you'd feel exactly the same way."

"If I had a fiancé, I would hope I'd take better care of myself for when he did come, than to put my life into the hands of a stranger."

"I'm not putting my life in Vic's hands. If things get bad, I can leave him and set out on my own."

Chris shook her head. "You're not thinking. What will you eat if you set out on your own?"

"I'll find something."

"Where? Berries on trees?"

"God will provide," Deni said.

Chris groaned. "You're testing God, Deni. You're not expecting provision, you're demanding it. You know it isn't God telling you to do this."

Deni didn't want to hear anymore. "I've got to get the water home." She dragged it across the grass.

Chris kept standing there, hands on her hips. "Deni, you need to pray about this."

Deni spun to face the girl. "I've been doing nothing *but* praying. Praying the outage would be over. Praying I'd hear from Craig. Praying that my family would stop driving me crazy. Praying that they'd find the killer. God isn't listening to my prayers."

"Deni, you're going to regret this."

"No, I'm not." Water sloshed out of the garbage can onto her legs as she pulled it to the street.

Chris crossed the grass and stepped in front of her. "Will you at least tell me before you go?"

"Maybe. If there's time." Deni wished Chris would just get out of the way and leave her alone. But she wouldn't budge.

"I don't want you to go. I'll miss you. Who am I going to hang out with?"

Deni softened then. "It's not like we've had a lot of time on our hands. I'll write. Maybe they'll reinstate the Pony Express."

"It's not the same."

Deni tried to smile. "Hey, it's not like we've kept in touch all these years, anyway. Until the outage, I hadn't seen you in a year."

"That was different. I always knew I could get in touch with you if I needed to. But now ... if someone's not right down the street ..."

Were those tears in Chris's eyes? Surprised, Deni stopped trying to get by her. "Chris, don't cry."

Chris just looked at her. "We used to be best friends, Deni, and I still think of you that way, even if you *didn't* ask me to be in your wedding."

Deni felt like a heel. She'd only asked sorority sisters and had forgotten all about Chris.

"I don't want you to go, not just for selfish reasons. I don't want you to do it because it's stupid."

Deni sighed. "You know, I haven't even decided for sure yet."

The grim look on Chris's face told her she didn't believe her. But she didn't say so.

"Just promise you'll tell me first."

That wasn't a promise Deni wanted to make. But she supposed she didn't have to keep it. "Okay, I promise."

Chris just looked at her, clearly not buying a word of it.

Deni didn't want to talk about it anymore. "I have to get home now. My parents are waiting for the water."

Chris stepped out of the way. Deni rolled the garbage can past her, aware that she hadn't fooled her for a moment.

FORTY

THE SCREAMS ALMOST MADE DOUG JUMP OUT OF HIS SKIN. They echoed over the neighborhood, and Doug dropped his shovel and grabbed his rifle from the patio table. It was broad daylight. Surely the killer wouldn't strike now! Doug stood still, trying to determine the origin.

Kay grabbed Beth and Logan and hurried them to the house. "Inside. Now!"

Deni and Jeff just stood there.

"Dad, which house is it coming from?" Jeff asked.

Doug shook his head. "Not sure. Both of you, go inside. Jeff, stay on guard in case anything happens. I'm going to find out."

Deni caught her breath. "Dad, no. You might get shot."

"I'll be careful. But somebody needs help."

As Jeff pulled Deni into the house, Doug saw Brad crossing the yard. He still limped, and that wound on his head hadn't yet healed. "You hear that?" Brad asked.

"Yeah, I hear it," Doug said. "Come on, let's go see what's going on."

Brad followed him between the houses behind him, and as they came out on the other street, they saw Hank Huckabee, who lived across the street from the Morton's, heading for the front door.

The screaming grew louder as they got closer. "That's it," Brad said. "It's the doctor's house."

Hank banged on the door, and the screaming stopped. They all looked at each other.

Finally, the door swung open, and Derek looked out. "What?"

"We heard screaming." Doug looked past him into the dim house, and saw Cathy standing there, her red face wet with tears. She was gasping sobs. "See? They think you're a killer! Sneaking around at night, lying about it—"

Doug tightened his grip on his rifle as he stepped inside, but Derek didn't seem to be armed—either physically or emotionally.

"Cathy, please calm down," Derek pled. "I know you're upset, but—"

"Let them arrest you! Let them lock you up for something you haven't done. You deserve it for what you *have* done!"

"What's going on?" Brad asked her. "Did he hurt you?"

Cathy's rage seemed to melt into sorrow. "Did he *hurt* me? Ask him!"

Doug, Brad, and Hank turned to Derek as he slowly sank onto his couch, his hands on his face. "Derek?" Doug said.

Derek slid his fingers down his jaws. "This is a personal matter, guys. I'm sorry we were so loud."

Doug looked at Cathy. "It sounded like screaming."

Derek nodded. "That's because she was really upset. She thinks ... that I've been cheating on her."

"*Thinks?*" Cathy spat out the word. "I don't think it, I *know* it. When I took him back the last time, he swore he'd be faithful. But I knew in my heart he wouldn't. And then I heard those girls talking about him being the killer because he's been sneaking around at night while he thought I was asleep. He's not a killer, he's a *cheat*! A stupid, lying cheat! And here I am, five months' pregnant!"

She punched a fist into the cushion next to him. "What's the matter, Derek? Am I so fat and ugly now that you have to look for someone else?"

Doug wished he hadn't come. The last thing he needed was to be smack-dab in the middle of a domestic squabble, refereeing a marriage. Brad was shaking his head, and Hank was backing toward the door.

"I'll bet these men don't cheat on their wives. I bet they thought their wives were beautiful when they were pregnant!"

The woman needed comfort. He'd have to send Kay to talk to her. And if he could get Derek alone, he'd throttle him.

"Cathy, I'm sorry," Derek said. "I was just going to talk to her. Nothing happened."

"You thought you could get away with it. I should have known when I found out we'd moved into *her* neighborhood! I should have left you while I still had a way to do it."

As disgusted as Doug was at the man, he could see the remorse on Derek's face as he stood up to face her. "I don't want you to leave, Cathy. I love you."

She reared back and slapped him. Derek stumbled back, his hand on his face.

Cathy's eyes flashed. "How dare you tell me you love me? How dare you say those words to me?"

A knock sounded on the door, and Hank's wife stepped into the house. "Cathy? Honey, I couldn't help hearing ..."

Relief washed through Doug. Thank goodness. Maybe Stella could calm the woman down, while he took Derek outside to talk.

Cathy fell into the woman's arms, weeping over her dying marriage.

Doug looked down at Derek. "Want to go out back and talk?"

Derek nodded.

"Look, I'm not comfortable getting in the middle of a fight," Hank said. "I think I'll just go."

Doug waved as Hank slipped out the door.

Derek led him and Brad into the backyard. Closing the door behind him, he said, "We should have closed the windows and doors before the screaming started. Didn't mean to alert the whole neighborhood."

"Well, we're a little on edge these days." Brad's words were weighty, given his obvious injuries.

"I knew I was in trouble when the sheriff questioned me about sneaking around at night." Derek rubbed his jaw and looked into the pool. "Man, I must be the stupidest idiot on earth."

Doug sat down in a patio chair. "What did you tell the sheriff?"

"I told him the truth. That I was going to see another woman." He looked from Doug to Brad. "I told him her name. He confirmed it. But if you don't mind, I don't really want to broadcast it to everybody. She's married. I don't want to break up her home."

Brad shook his head. "You should have thought about that before you did it."

"Tell me about it." Doctor or not, Derek reminded him of Jeff the day after he'd caught him drunk.

"Don't worry, I've learned my lesson. I'm not seeing her again."

Doug wasn't convinced. "Sounds like you've had this lesson before, and didn't learn it then. Cathy has every right to leave you, you know."

Derek nodded again. "Maybe she won't. It's really hard right now. Nowhere to go. Her parents aren't in town. I guess I at least have that going for me."

"Wait a minute," Brad said. "Do you really want to save your marriage?"

Derek looked up at him. "Well, yeah. I mean, I do love her."

"Man, you got a funny way of showing it."

"I know! I told you I'm stupid. I'm twenty-nine years old. I know better."

Doug struggled for something positive to say. "You know, Derek, your wife is going to need some grand gestures. Some assurances. She's going to be angry for a long time. She won't trust you. If there's any hope of saving your marriage, you're going to have to change."

"I know. And I will."

Doug knew he meant it ... right that moment. But it was doubtful that his resolution would last. "Having your wife stay with you out of hardship and limited options hardly makes for a solid marriage. But I guess it's a start. You have a baby on the way. Be a man, why don't you? Start being a good father by loving your baby's mother."

Derek assured them that he would, but Doug didn't have much hope.

As he and Brad started back home, Brad looked over at him. "You believe all that?"

"What? That he was having an affair?"

Brad nodded. "Yeah."

"Well, of course I do," Doug said. "He came clean. Confessed it."

"Something bothers me about it." Brad looked down at the ground as they walked. "I mean, the whole fight was because Cathy *assumed* he was sneaking around because he was having an affair. What if she assumed wrong?"

Doug wasn't following him. "Well, didn't he say the sheriff confirmed it?"

Brad seemed to think that over. "Yeah, he said that. But do me a favor. Ask the sheriff, to make sure."

Doug frowned. "Okay, but why can't you ask?"

"Because I think Scarbrough's got it in his head that I'm still a suspect."

"No, he doesn't. He knows you didn't kill anyone."

"Oh yeah? Then why didn't he arrest our little vigilante gang? It's because the sheriff thinks they did the right thing."

Doug wished he could reassure Brad, but how could he when he suspected the man was right? "Then we'll just have to find the real killer."

"Oh yeah," Brad said, a note of determination in his voice. "I'm highly motivated to find him and prove that the black neighbor had nothing to do with it."

FORTY-ONE

"WHY DID I LET YOU TALK ME INTO THIS?" SOAKED WITH
sweat, Kay leaned all her weight into the Expedition, pushing it the last of the four miles home. Logan sat behind the
wheel, steering it as the rest of the family pushed. "It's not
like we don't have anything else to do."

"I'm dying! We have to stop." Beth looked close to faint-
ing. "Can't I drive for a while?"

"Sure." Doug called up to Logan, "Son, swap places
with Beth. Let her drive for a while."

Logan put on the brakes and hopped out. "Glad to. I've
never seen anything move so slow."

"Oh right, Twerp," Deni said. "If we'd only had your
help we could have gotten home an hour ago."

"I wouldn't have had to stop so often. You girls are such
wimps."

Deni was clearly too tired to fight back. "Just shut up
and push."

Jeff shoved with all his strength. "It wouldn't have taken
so long if all these stupid cars weren't in our way."

It was true. Several times along the way they'd been
unable to get past without moving other people's cars out of
the way. Since most of them had been left in "drive" when
they stalled, it proved to be easier than they expected.It had
taken them all morning to move it this far. They'd had to
stop every fifteen minutes to rest and catch their breath, and
Doug and Jeff had needed the rests as much as Kay and the

223

girls had. The uphill roads were a nightmare. And the uphill roads with cars blocking them were worse still. Thank goodness most of the trip was downhill.

Though having the car at home served no purpose, Doug claimed he would just feel better with one of their vehicles in their possession. He'd insisted that it would help the community if people moved their cars out of the streets. Then their bicycle paths would be less hindered, and life would be grand. Or something like that.

When they finally reached the Oak Hollow sign, Kay wanted to weep with relief. They turned the car into the neighborhood, rolling it the last few yards to their driveway. She couldn't wait to get some water.

Brad's wife, Judith, was in their side yard, hanging out wet laundry on a line she'd strung up between two trees. She looked at them like they were insane as they rolled the Expedition past. Kay took the opportunity to quit pushing and went to talk to her.

"How far'd you push that thing?" Judith asked as she approached.

Kay shoved her sweat-soaked hair back from her face. "Four miles. Oh yeah, it was fun. You should try it. Gotta have it home, you know, so you can look at it each day and remember the good ole days."

"I don't think so. Ours are each twenty miles away."

Though the sight of the family struggling to get it into the uphill driveway should have been amusing, Judith's eyes were dull.

"Hey, are you okay?"

"Yeah, I'm fine. Just a little jumpy."

"Brad doing better?"

"For now."

It was clear Judith was depressed. She couldn't blame her.

Kay pulled a wet shirt from the laundry basket. "So how'd you wash all these? I've been putting it off, but I'm going to have to do it this afternoon."

"Did it down at the lake. Wasn't fun, I can tell you that. There must be a better way. And I don't have clothespins, so I'm using hangers, and bending the hooks closed so they won't blow off."

"Whatever works."

"We'll see if it does." As Judith reached high to hang a pair of drawstring pants, her shirt rose slightly. Kay noticed what was hanging on her hip.

A pistol in a belt holster.

"Where'd you get that?"

Judith wiped her face on a towel. "Get what?"

"The gun."

Judith patted it. "It's Brad's .22. He wants me to carry it wherever I go."

Kay's mouth went dry. Hadn't Doug said it was a .22 that had killed the two couples? And that it was probably a pistol with a silencer? "Oh. I thought you guys just had the rifle."

"No, Brad bought this about six months ago. Being a lawyer, you never know when your disenchanted clients are going to turn on you."

"I can imagine." She suddenly found it hard to breathe. But that was crazy. Brad wasn't the killer, and he had every right to own a pistol. Didn't he?

"I'd better go in and get some water," Kay said. "I'm starting to feel light-headed."

"Don't have a heatstroke, now."

"Yeah, that's all I need."

Kay hurried back home, her heart racing. The family had gotten the vehicle into their driveway, and everyone was heading in. She followed them in quietly, thankful to get out of the sun, even though the house was almost as hot. As she drank a glass of water, she told herself she was jumping to conclusions. Just because Brad's family had a .22 caliber revolver didn't mean that he was the killer. Of course he wasn't. Lots of people had pistols, and the .22 was a common caliber.

But Brad *had* been seen out at night so many times, by so many people.

She tried to put the thought out of her mind, and lay down on her bed to rest from the morning's grueling task.

Doug came in and collapsed on the bed next to her. "We can't just lie here," he said. "We have too much to do. I have to figure out something to do with all our garbage. We have ten bags in the garage. We're going to start attracting rodents."

"And I have to wash clothes. I've put it off long enough."

They both lay there, unable to move.

"Doug, did you know the Caldwells had a .22 caliber pistol?"

He rose up on an elbow. "No, not a pistol. They have a rifle."

"Judith is carrying a pistol in a holster on her belt."

Doug frowned and dropped back down. His eyes settled on the ceiling. "Well, that doesn't mean anything."

"I know it doesn't. It just surprised me, that's all."

Silence followed, ticking off the minutes. Finally, Doug spoke again. "Brad is innocent, Kay."

"I know."

More silence. After a while, she decided to change the subject. "Any ideas how I could go about washing the clothes? The lake water seems so dirty."

"What about the washing machine? Maybe you could filter the lake water like we have to do with the drinking water, and fill the washing machine up. Even though it doesn't work, it's better than washing them at the lake."

She sat up, envisioning it. "Maybe. I have plenty of detergent for now. Maybe I could put the clothes in there to soak, then scrub them one by one. How would I rinse?"

"You could filter some more water and fill up one of the garbage cans with it."

She thought that through. "I guess that could work."

"I don't see why not."

She sat up. "Guess I'd better go get the girls working on it."

Doug blew out a long breath and got up, too. "Yeah, and I'll get Logan and Jeff digging holes to bury the garbage."

"They'll love that."

Doug's plan for washing clothes had seemed sound as Kay and the girls soaked the garments in the washing machine, then scrubbed the dirt out of them with a scrub brush. The problem came with rinsing. They filled the garbage can with lake water they'd filtered through towels, but after they rinsed the first few things, it was full of soap.

"This is hopeless," Deni said. "We're never gonna get the soap out, and even if we do, the lake water is still not clean enough. It's just making the clothes dirtier."

"Mom, I told you we needed a swimming pool," Beth whined. "If we had a pool, we'd have cleaner water to use for all sorts of things."

"Well, I wish we had one, too." Kay wiped her sweating forehead on her sleeve. "But we don't."

"We could at least do it outside, where there's a breeze," Deni said. "It's sweltering in here."

"Stop complaining, would you? You're making it worse." Kay looked at the washing machine. "Let's just drain it and put some cleaner water in. We can rinse with that."

Deni went to the machine and peered in. "So how do we drain it?"

Kay froze. "I don't know, but ... there must be a way." She turned the dial, but nothing happened. She went behind the machine and looked at the tubing going through the wall. "It could go out that hose there. If we could just ... make the drain open. Beth, go get your father."

Beth seemed thankful for a brief reprieve as she hurried out, and a few minutes later she came back with Doug.

"How do you drain this thing?" Kay asked him.

He moved the washing machine out and studied the hose. Then he looked inside the tub, and shook his head. "Got me."

She grunted. "Then what are we gonna do? It was your idea to fill it up with water."

"I didn't think about draining it."

"Great." She slapped her hand on the machine. "So we either have to leave the water in there or bail it out?"

Doug shrugged. "I guess so."

Deni ground her teeth together. "Unbelievable! Like we don't already have enough to do."

Doug glanced out the window at the guys who were digging in the yard. "They've got that under control, so I'll help you bail. Deni, go find some buckets."

Groaning, Deni left the laundry room and came back with a bucket and three small plastic waste baskets.

Doug emptied the garbage can into the nearest bathtub, so they could use the dirty water for flushing. Then they bailed water out of the washing machine until the garbage can was full again.

He emptied it a final time, then brought the empty garbage can back. "Okay, now I'm going back out."

Kay didn't want to see him go. "Doug, can't you help us rinse these clothes?"

"Okay, if you want me to stop working on the garbage."

She wanted to kick something. "No, that has to be done. Just go back to work. We'll figure something out."

"I'm sorry I didn't think of this happening, but I can't think of everything."

"Neither can I." She racked her brain for another solution. "Come on, girls. Let's load up the soapy clothes and take them down to the lake."

"No!" Deni cried. "Mom, I have underwear in here. I don't want people seeing it! And what about our whites? They'll all turn brown!"

"Come up with a better idea and I'll consider it. Otherwise, do what I said."

"This stinks!" Beth cried.

"Not as bad as your laundry," Kay returned.

Deni hit the washer. "I *hate* my life!"

The girl's declaration almost sent her over the edge. "Just do what I said."

As the girls rolled the sloshing garbage can out of the house, Doug had another bright idea. "What if you asked Eloise for advice? She probably remembers how they washed clothes before washing machines. I'll bet she has some good tips."

Great, Kay thought. So now she got to look like a fool to her neighbor. Still, she supposed she had no choice. She really did need advice.

She left the girls grumbling and scrubbing the rest of the clothes before taking them down to the lake to rinse, and rushed across the street to consult with Eloise.

Her neighbor looked pale and weak as she answered the door.

"Eloise? Are you all right?"

"I'm fine, hon. Just the usual fatigue after the treatment."

Dr. Morton had managed to bring home an IV bag of her chemo treatment a few days ago. Kay supposed he was a decent doctor even if he was a lousy husband.

He hadn't promised he'd be able to do it again when her next treatment was due in three weeks. The hospital was running short, he said, and with no transportation it was unlikely they'd be getting any more supplies soon. Kay only hoped something would change before then.

"Eloise, are you eating? You look like you've lost weight."

"Oh, honey, I'm fine."

Kay breathed a laugh. "You can't be fine. None of us is fine. We're all desperate, hungry, scared ... and tired." As she spoke, she followed Eloise into her living room. The back patio door was open, and she saw Jeremy and Drew Caldwell in the backyard.

She stopped. In a low voice, she asked, "What are they doing here?"

"They're sweet boys. They're helping me get a composting pile started."

"Good," Kay said. "That's nice."

"Here, let me offer you some water. I was getting some myself."

Kay followed her into the kitchen, and saw Brad there, standing at the open pantry. "Hey, Kay," he said. "What's up?"

"Not much," she said. Eloise had a little more in her pantry than they did, probably because she didn't have so many mouths to feed. What was Brad doing?

He closed the door. "I was just looking to see what Eloise needed. But she's better set than we are."

Kay just stood there, staring at him. Was he thinking of taking from Eloise? She thought of that pistol on Judith's hip, and swallowed hard.

Eloise seemed undisturbed. "So what brings you over here, Kay?"

She shook her thoughts back to the matter at hand. "I needed to talk to you about washing clothes. I don't even know how to begin." She glanced back at Brad, saw him looking through each of the cabinets.

She tried to focus. "I mean, first of all, if we're getting water out of the lake, won't it make the clothes dirtier? Isn't there something I need to agitate them? I have to save what little bleach I have left for sterilizing our drinking water."

Brad finished going through the cabinets and headed back outside.

"Have you tried washing them at the lake?" Eloise asked.

Distracted, Kay went to the window and looked out at them.

"Kay?"

Swallowing, she turned back. "What? Oh, the lake. No, I haven't tried that. Doug had the bright idea to fill up the washing machine with water, but I can't drain it out. We had to bail the stupid stuff. And we can't keep the water clean enough for rinsing. I don't know what to do."

Eloise laughed softly. "Come on, honey, let's go over to your house, and I'll see what I can do. You've got that beautiful home and all sorts of stuff you can use. You just have to be creative."

"But that's just it. I'm *not* creative. I look at everything and just see what we don't have, what doesn't work!"

"Then you need to change your thinking."

If only she could.

"Just let me tell the boys where we're going."

Kay stopped her. "Eloise, I don't think you should leave your house with Brad and his boys here."

"Oh, don't be silly. They'll be fine. I won't be gone that long."

Kay wished that tension in the pit of her stomach would melt away. As they started to the door, she looked back over her shoulder. The Caldwells were working hard to help Eloise.

What was wrong with her? She had no reason to suspect Brad in any way. All he was doing was helping a neighbor in need. She and Doug should have been doing it, too.

She almost wished she hadn't seen that gun. It was coloring her thoughts, and making her suspect a decent man.

She decided to push it out of her mind.

She followed Eloise as she slowly made her way to the front door. As her neighbor closed the door behind her, Kay looked across the street at the beautiful home she'd been so proud of. The flowers still bloomed in the front yard as if they'd been nurtured and cared for, as if nothing had changed. But other than providing shelter, the house with all its bells and whistles was now a huge white elephant. And so were all the hi-tech appliances they had had built into it. How much money had they spent on those useless items?

When they went in, Kay led Eloise to the laundry room, where Deni and Beth were still scrubbing clothes. They were both soaking wet, and water was all over the tile floor.

Eloise chuckled.

"Miss Eloise, please tell Mom a better way to do this," Deni said. "This is ridiculous."

"I'd do it down at the lake," Eloise said. "Do the soaping and the rinsing there, and it'll save you a world of trouble."

Deni grunted. "But my whites'll turn brown!"

"They'll be a little dingy, but it can't be helped. Trust me, it's the easiest way."

"But we have a ton of clothes," Kay said.

"Then you do it more often so you'll have smaller loads."

It sounded so simple when Eloise said it. Kay sighed. "With all our intelligence, all our technology, it seems like we could come up with something better than this."

"I know, honey, but this is what you've got." Eloise stepped into the kitchen and looked out the window, saw Logan and Jeff digging out in the yard. They were covered with sweat. "What are the boys doing?"

"Doug has them digging a hole so we can bury our garbage. Things are backing up, and we've got to figure out what to do with it. We have ten bags."

"Can I see it?"

The question surprised her. "Well, sure." She led the older woman into the hot garage and opened the door to let some light in.

"The smell is awful," Kay said. "We haven't had any way to dispose of anything since all this started."

Undaunted, Eloise opened one of the garbage bags, then shook her head. "You're throwing away stuff you shouldn't ought to throw out. There's a lot here that's salvageable." Eloise pulled out a milk carton, set it on the concrete, then sifted through and pulled out a coffee can, a plastic jug, and a couple of plastic butter tubs.

"All this can be used, child. You can wash these up and you'll be surprised how handy they'll be."

Great. More work. Kay took one of the empty milk jugs from Eloise. "I just don't have any place to put them. And I'm sick of washing things."

"Darlin', you have to use what you've got. You've got a whole refrigerator there with plenty of shelves. Use them for things like this. Just go wash them out and put them in there for when you need them again. And if you need to, just stack them on the counter. May not look pretty, but there's no sense in wasting things that I guarantee you'll have need of later."

Eloise kept salvaging, pulling out what she thought they could use—empty cans, two-liter bottles, and other recyclables.

"Remember, when you need something, you can't just pop over to the store and buy it. You have to think ahead. Anything that might be useful some day, you keep. They didn't invent recycling in the last couple decades. People have been doing that for centuries."

"I've never recycled," Kay said. "It seemed like a waste of time."

"Well, it's not. Darlin', you need to develop a whole new set of eyes, start looking at things as possibilities. Instead of throwing something out, think, 'What can I use this for?' And if you can't think of anything but it still washes and cleans up, then save it 'til you do. That way, you don't have as much garbage to bury. Cuts down on a whole lot."

Maybe Eloise had a point. Slowly, Kay joined in, sifting through the bags and pulling out everything that could be used.

When they'd finished, she'd condensed the trash down to half of what it was.

But Eloise wasn't satisfied. "That's still too much to bury in your yard."

"Well, what do I do with the rest of it?"

"You'll need to start composting. If this outage goes on as long as they're saying, you'll need to plant crops for food, and you might as well start your compost now. Throw any old food in there, anything perishable. That will cut the garbage down even further. I showed Brad and Judith how to do it. That's why they came to help me with mine. Come on out with me, hon, and I'll show you what to do."

Kay followed her back through the house, and looked toward the laundry room. The girls needed her help. They'd have to get the clothes to the lake soon to rinse them out. She'd rather learn one thing at a time, but she couldn't insult Eloise.

Kay followed the frail woman out to the back of their yard, listening as Eloise told her how she needed to build a pen for the compost. She supposed she could get Doug to work on it. Then, when she got back from doing laundry, she would sift through the garbage for the stuff with compost potential. The thought made her sick. Sick of working, sick of dirt, sick of everything being so hard.

What she really wanted to do was go get her hair done and sit for a manicure. She wanted to read *Family Circle* while a woman who didn't speak English gave her a pedicure. She wanted to be behind the wheel of her Expedition, sipping on a Diet Coke and heading to a soccer game.

Grow up, Kay. You're as much a diva as Deni.

She could do this. She could change.

She called Logan over with the shovel, and Eloise marked out where the pile should be and told them how to get it started.

By then, Deni and Beth were dragging the garbage can full of wet, soapy laundry out the back door. They weren't happy campers.

Kay thanked Eloise profusely, though she wasn't sure she was grateful for the new work she had suggested. She walked her tired friend home, then hurried down to the lake to help the girls.

If this went on as long as Doug thought, she would die. It would literally kill her.

Lord, forgive me for being so spoiled. She'd never seen herself as superficial or materialistic before, but now she realized that real work wasn't something she was that familiar with. Would she ever adjust?

She couldn't let the girls see her in such a negative state, because their whining was even worse than her own. Somehow, she had to let them think that she was up to the tasks. That they all were. Somehow, she would grit her teeth and act like she was strong.

BY THE TIME THEY'D GOTTEN BACK WITH THE CLOTHES AND HUNG them on a line strung across the backyard, Deni was exhausted.

Deni kicked off her wet, dirty shoes and went barefoot into the house. The kitchen floor was filthy because of all the sloshing water and the dirt tracked in, but there were more pressing things to do than mop. Her mother expected them to go sort through garbage now. "I'm sick of this. And I am *not* digging through that garbage. Let the boys do it."

"Would you rather be out there digging holes like your brothers?"

"No. None of this is right. It's all just incredibly stupid."

"Tell me about it. But you *are* going to sort through garbage. And then we have to go in and make supper."

"Supper? Mom, give me a break! Can't we just have sandwiches?"

Kay sighed. "You know we don't have bread."

"I don't want to stand over that hot grill out in ninety-degree heat. This is ridiculous. How much can a person cram into one day?"

"So what do you suggest?" Kay asked.

"We can eat Pop-Tarts."

"We're *out* of Pop-Tarts."

"Then we could open cans and have cold beans or something."

Kay shook her head. "We need to do better than that, Deni. The men have worked hard."

"The men? What about *us*?"

"Us, too. I'm starving. The family deserves a decent meal. If anyone had had time to go fishing today, we'd have some protein, but since they didn't, we'll have to boil some noodles."

"I'd rather starve."

Kay rolled her eyes. "Fine. Starve then. If you don't help with dinner, you don't eat."

Deni huffed and sighed, but she didn't opt out of dinner. "All right! But just so you know, we have slavery laws in this country."

Kay set her hands on her hips and looked at her whining daughter. "You know what? I agree with you. It is hard. I'm not thrilled about working like a slave, either. But it's not just you and me. Everybody in this family is exhausted. So all we can do is get over it."

When it was finally time for dinner, everyone came inside. The guys reeked of sweat, but they were too exhausted to clean up, and Kay didn't have the heart—or the energy—to force the issue. They all sat at the table eating noodles, no one saying a word.

Then came the tedious task of cleaning up.

Sundown was a relief, marking the end of a day that had worn them all out. Kay had no trouble getting the kids to bed early. Even Jeff was glad to get some rest before he had to get up with the sun and do it all again.

But Deni had other plans. "I'm going over to Chris's to commiserate a little before I go to bed. I won't be more than an hour."

Kay looked at Doug. "Do you think it's all right?"

He shrugged. "I guess so. It's not completely dark yet. But, Deni, I want you back before dark."

"Don't worry," she said. "No way I'm making myself vulnerable to the crazies around here."

Doug got Jeff's shotgun and handed it to her. "Take this with you, just in case. And be careful with it."

Kay didn't like it. "Doug, do you really think she should go? I don't like her carrying a loaded gun."

"Come on, Mom. Dad taught me how to use it."

"She can handle it," Doug said.

Kay didn't protest further, but as Deni hurried out, she prayed silently that God would watch over her.

FORTY-TWO

DENI DECIDED TO LEAVE HER BIKE AT HOME AND WALK THE four blocks to Chris's house. Neighbors loitered outside, their lawn chairs in the middle of the street. The sound of laughter and friendly chatter lilted on the breeze.

It looked like a block party in Mayberry.

She found Chris sitting in one of those circles, visiting with her neighbors.

"Deni!" Chris sprang up as Deni approached. "I was thinking of coming over."

"Don't have to. Here I am." She looked around and spoke to each of the neighbors, most of whom she'd met at the lake.

Chris took her hand and pulled her away. "My parents are driving me crazy. You won't *believe* what I've had to do today."

"Couldn't be worse than what I did," Deni said. "First I helped push our Expedition four miles. Then I had to wash clothes by hand, then sort through garbage for recycling and composting. It was a lovely day."

Chris looked at Deni like she'd stolen her thunder. "Okay, that's bad. Maybe yours was worse. But my dad made us all walk to the apple orchard we own five miles away and pick apples. We had to carry back huge bags of them. It took all day long. But I guess it was worth it. We're hoping we can use them to trade for some of the things we need."

Deni longed for the taste of a Granny Smith on her tongue. Their food for the last couple of weeks had been tasteless and utilitarian. "Can I have one?"

Chris shrugged. "Okay, come on in. But just one. They're all the currency we've got."

Deni went in, and Chris gave her a small one. She bit in. Flavor exploded on her tongue, almost bringing tears to her eyes. "That's the best thing I've ever tasted. No kidding. It's like ambrosia."

"I know. And to think I only ate about one a month before."

They heard a cheer outside and went back to the open front door to see what the fuss was.

A fluorescent green Volkswagen bug was rolling up the street, pulled by two horses.

"Look at that!" Still holding the apple, Deni went back to the street. Neighbors were moving their chairs out of the way, laughing and high-fiving the driver through the windows.

"Who is that?" Chris asked.

Deni pushed through the crowd to get a better look. "Mark!"

Mark Green held the horses' reins through the hole where the windshield had been. "Hey, Deni! Chris! Hop in!"

Deni ran around the car and got in. Chris piled in next to her.

Deni felt like a beauty queen in a parade as the neighbors stood on the side of the road letting them pass. Mark laughed and waved like the conquering hero.

"How did you do this?" Deni asked.

"Just a little ingenuity, my friend."

Oh yeah, he was getting cocky. The attitude looked good on him.

Deni looked out the window as they passed Vic's house, and he came running out.

"That's my boy!" he shouted.

Mark beamed with pride. "It worked, Dad! You were right."

Vic laughed and high-fived a neighbor.

"Where'd you get the horses?" Sam Ellington asked as he ran along beside them.

"Traded my motorcycle. The guy figured it would be a good deal when the lights come back on." He lowered his voice and looked at Deni. "The guy's a conspiracy theorist. He'd read the president's letter, but didn't believe it."

A few of the neighbors asked him if he could rig the horses up to their cars to get them home.

"That's just great," Deni muttered. "Someone figures this out *after* we spent all morning pushing our car."

"This is gonna catch on big-time if the outage lasts," Chris said.

"Yeah, if people can get horses," Deni said. "Hey, Mark, you could rent them out, make a fortune."

Chris leaned forward to look at him. "You wouldn't trade one for a bushel of apples, would you?"

He laughed. "I'm keeping these babies."

He reached his driveway and carefully guided the horses into his yard. The VW rolled behind them into the grass. Several of the neighbors were waiting when they got out of the car. They descended on him, examining his design, trying to determine if they could copy it.

When Vic came up, he put his arm around Deni and whispered in her ear. "I'm almost finished building my wagon. It'll be a nicer ride than this to Washington, if you're game."

Mark heard that, and turned from the neighbor who was on the ground, looking at the changes he'd made to the car. "What did you say, Dad?"

Vic just grinned. "Never mind."

Mark looked troubled, but he was polite as the neighbors questioned him. Finally, when they had all gone home, he turned back to Deni and Chris, then glanced at his dad. "How do you know each other?"

Chris shrugged. "Your dad's a trooper. He's been letting us swim in his pool."

His eyes drifted up to his father. Something flashed between them. "Well, that's nice. You should have told me. I'd have come over, too."

Mark's mother came out to admire the vehicle, so Vic headed back home. It was clear there was bad blood between them.

When everyone had left them alone, Mark unhooked the horses and led them into his fenced-in backyard. The horses began to graze in the tall grass. Mark unbridled them, then tossed the gear onto the patio table.

"So, Deni, what was my dad saying about going to Washington?"

Deni hesitated, but Chris nudged her. "Tell him."

Deni didn't know if it was wise to share it with him, but she couldn't see her way out now. "Your dad offered to take me to D.C. to be with my fiancé, when he leaves in a few days. I'm still thinking about it."

Mark chewed on the corner of his lip. "Did, huh?"

"Yeah, but I can't decide if I should or not."

"I've told her she needs to stay here," Chris said.

Mark's lips tightened. "I agree with Chris. You don't need to set out across the country with my dad or anyone else."

"But he says he has money and provisions. And he's building something to take us there."

"Yeah, I've seen what he's building. It'll work. But, Deni, it's dangerous out there. You're better off waiting here. If this guy you're marrying has any sense, he'll come for you. I would if I were him."

That surprised her. "Thank you, Mark. That's really sweet."

A hint of red seeped into his cheeks. "Not trying to be sweet, just stating fact. If a man loves a woman, he wants to be with her no matter what. If he doesn't come, you should dump him."

Her smile faded, and she shot Chris a look. "What did you do? Tell him to lecture me, too?"

Chris's eyes took on that pleading look again. "I didn't have to tell anybody anything, Deni. It's a no-brainer. You don't need to go with Vic."

"I'll think about it," Deni promised. But the truth was, the more they tried to talk her out of it, the more she wanted to go.

THAT NIGHT, AS DENI LAY ON HER BED, WRITING TO CRAIG BY THE light of the candle, she counted up the days it might have taken for him to come. He could have been here days ago if he'd really wanted to get to her.

She thought of Mark's words tonight.

If a man loves a woman, he wants to be with her no matter what. If he doesn't come, you should dump him.

Was Craig content with their separation? She didn't want to think that, but why hadn't he come? Wasn't he worried about her plane crashing? Wouldn't he move heaven and earth to make sure she was all right?

Unless ...

Maybe he was injured, unable to get to her. He might have been in a car accident when the power suddenly failed. Maybe he'd been injured, and they couldn't get an ambulance to him.

Maybe he was sick, unable to get medical attention.

Or maybe he'd been mugged for his bike on his way to her. He could be lying in a hospital calling out her name.

Whatever the reason, it had to be big. And if he couldn't get to her, then she should go to him. What if he was lying in a hospital bed and she never came? Maybe he was counting the days, praying for her arrival.

She thought of Vic's invitation again. He was building something to take them there. Something comfortable and creative, like Mark had done. Maybe going with him was the right thing to do. If she didn't, the course of her future might be changed. She couldn't take the chance of losing Craig forever.

FORTY-THREE

The next night, Brad brought the Brannings a real treat. Venison! He'd taken his boys deer hunting, and the outing had been productive. It was the first red meat they'd had in weeks, and everyone was grateful.

But Deni saw the tension on her mother's face as her dad invited the Caldwells to join them for dinner.

Deni couldn't help watching the interactions. The memory of Brad following her through the neighborhood the other night, hiding when she glanced back, kept running through her mind. And so many of the neighbors were suspicious of him. The stitches on his forehead were evidence of that.

She wondered, for the thousandth time, if the neighbors were right about Brad.

Kay and Judith cooked the venison on the Brannings' barbecue pit. Then both families sat at the patio table in the Brannings' backyard and feasted until they were full.

Deni was quiet, silently devising her plan of escape while everyone laughed and talked. The children scattered into the yard, playing as the sun set and the breeze cooled things down. She and Jeff stayed with the adults, simply because there was no place else to go. The house was getting dark.

Her father seemed more relaxed than she'd seen him in weeks. "I want to talk to you guys about something," he said as he picked his teeth with a toothpick.

"Go ahead."

"I was thinking of having church on Sunday."

Brad, who sat leaning back in his patio chair, looked at Doug like he was crazy. "Church? How you gonna do that?"

"I was thinking of having it here in our house."

This interested Deni, because she knew that the Caldwells didn't go to church. Most Sunday mornings as her family loaded up the car, they'd see Brad and his family out washing their cars or playing ball in the yard. What was her father thinking, bringing this idea up to them?

Brad laughed. "Who's gonna preach? You?"

"I thought I would."

Deni sat straighter in her seat. "You, Dad? You've never even taught Sunday school."

"I realize that," he said. "But we need to worship, and our church is way too far away."

Deni leaned back in her chair again. So that was it … This was his way of being shrewd as a serpent and guileless as a dove, like the Bible said. He was worried about Brad and Judith's souls, so he'd probably been losing sleep over ways to talk to them about Christ.

She wondered if they realized it. Were they thinking how arrogant it was of him to be so blunt with his faith when it was clear they weren't of the same mind?

"Where do you plan to do this?" Judith asked. "Out in the yard?"

"No. If it's not too hot, I thought I'd invite everybody who wants to come into our house, so we can sit and be comfortable. Outside, there are too many distractions. And inside, Kay can play piano—"

"Me?" Kay sprang up. "Doug, I haven't played in years."

"You have a few days to practice."

Everyone laughed.

"And Jeff can play guitar."

Jeff shrugged. "I could do that."

Deni was glad she'd never mastered an instrument. She hoped her dad wouldn't volunteer her to sing.

"You play guitar, too, don't you, Brad?"

Brad started to chuckle. "Oh, I don't know, man. I'm not much into hymns."

"We could do praise choruses," Jeff said. "They're real easy. We could practice for an hour and have it down."

Brad leaned forward, planting his elbows on his knees. "Look, man, I don't want to be a wet blanket. But the fact is, I'm not really into church. And I sure don't want to sit there acting all charitable to the others who might come, when most of them still think I'm the killer."

Doug shook his head. "Brad, I think you're wrong about how many people think that."

"Easy for you to say."

Tension mounted again, but finally, Judith spoke up. "The boys and I will come. I've been thinking for a long time that we needed to start going to church. I think it's a great idea. We'll come with or without Brad."

Brad shrugged. "That's fine. I have no problem with that. But I'm staying home."

Deni saw the disappointment in her father's eyes, but he didn't let it dissuade him. "Great. Now all I have to do is come up with a sermon. We'll get the kids to make signs to go all over the neighborhood, inviting anyone who will come."

Deni rolled her eyes. Great. She'd be a human Xerox machine for the next several days. Oh well. That was a step up from laundry and compost girl.

Beth heard the conversation and came back to the table. "Dad, are you going to do this every week?"

"I was thinking I would. Even if nobody comes, at least *we* can worship on Sundays. We've been working too hard. We need a day of rest and thanksgiving. And we need to set that day apart like we're supposed to."

Thanksgiving for what? Deni couldn't think of a single thing to be thankful for.

"So, Deni, what do you think about all this?"

She knew better than to say what she thought. Forcing a smile, she decided to lie. "I think it's a great idea, Dad. I've missed going to church."

But even as she said the words, she hoped she could convince Vic to leave before Sunday.

FORTY-FOUR

LATER, WHEN SHE KNEW HER FAMILY WOULDN'T MISS HER, Deni rode her bike to Vic's house and knocked on his door. She waited with her chin thrust defiantly in the air, arms crossed. On the other side of the door, Scrappy barked, and she heard Vic trying to quiet the dog down. The door opened, and he smiled. "Deni! Come on in. I was just cleaning out the pool."

She didn't answer his smile. "I didn't come to swim. I came to take you up on your other offer."

Vic picked Scrappy up so he wouldn't dart outside. "My offer? The one about taking you east?"

"That's the one, if it still stands."

He laughed. "Of course, it does. I'll take you all the way to D.C. Deliver you to the door of the church and walk you down the aisle if you want me to. Come in the garage and I'll show you the rig I've been working on."

She stepped into his tiki bar living room and followed him through to the dark garage. He pulled up the door to give them some light, and she saw what would take her to see Craig.

He'd built a wagon out of wood, but instead of a wooden bench seat, he'd put in two captain's chairs like those one would find in a van. Instead of wooden wheels, like they'd had in the old days, he'd fitted the wagon with four Goodyear tires.

"I got four horses to pull us," he said. "It'll be a smooth ride, all the way."

Deni couldn't help grinning. "It's creative, I'll say that. I never would have thought of using a car's tires."

She glanced at his van, parked in the adjoining bay. It still had all four tires, and the seats were still intact. Had he stolen those on the wagon from stalled vehicles?

Well, it was none of her business.

"So you can see we'll be comfortable, and we'll make good time."

Hope spiraled up in her heart. She could be in D.C. in a matter of days. She imagined the look on Craig's face when he saw her. She couldn't wait. "When do you think you'll be ready to go?"

"I had already planned to leave this weekend. That okay with you?"

Deni sighed. "You can't leave earlier?"

"No, I still have some work to do on the rig. I want to put some kind of roof over it, to keep the sun from baking our brains, and protect us and our stuff from rain. Plus I won't be able to get the horses until Saturday. I'll be ready to leave Sunday."

Deni thought of that church service her family was planning. If she wasn't going to leave until Sunday, she at least needed to sit through her dad's sermon. Otherwise, he'd be so distracted by her absence that he might not be able to concentrate. "Do you think you can wait until after lunch Sunday? My dad's doing a church thing that morning, and I really don't want to freak him out before-hand. He's going to be nervous enough."

"Sure, honey. I can take my time loading up the wagon."

"What are you taking with us?"

He shrugged. "Just some inventory for my stores."

"What kind of stores did you say you owned?"

"Bookstores."

Deni frowned. That was odd. He didn't strike her as a book lover, but then, she didn't know him that well. There were no bookshelves in his tropical living room, and in all the times she'd come to swim, he'd never been reading to pass the time.

"Don't worry, I don't plan to spend much time at each place. Just long enough to meet with my managers and make sure they get the stores opened back up for business."

Deni didn't tell him that no one was going to use their precious cash for books, when they were scraping for food. No point in talking him out of the trip. "Thanks. And I'd appreciate it if you wouldn't tell anyone I'm going with you. I don't want my family to stop me."

"Sure you don't want to tell them? I don't want anybody accusing me of kidnapping after we're gone. I have to come back and live here."

"If I tell them, they won't let me go. But I'm an adult, and I have every right to do what I want. I'll leave them a note so they'll know I went on my own free will, but the less they know, the better."

"What about Mark and Chris?" Vic asked. "They heard us talking about it."

"I'll talk to both of them and convince them not to tell." She stooped down to pet the dog, and he nuzzled into her hand. "What are you going to do with Scrappy? Take him with us?"

"No, he's too delicate. Not the kind to rough it. I'm gonna leave him with one of my sons."

Deni wondered if *she* was up to roughing it. But for Craig, she could do anything.

As she rode her bike home, a sense of trepidation fell over her, but she forced it away. She would not let guilt or fear keep her from her plans. She was going to be with Craig, and nothing was going to stop her.

FORTY-FIVE

EARLY SUNDAY MORNING, A GUNSHOT JERKED DOUG FROM
a dead sleep. He lunged out of bed and grabbed his rifle. Kay
sprang up beside him.

"Doug!"

He held a hand out to keep her from following him.
"Stay here!"

"But Jeff's in there!"

He led with his gun, stepping toward the lamplight flickering in the kitchen. Rain pounded on the windows, and
thunder cracked overhead.

What if Jeff had been shot? The killer could be in the
house right now, heading up the stairs to his children.

"Dad?"

It was Jeff's voice, and Doug was able to breathe again.
"Jeff, are you all right?"

"Yeah, Dad. It was a mistake."

He saw his son then, standing at the french doors leading
out onto the patio. A pane of glass had been shattered by the
gunshot. "What do you mean, a mistake?"

"I heard something. I'd kind of dozed off, and the sound
scared me. Then I thought I saw something outside, so I
fired."

Jeff's hands were shaking as he held his shotgun.

Doug pointed the barrel of his rifle through the glass.
"What did you see?"

Jeff didn't answer right away. "After I fired, I saw a raccoon running off."

Doug lowered his gun. "A raccoon? Are you kidding?"

"No, Dad. I wish I were. I just got spooked and overreacted."

Doug turned to look at his son. "Jeff, you're never supposed to fire that gun unless it's an emergency. A raccoon is not an emergency!"

"I know. I feel like an idiot, okay?"

A knock sounded on the front door, startling them. They both swung around. It had to be three in the morning. Who would be knocking on the door?

Thunder cracked again, and the rain pounded harder against the windows. Doug went cautiously toward the front door. "Who is it?" he called through.

"Brad. I heard a gunshot. Is everything all right?"

Breathing a sigh of relief, Doug opened the door. Brad was soaking wet.

"It was a false alarm," Doug said. "A raccoon."

Jeff shrugged. "I thought it was somebody breaking in, but it wasn't."

"Well, that's a relief."

"You got that right," Doug said. "Come on in."

Brad looked down at his muddy Reeboks. "No, I don't want to track anything in. Besides, I don't want to leave Judith and the kids alone. I just wanted to see if you needed help."

"Thanks for checking." Doug closed the door as Brad stepped off the porch. He turned to see Kay standing in her gown.

"Jeff?"

"It's okay, Mom. It was just—"

"I heard," she cut in. "But do you see how you could have killed someone? You can't just go firing at random like that! What if it had been one of us?"

"I wouldn't have shot just anybody, Mom. I heard something. It was real. It happened to be a raccoon this time, but how could I be sure?"

"Mom? Dad?" It was Deni, halfway down the stairs. "Is everything okay?"

"It's okay. Come on down." Doug filled her in on what had happened, and sent her back to bed.

But Kay was still a wreck. Doug was too tired to argue this out tonight. "Look, we'll talk this over tomorrow. It was a mistake. Nobody got hurt."

"Not even the raccoon." Humiliation flattened Jeff's tone.

Doug took his son's shotgun. "Help me tape up the window so the rain doesn't blow in, and then go on to bed."

"No, Dad. It's my watch. You have to preach a sermon later. You need your sleep."

Doug shook his head. "You're too tired. That wouldn't have happened if you hadn't dozed off. You can't keep guard if you fall asleep and wake up firing."

Jeff looked as depressed as he'd been the day he was hit in the head at Wal-Mart. But Doug couldn't worry about that now. He taped a piece of cardboard over the broken glass, then sent Jeff to bed.

Kay waited until Jeff was gone. "Doug, I had a bad feeling about Jeff getting so much responsibility. He doesn't need to be put in a position where he can fall asleep with a loaded gun!"

"What do you want me to do, Kay? I can't give up sleep entirely. I need his help."

"Then let me take turns with you. Jeff is sixteen. He's not mature enough to make the right judgments."

"Yes, he is. He just made a mistake."

"Doug, we can't have him firing whenever he hears something!"

Doug sighed. "I know that. I'll talk to him tomorrow. We'll figure out something."

Kay finally went back to bed, and Doug sat on the couch facing the french doors, his gun aimed at the exact spot where the cardboard was taped. The rain kept pounding down. He hoped it was keeping the killer at home tonight.

Quietly, he prayed that God would help them find the killer soon. He didn't know how much longer his family could go on like this.

THE RAIN STOPPED AS DAYLIGHT CAME, AND DOUG WENT OUTSIDE to clean up the glass.

But before he started sweeping, something caught his eye.

Several muddy footprints led up to his door, then headed out toward the grass. He stooped down and studied the print. Were they his own? Jeff's?

There was a zigzag pattern on the print. Doug checked the bottom of his sneakers. The pattern was different.

He stood up, wondering if there had been someone here last night, after all. He went back in, and saw Jeff's sneakers lying on the floor by the couch. He picked one up, turned it over. No, his hadn't made the prints, either.

Fear lodged in Doug's throat as he thought back over last night's events. Jeff had been sure he'd heard something. He'd fired into the dark.

Just because a raccoon had dashed by didn't mean no one was there. Maybe the gunshot had frightened the intruder off.

He stepped out into the yard, looking for more evidence. The rain had erased any prints that might have been left in the yard. Still, he walked around the house, searching for anything the would-be intruder might have dropped. He saw nothing.

Finally, he got to the front of the house and stepped up onto the porch. Standing there, he scanned the yard. Had someone been there? Had Jeff saved their lives?

The front door opened, and Kay leaned out. "There you are. What are you doing?"

He wondered if he should tell her. Slowly, he stepped toward her, looking at the ground and trying to decide ...

And then he saw them. More footprints, exactly like the ones in back. But he knew who had made these.

Brad Caldwell.

Doug suddenly felt sick.

"Doug, what is it?"

He looked toward his neighbor's house. "Jeff didn't shoot at a raccoon last night," he said finally. "He really did hear someone. They left prints. The same ones as these."

It took Kay a moment to follow what he was saying. "Are you saying ... Brad?"

Doug felt the blood draining from his face. "I can't say for sure. But maybe we need to talk to the sheriff."

Not wanting to waste a moment, Doug rode his ten-speed to the sheriff's office, but it was closed. Since he wasn't sure where he lived, and it was getting close to time for his church service, he decided he'd have to tell him about the prints later. He hoped the people who came wouldn't walk all over them. To make sure they didn't, he turned a clay pot upside down over one of them. He hoped that would preserve it until the sheriff could see the evidence.

FORTY-SIX

ONLY A FEW PEOPLE SHOWED UP FOR THE SERVICE, AND DENI wondered what the point was. Her parents had been whispering like crazy all morning, and instead of treating Jeff like a loser for shooting at a raccoon last night, they'd bent over backward to make him feel better. Her parents seemed preoccupied as they'd prepared the house for company.

It was just as well, since it kept them from coming upstairs. She didn't want them to find her packed suitcase.

When the guests arrived, they sat around the dimly lit family room like Tupperware ladies, and her dad preached from a dining room chair he'd brought in. As he spoke, Deni's eyes swept from one face to another—from Judith, who'd come without Brad, to Chris's family, to the children lined up on the floor, to Mark and Vic Green.

She'd been startled to see her rescuer coming to the service, since he hadn't told her he'd be there. She tried not to make eye contact with him as her father preached. His presence seemed like an act of defiance, a thumbing of his nose at the family who would be reeling and upset when they discovered her missing in just a few hours. He was going to take her away, and it might be months before she'd be able to see them again.

She hated being deceptive. But in her heart she knew that her life was not here. It was in a big city, the nation's capital, where she knew things *must* be better than they were here.

She had a life, a future with Craig, and she intended to start it as soon as possible. No way would she accept things the way they were.

Out of the corner of her eye she saw Vic looking at her, trying to catch her eye, but she kept her gaze fixed on her dad.

"'I know what it is to be in need,'" he read from Philippians, "'and I know what it is to have plenty. I have learned the secret of being content in any and every situation, whether well fed or hungry, whether living in plenty or in want. I can do everything through him who gives me strength ...'"

Content. She wished she could be content, sitting here with her family, waiting patiently for something to change. But that wasn't in her nature. She had to make things happen.

Her dad waxed poetic about the ways God had provided for them through the outage. He encouraged them to find the blessings in their situation, to trust God to continue to provide, to depend on Him to have a plan even in this. He encouraged each of them to reach out to neighbors who might have no hope.

And then, just as she'd expected, he launched into the reason for his hope, shamelessly hitting the small congregation with the Gospel in all its glory.

She hoped no one would be offended.

When the church service was over, she walked outside with her family to thank everyone for coming. Vic cornered her. In a low voice, he said, "Meet me just outside the neighborhood as soon after lunch as you can. My rig's gonna draw a lot of attention, so you won't want to be with me as I ride out."

"Okay. Give me an hour or so."

"Do me a favor. When you leave your folks that note, don't mention you left with me. I really don't want them mad at me."

"I won't," she said. "Don't worry. They have no reason to think of you."

"Bring a sleeping bag," he said. "And pack light."

"Will there be room for my bike? I was thinking that it might be handy in case we decide to part ways."

He frowned. "Why would we want to do that? I told you I'd deliver you to Craig's door. But there isn't room, anyway. I'm taking a lot of stuff with us."

"Okay." Her chest felt tight as she looked back at her parents, talking with people, oblivious to what was about to happen. They would see this as a tragedy, maybe even treat it like a death in the family. If there was a National Guard to call out, they'd have them after her by nightfall.

She didn't like the way this would hurt them, but she had to think of herself.

That afternoon, after a sparse lunch, Deni went upstairs. Quickly, she finished packing, then dropped her sleeping bag and suitcase out the window, and watched them thud onto the grass. She turned back around and took one last look at her room. Her wedding dress hung in a plastic bag on her closet door, and her heart plunged. When she made it to D.C., she intended to elope with Craig. That meant she wouldn't have the church wedding she'd dreamed of, with her father walking her down the aisle, her bridesmaids jealous that it was her and not them, her mother crying from happiness.

And she wouldn't be able to wear the dress.

She crossed the room and unzipped the bag, pulled out the train. It was so beautiful. It was a Vera Wang gown that was way too expensive. She'd seen it hanging in the store and had begged her mother to let her try it on. Her mother agreed, though she warned Deni it was way out of their budget.

But the moment she'd stepped into it, she knew it was the one. Nothing else fit her this way. Nothing else gave her that feeling of being a bride. Nothing else satisfied her fantasies.

Her mother finally capitulated and bought the dress ...

Deni supposed the money would be wasted now.

She stood there a moment, knowing she'd regret leaving the dress behind. But who said she had to? What if she took it with her?

The thought energized her. Yes, she could take it. In its bag, it would be protected. There had to be enough room in the wagon.

Quickly, she folded the train back into the bag, grabbed the plastic bag holding her veil, slipped it inside, and zipped it up. If Vic balked, she would explain how important it was to her, and dig her heels in.

She took it to the window, and thought of throwing it down with the suitcase, but it was too precious. So she folded it over her arm and took it downstairs with her.

Her dad had given the family the afternoon off from their chores, since they'd worked extra hard yesterday getting enough water to get through today. The whole family had gone outside to the backyard. Her dad sat on the patio swing, talking in a quiet voice to her mother.

"I left a note on the door," he was saying. "Hopefully the sheriff will come as soon as he sees it."

Her mother looked distraught. "I hope he hurries."

Deni's heart jolted. Did they know she was leaving? Were they already preparing?

There was one way to find out. "Dad, Mom, I'm going over to Chris's." The lie made her head hurt. "I'm taking my wedding dress to show her."

"Your wedding dress?" her mother asked. "Hasn't she seen it?"

More lies. "Every time she's come over I've meant to show her, but I've forgotten."

"Wouldn't it be better if she came here to see it? It weighs a ton. Besides, you don't want to get it dirty."

"I want to show her mother, too. Don't worry, I'll be careful."

Her mother shrugged. "Okay, honey, if you say so. Tell them thanks again for coming this morning."

Well, that answered her question. If they'd known her intentions, they wouldn't let her go so easily. She was home free.

So why wasn't she happy?

She stood there looking at them, wondering if she was doing the right thing. A surge of panic froze her in place.

Tell them what you're planning. At least give them the chance to talk you out of it ...

But that was the surest way to seal her fate. It wasn't as if they would remember being young and in love, and help her find a way to get to Craig. They would be rigid, unreasonable.

But knowing that didn't make this easier. Following a sudden, irresistible impulse, she bent down and kissed her dad on the cheek. "You did a good job this morning, Dad. I was proud of you. Thank you for being a good spiritual leader. And thanks for being a good dad."

He smiled up at her, clearly surprised. "Thank you, baby."

She turned to her mom and her heart jolted with pain. She'd wanted her mother with her when she got married, fussing over her hair and dress before she walked down the aisle. Now she would miss everything. But the family would get over it ... and so would Deni.

Tears filled her eyes as she bent over and kissed her mother. "Bye, Mom."

Her mother reached up and gave her a hug. "Bye, honey. Be careful."

The lump in Deni's throat almost kept her from speaking. "I will."

She tore herself away before the tears rolled down her face. She went around the house to where her suitcase and sleeping bag lay on the grass, and folding the dress three ways over her arm, she swept the suitcase up, balanced the sleeping bag on top of it, and cut through backyards and between houses to get to the meeting place with Vic.

He was waiting just outside the neighborhood, exactly where he said he'd be. He'd modified the wagon since she'd last seen it. It now had three walls with shelves inside that held the boxes of Vic's supplies and inventory. A blue tarp covered them to keep the sun and rain out. The four horses looked strong and healthy, and they grazed on the grass on the side of the road as they waited.

Vic saw her coming and hopped off to help her with her things. "Hey there, darlin'. You ready to go on our big adventure?"

She glanced back at the entrance to her neighborhood. "Yeah, I'm ready."

He looked down at the things she'd brought. "Are you bringing everything you own?"

"I don't plan to be back for a long time. It's a major move for me. You have room, don't you?"

He looked a little disturbed as he threw her sleeping bag in, then moved around some boxes to make room for the suitcase. As he did, she saw the boxes he'd stacked in the big wagon. She hoped some of them held food.

He turned back to her and nodded toward the dress folded over her arm. "What's that?"

She thrust her chin up, ready to fight. "It's my wedding gown. I have to bring it, because I'm getting married as soon as I get there."

"I'm not equipped to take care of a wedding dress. It'll get all wadded and crumpled." He took it from her, and felt its weight. "Can't you leave it here?"

"No. If it doesn't go, I don't go." She wasn't entirely sure she meant it, but she wanted him to think she did.

He sighed and lifted the tarp, then laid the dress bag over several boxes. "If it gets damaged, it's not my fault. You understand?"

"Yes, I understand."

He shook his head and muttered, "Her wedding dress, of all things."

She smirked. "I can hear you, you know."

"I know," he said on a sigh. "It's just crazy, that's all. Come on, let's hit the road."

Relieved, she climbed in the front of the wagon with him and settled into one of the captain's chairs. He got the reins, and slapped them on the horses' rumps, then let out a little yell to get them going.

As the wagon rolled smoothly on the rubber tires, Deni grinned. This was going to be fine. She was comfortable, and they had enough food to get them where they were going, and enough cash for whatever they needed along the way. Yes, she'd made the right decision.

Soon she would be with her beloved.

FORTY-SEVEN

IT WAS MIDAFTERNOON WHEN THE SHERIFF FINALLY CAME. When he'd examined the prints on the Brannings' back patio, he'd gone over to Brad's to look at his Reeboks and question him. Scarbrough came back later to report what he'd found.

"They were his shoes, all right. He said that after he heard the gunshot and talked to you at the front door, he went around back to make sure no one was there. That's why his prints were in both places."

"That's convenient," Kay said. "You didn't think he was going to give you a full confession, did you? Are you going to arrest him or not?"

Sheriff Scarbrough shook his head. "I can't. The evidence against him is flimsy, at best. A murder didn't happen here last night. His prints were just on your patio. I have nothing linking him to any of the other murders. He's a lawyer. If he's really guilty, and I don't go by the book, he'll get off on a technicality."

Doug just gaped at him. "So we're supposed to just wait for him to get caught in the act?"

Scarbrough clearly didn't appreciate that. "He knows we're onto him. If he's the one, he'll probably lay low to keep from drawing any more heat."

Kay ground her teeth. "Can you guarantee that? The man knows we accused him! He's got to be angry at us! How can you think we're safe now?"

The sheriff muttered something about staying alert and keeping their eyes open, then told them to come get him again if they found any more evidence.

KAY'S TENSION MOUNTED AS THE DAY WENT ON. HOW WOULD SHE stand another night like last night?

Her mind drifted to Judith. Did she know her husband was a killer, or was she just as blind as they had been? The other day she had explained his behavior, telling her of his childhood and the murder of his brother. Now Kay wondered if that trauma had turned him into a killer.

They considered calling on the gang of men who'd declared themselves watchmen of the neighborhood ... but it was Judith and the kids that caused their hesitation. What would this do to them?

And what if they were wrong?

Despite the disturbing thoughts rolling through her mind, Kay had to figure out what to feed her family for supper. The food portions were getting smaller and smaller. Kay opened her last jar of the Keegans' green beans to go with the fish Jeff had caught earlier that afternoon. He'd only caught three, so she cooked it and flaked the meat off of the bones, then divided it six ways so they'd each get a little protein. It was barely enough to whet their appetites, certainly not enough to fill them.

While she waited for Doug to get home, she sent Jeff to get Deni from Chris's.

He came back without her. "Mom, she wasn't there. Chris said she hasn't seen her since church this morning."

Kay looked up at her son standing in the doorway. "Do you think she came in and we didn't see her?"

"Got me. All I know is she didn't go where she said she was going."

It was the way of her children, to always call it to her attention when another of them disobeyed. They were legalistic when their siblings disobeyed, but expected grace and mercy when they were caught themselves.

Kay sighed. "I'll see if she's in her room. Maybe she came in and took a nap. Go tell Beth and Logan to wash up for dinner."

Jeff came in and looked over her shoulder at the meager offerings. "That's all we get?"

"That's all we have." She should be grateful for the provision. Yesterday, she'd wondered how they'd make it through today. Somehow they had. But it seemed they were always hungry, and the gnawing feeling of emptiness grew worse every day.

She left the food on the counter and went upstairs. Deni's door was closed, so Kay knocked, waited. No answer. She opened the door and stepped into the dark room.

Deni wasn't there. Her bed was made up, probably for the first time since she'd been home, and the room was unusually clean.

Something was wrong.

Downstairs, she heard the door close. Doug had probably come home. She heard him talking to Jeff.

She stepped toward the bed, and saw a note lying on the comforter. Slowly, she picked it up and went to the window to read it in the declining light.

Dear Mom and Dad,

I know you won't understand this. You're probably freaking right about now, so I guess I should go ahead and say I'm sorry to upset you. But you were never in my position when you were my age. You and Dad were able to start your life without a glitch. Once you decided you would marry, you were able to have the beautiful wedding you always dreamed of, move into an apartment together and start your lives. I want that, too.

I miss Craig and I miss the life we've planned together. I could stay here until the outage is over but I feel like my life is getting past me, and the longer I'm away from Craig, the further my hopes for my future drift away.

Okay, so it may sound a little melodramatic, but it's how I feel.

*Because of all that, I've decided I have to get to him.
Don't worry about me. I'm safe. I found a friend who could
give me a ride east. It will take us awhile to get there, but I'll
be all right.*

*This isn't good-bye. I know I'll see you again soon when
transportation is moving again.*

*Meanwhile, just pray for me. I'm going to marry Craig
as soon as I get to Washington. He'll take good care of me.
You don't have to worry. Please don't come after me. I don't
plan to come back. This is my decision and I pray you'll
understand.*

*Tell Jeff and Beth and Logan that I love them, and try to
explain my need to have my own life. If the post office starts
moving again soon, I'll write to let you know I'm okay.*

I love you,
Mom and Dad,
Deni

KAY BOLTED FOR THE STAIRS AND STUMBLED DOWN THEM. "DOUG,
she's gone! Deni's gone!"

Jeff was at the bottom of the stairs, and she almost ran over
him. "What did she do now?"

"She took off! Where's your father?"

"Out back," he said.

She raced through the house and out the back door. "Doug,
Deni's gone! We've got to find her!"

Doug was putting out the fire under the grill. He looked up.
"Gone where?"

"To *Washington*!" Her face twisted as the tears burned her
eyes. "How could she do something so stupid? How could she take
off without food or money?" She thrust the letter at him.

He read it quickly, the lines deepening in his face. "God help us.
How long do you think she's been gone?"

"Maybe hours," she cried. "When she left after lunch, and
kissed us and thanked us ... Doug, she was saying *good-bye*."

"But how? Who did she ride with? Did she take her bike?"

"I don't know." Kay ran to the garage. It was too dark to see the bikes, so she pulled open the door, letting in what was left of daylight. Deni's bike was still here.

Doug was behind her when she swung around.

"She didn't take it," Kay said. "What does that mean?"

Doug shook his head. "I don't know. She wouldn't have left on foot. Maybe she got a horse somehow."

Kay pulled the garage door shut. It clanged and vibrated throughout the garage. "Doug, you've got to go after her. You've got to stop her before she gets any farther!"

By now, Logan had come to see what was wrong. "Mom, what is it?"

She burst back into the house. "Your sister's run away."

"Why?"

Jeff answered his question. "Because she's an idiot. A complete moron."

Kay turned on him. "That's enough, Jeff! Your sister is in trouble."

His cheeks blotched red. "She *deserves* to be in trouble."

"I said, that's enough!" She turned to Doug, astonished that he was just standing there, staring into space.

Beth came down from her room. "What's all the yelling about?"

Kay swung around. "Have you seen your sister?"

"No, not since she left after lunch."

Kay grabbed the letter back from Doug, tearing a corner as she did. Her hands were shaking as she read again. "Doug, we have to *do* something."

"I am. I'm going to Chris's. She'll know something."

"Dad, I just went there," Jeff said. "She said she doesn't know where Deni is."

His eyes flashed. "She's lying. I'm going over there."

"I'm coming with you!" Kay turned back to the kids. "Jeff, stay here and eat, and take care of the house."

"I will." Even as he said it, he started for his plate. She couldn't blame him, really. He was starving, as were Beth and Logan.

But she had lost her appetite.

"Pray for Deni," she cried as she started out the back door, locking it behind her. "Pray God will help us find her."

THE LOOK ON CHRIS'S FACE TOLD KAY AND DOUG SHE KNEW EXACTLY whom Deni had gone with. But she wasn't telling.

"Really, I don't know," she insisted weakly.

Chris's parents had come to the door to see what was wrong. "Chris," her father said, "don't lie to them. If you know who Deni's with, tell them."

Chris's mouth trembled. "I tried to talk her out of it. I warned her it would be dangerous, but she wouldn't listen."

Kay took Chris by the shoulders and stared into her face. "Chris, you listen to me," she said through her teeth. "My daughter is with some stranger on her way to the East Coast with no food and no money. So help me, if you don't tell me who she went with, I can't be responsible for what I do!"

Chris's eyes widened, but she wouldn't budge. "She's okay, really. He isn't a stranger. And he has food and money."

"He?" Doug asked. "She went off with a *guy*?"

Chris looked as if she'd been caught, and she swallowed hard. "I don't know. I think it was a man. Maybe it was a woman . . ."

Kay shook her and screamed into her face, "Don't you understand she could be in danger? What is wrong with you? Don't you care about her at all?"

"Kay!" Chris's mother tried to get between them. "That's enough. Let her go."

Chris started to cry as Kay dropped her hands. "Of *course* I care! But I promised her—"

"You shouldn't have!" Kay screamed. "What kind of friend are you?"

Doug pulled Kay back, making her more angry. His voice was broken, raspy, as he appealed to Chris again. "Please ... I'm begging you."

Finally, Chris dropped her hands and looked down at her feet. "She went with Vic Green."

Kay gaped at her. "Vic? Mark's father? But—he was at our house this morning. Did they plan it then?"

Chris sucked in a sob. "No. They've been talking about it for a while. They went in this crazy-looking wagon he built, pulled by four horses."

Kay's face twisted as she tried to imagine that relationship. "I didn't even know Deni knew him. I thought today was the first time they'd met." She looked up at Doug, saw the anger pulling at his face. She felt the tremor of rage passing through him as he held her.

"Come on," Doug said. "We're going over to Vic's house. Maybe she's still there."

"She's not," Chris said. "I saw him leave hours ago. Not that long after church was over. He fixed this covered wagon up with Goodyear tires and captain's chairs, and everyone was rushing to see it when he rode out of the neighborhood. Deni wasn't with him. She must have met him someplace." Her father pulled her into his arms, and she buried her face in his chest. "I'm sorry, Mr. and Mrs. Branning. I should have told you when she started talking about it. I knew it was the wrong decision. I tried to tell her."

Kay found no comfort in knowing the truth. "Did Mark go with them?"

She shook her head. "No. He lives with his mom next door to where the Abernathys lived. But maybe he can give you some ideas about where they're going."

They left the girl weeping, and hurried off.

DOUG RAN UP THE STREET TO VIC GREEN'S HOUSE, KAY RIGHT ON his heels. "Doug, do you think he's dangerous? Shouldn't we get a gun?"

Doug jogged up the steps to the door. "I'm the one who's dangerous, Kay. When I get my hands on him—" He banged on the door, with no response. He knocked harder, unwilling to give up.

"Doug, he's not here."

He hammered with his fists. "Maybe he is. Maybe he's just a coward and doesn't want to answer it. Maybe I should just kick it in."

Kay stopped him. "That's a waste of time. Mark lives around the corner. Let's go talk to him."

Doug stopped banging and dropped his hands. Breathing hard, he turned and looked toward Mark's house. "All right, let's go to Mark's." He walked so fast that Kay could hardly keep up.

When they got to Mark's, Doug banged again. This time, Mark's mother, Martha, answered the door. "Doug! Kay!"

"We need to see Mark." Doug struggled to keep his voice even. "It's an emergency."

"Well, sure." Martha stepped back from the door. "I'll get him."

She led them into the darkening house, then walked out back and called her son. Mark was at the grill stirring a pot, but he came inside when his mother told him who was there.

"Mr. and Mrs. Branning. How's it going?"

"Our daughter is missing." Fear wobbled on Kay's voice. "Do you know anything about it?"

He frowned. "Missing? What do you mean?"

Doug met the boy's gaze. "Chris said Deni left town with your father."

"Oh no." Mark's mother brought her hand to her mouth. "He *didn't*. Mark, did you know about this?"

"No!" The look of disgust on his face looked genuine, but Doug couldn't be sure. "I mean, Deni told me she was thinking about it. But I thought I talked her out of it."

"Then you knew your father was leaving town?" Doug asked.

"Well, yes. I saw the rig he was building. He had business to do … I heard him invite her one time, but I didn't think she took it seriously."

"Heard him?" Kay asked. "Where?"

"They were both over here looking at my car. She'd been swimming at his house a lot, and they'd gotten to be friends."

Martha's lips were tight against her teeth. "That lowdown, sorry excuse for a man! How *dare* he?"

Her indignation didn't make Doug feel any better. He could feel Kay's body trembling next to his, so he unclenched his fists and put his arm around her. "Mark, we need you to tell us where your father was going, when he left, and how far you think he could have gotten by now."

"I don't know," Mark said. "He owns a chain of bookstores across the south. I guess he was going to stop at each one."

"Do you have a list of the stores?" Kay asked. "A map of where they're located?"

"No. I try to stay out of my dad's business."

Martha's eyes were filling with rage. Doug wondered if they were tears of anger or compassion. "My ex-husband is not the most scrupulous man in business. I've never wanted Mark to be that involved with him."

"You must know something that could help us," Doug said. "Do you have a key to his house?"

Mark's eyes widened. "Yes, I do. I'll go in and see what I can find. Surely he has a map in his office or a listing of his stores."

Finally, some hope. "Yes," Doug said. "Please, hurry."

Mark got the key and pulled on his shirt and shoes, then led them back to his father's house. He unlocked the door, and they followed him in.

The décor of the house would have been comical if Doug hadn't been so worried. It looked like something one of those crazy TV decorators had put together. Vic had left an empty beer can on the table and a wadded napkin next to it. Beside it was a notepad with what looked like a packing list.

"His office is upstairs," Mark said. "Come on, you can help me look."

All the doors on the second floor were closed. That was odd. If Vic lived alone, why would he need the doors closed, especially when the heat was so intense? Wouldn't he want to keep the upstairs windows open and the air circulating?

Mark went to the second door down the hall and pushed it open. Doug and Kay followed him inside.

Kay gasped. The office was decorated with lewd photos, and on the floor around his desk were several boxes filled with pictures and porno magazines.

"I'm gonna be sick." Kay backed out of the room.

Doug took in the images around him. His pulse hammered in his temples, making his head throb. What kind of man was Deni with? "What business did you say your dad was in?"

Mark hesitated. "Bookstores."

"What *kind* of bookstores?"

Mark glanced at the boxes. "I don't really know, but ... I have a good idea."

Doug felt the blood rushing from his head. *Hold on*, he told himself. *Think!*

Mark pulled out the drawers on his father's desk and looked through them, but he didn't find what he was looking for. "I'll look in his bedroom. I think he has a file cabinet in there."

He went back out in the hall, and Doug stepped out of the office. Kay was sitting on the floor, her head in the circle of her arms. He started down the hall to follow Mark, but as they passed another closed door, he paused. Opening it, he looked inside.

And then he saw it. Boxes and boxes of food. Cereal and canned goods and soups and bottles of juice ...

"Where did he get all this?"

Mark came back and looked inside. "I don't know. We've been running out down at my house, and he knew it. He didn't tell me he had this."

He went to open the drapes so he could see better. The light spilled in.

Doug started going through the boxes, and saw some bags with a survivalist imprint on the front. He'd considered that brand of dried food when he tried to prepare for the year 2000 and the crisis they had expected.

"Mark, was your dad a survivalist?"

"Not that I know of."

Doug didn't know anyone who was ... except for the Whitsons. Hadn't Ralph admitted it at one of the meetings?

"I've been stockpiling this stuff since Y2K."

A chill ran through him, and his mind raced. What was in those other rooms? He pushed past Mark, out into the hall, and opened the next door down.

The room was full—three flat-panel TVs, a Bose stereo system, five car stereos ... Mark looked as shocked as Doug to see the stuff. "He didn't have all this before."

Kay got up and pushed between them, and Doug saw the look of terror darken her face. "Doug ... is he the one?"

His throat closed up, and he couldn't catch his breath. His hands trembled as he went to a small black velvet box sitting on a table. He lifted its lid.

Twenty or thirty loose diamonds lay on the velvet.

The blood seemed to flush from his head, and he felt as if he stared through a fog.

He heard Kay's choked gasp behind him. Covering her face, she cried, "Randall Abernathy sold diamonds! Vic killed them!"

Mark swung around, stricken. "No way! Not my dad. That's not where he got them."

Kay started to crumble, and Doug felt a numbness crawl over his body, weakening his arms, his fingers ... blurring his thoughts.

"My dad probably bought them. He's always buying things. Thinking of new enterprises. He just ... got these somewhere ..."

"I want to get out of here." Kay couldn't catch her breath.

Doug pulled her into his arms and held her as he stared at Mark. The young man was going from box to box, declaring his father's innocence. But his voice was growing weaker.

As he did so, Doug watched him slowly wilt from a state of confidence to trembling realization. When he got to the Bose DVD player, he fell to his knees. "Aw ... no!"

"What?" Doug watched him pull out a box that was behind the system. It was full of DVDs. Mark's fingers were clumsy as he grabbed some out. The Telletubbies, the Wiggles, *Stuart Little.* On the back of one was a child's crude handwriting: "Propity of Michael Whitson."

The Whitsons' six-year-old son!

Kay let out an anguished moan, and Doug tried to keep her from falling. But he wasn't sure he could stay upright, either.

Vic Green was a cold-blooded killer.

And Deni's life was in his hands.

FORTY-EIGHT

THE HIGHWAY WAS A WASTELAND OF STALLED, STRIPPED CARS with shattered windshields, the doors left open by hurried bandits. The useless vehicles stood in the way, slowing Vic's wagon, and Deni had the urge to get out and walk ahead, closing the car doors as she went.

The heat was oppressive, beating down on the sweating horses and dehydrating her. Every couple of hours they stopped so Vic could let the horses drink. They were moving much more slowly than she'd hoped, and the jostling ride, even in the captain's chairs, was miserably uncomfortable. The sun was setting behind them, and soon it would be dark. Deni had no idea where they would sleep.

Vic had been drinking beer—one after another—as they rode. He passed the time singing the songs from *Les Miserables*, in a voice that wasn't half bad. When he'd covered every song, he moved on to *Fiddler on the Roof.*

Just as well, since it kept them from having to make conversation—and she didn't have to pretend she was listening.

Finally, he quit singing. "What's the matter, darlin'? You've been awfully quiet."

"Just the stress. Plus I'm a little frustrated that we're moving so slowly. If I'd ridden my bike I'd have covered three or four times more ground."

"But then I couldn't have carried all this stuff. Had to be a covered wagon."

Deni looked back over her shoulder. There were so many boxes piled in there that she didn't know why the whole thing hadn't collapsed. "What all do you have back there, anyway?"

"Products, I told you."

"Like books? Anything I could read?"

He hesitated a moment. "I don't think so."

"You don't think so ... what? That they're books or that they're anything I can read?"

"They're books, but nothing you'd like. Best if you stay out of those boxes. I don't want the books to look used when I stock them."

She might have known. Why hadn't she brought her own reading material?

"Few more miles," he said, "and we'll stop and take a rest."

"Again? Why? We're never gonna get there at this rate!"

He looked disappointed in her. "The horses have to be watered, you know. Road's hard on their joints."

Deni couldn't believe this. She could make the 750 miles from Birmingham to D.C. in thirteen hours by car. Of course, they were moving slower—maybe twenty miles an hour instead of seventy. That meant it would take ... what? Thirty-plus hours to get there?

Except she wasn't sure they were going twenty. They might be going ten ... or even less.

"How much sleep do horses need?"

"They need nights, just like you and me."

She groaned. "So I guess we can't expect them to travel all night?"

He bellowed out a laugh. "No, darlin', we're not traveling all night."

Deni didn't like the idea of stopping to sleep. She had no idea what the arrangements would be. Would they sleep on the ground? What about rodents, bugs, snakes?

Maybe she'd just recline the captain's chair and curl up on that. She should have brought warmer clothes for the night's drop in temperature, but she supposed she could cover up with her sleeping bag.

Her biggest mistake, though, was not bringing enough sterilized water. Instead, she'd brought Beth's flat iron and hair dryer, since hers were still in the car at the airport. She'd also brought her lighted makeup mirror, so that if the power miraculously returned, she could find an outlet and fix her hair and face. And she'd brought her credit card, which might be her salvation if she was able to find an ATM machine or an open bank.

But from the looks of things, civilization was just as dead here as it was at home. It looked like Hank was right.

She wanted more than anything to guzzle a gallon of water, but she had to conserve the bottle she had. She wondered how she'd replace it when she ran out. She'd need to sterilize any she got before she could drink it, but how in the world would she do that? Vic might have water in the wagon, but if he did, he was keeping it for himself.

She should have thought things through, but she hadn't bothered with details.

Earlier, she had managed to convince Vic to travel on Highway 78, which ran parallel to I-20, in case her father came after them. She knew her dad would look for them on I-20 first. When they stopped and watered the horses for the umpteenth time that day, she got out and tried to get her blood circulating. Every muscle in her body vibrated, and she dreaded getting back into the wagon. How had people traveled like this in the old days—without the plush chairs and the rubber tires? Maybe it was easier when you didn't have anything else to compare it to.

When darkness began to fall and they came upon a brook, Vic pulled over for the night. He led the horses down to the water, and Deni drank her fill of it as well, feeling life seeping back into her body. Vic started a fire and set cans of kidney beans over it, then opened a couple of cans of Spam. Deni devoured the food.

Next, Vic opened a bottle of Scotch. "You okay, hon? Or are you thinking you got more than you bargained for?"

"It's worth it, as long as I get to Craig."

"Traveling this way is not for wimps," he said. "That's for sure."

She turned and looked back at the horses where they were tethered and grazing. "I was just thinking ... you wouldn't let me take one of the horses and ride the rest of the way on my own, would you?"

He laughed. "No offense, but you don't look that stupid."

She groaned. "I just want to go faster. I didn't think this would take so long."

He took a long drink. "I need all four horses to pull the wagon. Here, drink some of this. You're wound too tight."

She pushed the bottle away. "I don't need booze. I need faster transportation."

"Well, I'm all you've got."

She sighed. "How many miles do you think we covered today?"

"About eighty, give or take."

She got up and walked to the dark road, peering east. This was absurd. "It's about 670 more miles to Washington. At this rate, it'll take eight or nine days to get there."

Vic laughed as if she was the best entertainment around. That laughter was really starting to get on her nerves. "Most days we'll get more traveling in, but we got a late start today. I told you I'll be stopping along the way, taking care of business. You might as well relax and be patient."

She wanted to scream. Instead, she walked out to the middle of the dark road. An old Pontiac was abandoned there, and she reared back and kicked its tire. "Okay, so I made a mistake. This whole thing was a horrible idea. Maybe I should just go back home."

Vic had almost finished off the bottle. He belched. "How do you plan to do that?"

She took a few steps toward him, then stooped down in front of him. "Maybe you could take me back?"

Again, the laughter. "Nope. I'm not going back." He bottomed his bottle, then flung it toward the woods. Then he reached out for her hand. She let him pull her next to him, and wearily sat down on the grass. He reminded her of her dad, amused at her ranting, tolerating her tantrum.

He put his arm around her, pulled her against him. "I'm telling you, you need to relax. So you don't like Scotch. Do you want beer? Wine?"

She stiffened. "You have all that?"

"Hey, I brought what I need." He swept her hair back from her eyes, and her heart jolted. He was too close, and she could smell the alcohol on his breath—that sour, medicinal smell that mingled with his body odor.

She pulled away and got up. "I don't drink. I just want water."

"Behind your seat, I got Sprite, Coke ..."

She climbed up in the wagon and tried to see into the back. Which box held the Cokes?

Suddenly, he was beside her. "I'll get it. I don't want you digging through these boxes." His voice had a sharp edge.

"Sorry." She got off the wagon and waited as he dug through.

He tossed her a bottle, then threw down her suitcase. "That thing weighs a ton."

"I'll get rid of it if it means we'll travel faster," she said. "None of what I brought is important except for the wedding dress. What could *you* get rid of?"

"Nothing. My inventory's crisp ... crick ... *critical* for this trip."

Deni tried not to smile at his slurred speech.

"I'm doing you a favor, 'member?"

She sighed. "I know you are."

"Then why don't you ac' like it?"

He looked genuinely hurt as he pulled out another bottle of Scotch.

Was he for real? "Are you gonna drink that? You've been drinking all day! And you just finished off that other bottle."

"It wasn't full. Besides, I can hold my liquor. Do I seem drunk?"

"Yes, actually. Do you drink this much at home?"

He waved her off. "You sound like one of my ex-wives."

"Well, maybe you should listen to them." She sat down on the dirt, watching him open the bottle. For him to drink as much as he had so far without falling over drunk, he had to be a heavy drinker. She had friends from college who drank so much that it took more and more to get a buzz.

She wouldn't have come with him if she'd known about this. It was one thing to leave town with her friend's dad, and another thing entirely to go with an alcoholic.

Why hadn't she listened to Chris?

He unrolled both sleeping bags, stretched them out next to each other on the grass. In the flickering glow of the campfire, he stretched out, leaning back on his elbows.

She stayed back, arms crossed, keeping her distance. Surely he didn't expect her to lie there beside him!

"Speaking of exes, did you know my first love was a girl who looked a lot like you?"

She swallowed. "No."

"Beautiful girl. Soft, big brown eyes. You looked into them and felt like you were underwater, gasping for breath." He took a drink. "She was feisty like you, too. Hard to please. Made you try harder."

Deni sighed and looked back toward the road. It had been a mistake, getting off the main interstate. She'd been so determined to avoid her father if he came looking for her, but now she'd jump up and dance if he came along.

Vic turned over and crawled across the bag toward her. Again, he was too close.

"She used to wear her hair like yours." He reached out and took a strand. She pulled it out of his hand. "Sometimes she wore it up, like this." He pulled it up, piled it on her head.

She closed her eyes. "Don't."

"Don't be afraid of me." His voice came on a whisper. "I know you're tense, but I can help you relax."

Deni slipped out of his reach and got up. She grabbed her suitcase and put it between them.

"You're not mad at me, are you?" he asked.

"No, I'm not mad."

"Then come here."

"I have to get something." She unzipped the suitcase and dug through, as if looking for something. Her mind raced. What should she do? She wasn't safe with him, not when he was drinking. But where would she go?

"I know you're worried about being faithful to Craig." His voice was still soft. He got up and came around the suitcase, close to her again. "It's lonely out here, and we gotta long way t'go. Nobody knows what we're doing. As they say in Las Vegas, 'What happens here, stays here.' "

"Nothing's going to happen. Here or anywhere."

"Well, it could, y'know. No reason either of us has to be lonely."

She looked up at him, struggling to keep her revulsion from showing. "Vic, I appreciate your bringing me with you, but if you did it so that you and I ..." She couldn't utter the words, so she looked away. "Well, you just need to forget it. I'm not interested."

Silence pulsed between them, and suddenly he grabbed her arm. She swallowed a scream and looked up at him.

His eyes were razor sharp. "Don't get haughty with me, Miss Debutante."

She shivered, and tried to level her voice. "I'm not getting haughty. I just didn't think there were strings attached."

"You wouldn't have run away with me if you didn't like me. I been 'round the block enough to read th' signals. You might 's well wave a banner."

She jerked back as if he'd slapped her. "I haven't given you signals! I thought you were a nice man. I *trusted* you."

"And I trusted you to show the proper gratitude. I trusted you not to be a tease."

She caught her breath. "A tease? That's ridiculous."

"Comin' over to my house in your bikini, swimming in my pool ..."

She needed to throw up. She backed away, but he came toward her. "Leave me alone!"

"I don't like being shunned," he said through his teeth.

Why, oh *why* hadn't she brought a gun? What had she been thinking? She needed to get away from him. But how? She couldn't even make it back home without transportation. They'd come too far.

But she refused to be trapped. She'd worry about the consequences later. She bent over and zipped up her suitcase. "If this is what you want, then I've traveled far enough with you."

He laughed bitterly. "You going to the bus station, the airport? You going to rent a car?"

That made her angrier. She stood the suitcase up and pulled out the handle. "I'm leaving."

"Darlin', you can't leave. You're stuck with me."

She ground her teeth together. "Oh, yeah? Watch me!"

With that, she stepped up into the wagon and jerked out her wedding dress. She threw it over an arm and, rolling her suitcase behind her, started off down the street.

She could hear his drunken laughter in the night behind her. "I'll be here when you come to your senses, darlin'!"

She walked faster, the suitcase bumping along the highway. The dress was getting heavier, so she draped it around her shoulders.

The night was so dark that she almost couldn't see where she was going, and fatigue fell over her with a vengeance. She had to go so far that he couldn't find her easily, but she needed sleep, too.

Tears burned her hot face as she walked. *Please, God ... don't let him follow me ...* Surely he wouldn't take the chance of leaving the horses and all his stock. With all her heart, she wished she hadn't come. She had been so sure she was doing the right thing—and now look at her!

Sudden realization struck her. She hadn't grabbed her bottle of water when she'd left! How stupid was that?

She walked between the stalled cars until she was crying so hard that she couldn't go any farther. She leaned against a truck that had been stripped of its wheels, looked up at the sky, and wept.

She was so tired. If she could only lie down and sleep. But she feared sleeping on the ground with nothing to protect her from rodents or snakes ... or evil people.

She looked at the cars around her. She could climb into one of them and curl up comfortably for the night.

If she could just find a car that didn't have glass all over the seats ...

In the darkness, she walked on, checking each car. Finally she came to a van that seemed relatively intact, except for one window that someone had smashed to get inside. She got in, and looked through the vehicle. Though it was dark, it looked like the back bench seat was clean of glass fragments. Relieved, she pulled her suitcase in. She lay down on the backseat, covered herself with her wedding dress, and used her arms to pillow her head.

She felt almost safe.

She cried herself to sleep, praying that God would protect her from vandals and animals ... and Vic Green. Praying that He would help her figure out what to do tomorrow.

As sleep overtook her, she imagined Craig getting his first glimpse of her as she rode into town, running toward her, spinning her in his arms ...

Then the mist of her dreams dragged her back to Crockett, and she saw Brad Caldwell sneaking behind the house as he watched her ... the Abernathys lying on the floor in their blood ... her brother Jeff with a gash on the back of his head ...

Evil played its sharp refrain in her mind as she drifted off, lulling her into dreams of darker terrors than those she'd left behind.

FORTY-NINE

IT TOOK MORE THAN AN HOUR FOR ONE OF THE NEIGHBORS
to locate the sheriff and bring him and several deputies to
Vic Green's home. While Doug waited, he imagined Vic and
Deni traveling farther and farther away. Darkness might
have brought his daughter into even greater danger. Vic was
a killer, and there was no possibility he'd had good intentions when he lured Deni away.

Doug heard Kay throwing up in Vic's bathroom, and
wondered why he wasn't doing the same. Instead of nausea,
he struggled with a simmering, volcanic anger that rumbled
and smoked inside him, threatening to erupt with a vengeance. He was glad Mark had stayed out of his way since
they'd made the discoveries. The boy was downstairs with
his mother and stepfather, ranting about his father. The
emotion in his voice suggested Mark wasn't involved, but
Doug didn't trust him.

And if the boy came within striking distance, Doug
wasn't sure he could control himself.

When the sheriff arrived, Doug showed him what they'd
found. It was indisputable evidence and, according to the
sheriff, offered ample probable cause to make an arrest. If
only they knew where to find Vic.

While Sheriff Scarbrough interviewed Mark, Doug took
Kay home.

He walked her inside, updated the kids on what they'd learned, then grabbed a box of ammunition and started back out, rifle in his hand.

"Where are you going?" Kay's words sounded hollow.

"I'm going back to that house to wait for the sheriff to figure out where they went. Then I'm going after our daughter."

Kay didn't argue. "Doug, please be careful."

When he returned to Vic Green's house, the sheriff was still questioning Mark. Mark's face was wet with tears and glowed red in the light of the oil lamp. His mother paced behind him.

Shadows flickered around the room, like demons wanting to play. Doug couldn't wait to get out of this place.

"My brothers know where he went," Mark said. "Larry and Jack are tighter with him than I am. They work in the family business."

"Did you know your father dealt in pornography?"

Mark studied his feet for a moment. "I knew something wasn't right. I'd found some of his magazines before ... And I knew he had picked up a lot more web-based business in the last few years. He kept all this from me, probably because he knows I'm a Christian and would have been disgusted."

Doug watched Mark's face, wondering if the kid was for real. Maybe it was just a cleverly hatched story that he and his father had prepared in advance. Vic had no qualms about feigning Christianity when it suited his purposes. How could they be sure Mark wasn't the same way? Doug's blood boiled as he thought of Vic sitting in his living room this morning, singing hymns and praying like he meant it.

Mark seemed to read Doug's thoughts. The boy looked up at him, his face twisted with despair. "Mr. Branning, I should have suspected his intentions when I brought him to church this morning. I thought the Holy Spirit was moving him. I thought he was finally coming around."

"I *told* you he wasn't." Martha blew her nose on a handkerchief. "That man is evil. Pure evil. And so are his other sons."

Doug couldn't sit down; he stepped into the light of the lamp and fixed Sheriff Scarbrough with a look. "You need to get over there and interview those boys. Every minute that passes puts my daughter in greater danger."

The sheriff got to his feet. "I agree with you. Give me their addresses, Mark, and we'll head over."

"I'll do better than that. I'll take you there myself. I want to hear what they have to say."

"Mark, no." Martha grabbed her son's arm. "I want you to stay home."

Mark spun around. "Mom, Deni is in trouble. There's no time to waste. I don't want to upset you, but this is something I have to do. They're my brothers. He's my father. And Deni's my friend."

If Mark was faking his concern, he was giving an Oscar-caliber performance. "I'm going, too," Doug said. "I can't go after my daughter until I know where they went."

Sheriff Scarbrough acquiesced. "All right, you can both come. But don't interfere. You let us do the talking. No heroics, no vengeance. We do this according to the law, which still applies, outage or not. No grandstanding. We go smart, so Green won't walk free on a technicality. Got that?"

Doug agreed. "Got it."

They mounted their bicycles, and Mark took the lead.

The two brothers lived a few miles away, both on the same street. Doug and the others found them both at Larry's house, sitting out back, smoking cigars and drinking beer. Doug wondered if the beer had come from the Abernathys or the Whitsons.

The sons bore a striking resemblance to their father, especially in their demeanor. They exuded arrogance as the police identified themselves and asked where their father was.

Larry took a long drag of his cigar, then took his time blowing the smoke out. "Don't have a clue. Why are you looking for him?"

Sheriff Scarbrough was playing it nonchalant. "We have reason to believe he left town with this man's daughter. We need to find her."

Larry and Jack exchanged looks and burst out laughing. Jack looked up at Doug. "Who's your daughter?"

Doug wanted to smash those grins off of their faces. "Deni Branning."

"Oh, *her*." Larry seemed genuinely delighted. "So she went with him, after all, did she? I didn't think she'd give him the time of day."

"Guess we don't give the old man enough credit." Jack high-fived his brother, and the two spat out more laughter.

The eruption hit, and Doug snapped. He lunged forward, intent on knocking that beer bottle out of Jack's hand and smashing the cigar down Larry's throat.

But the deputies grabbed his arms and fought him back.

"Where did he take her, Larry?" Mark demanded.

Larry's eyes glowed with mirth. "How would I know?"

"You know where his perverted stores are."

Larry's grin faded. "I don't know what you're talking about."

Sheriff Scarbrough held up a hand to stem Mark's questions. "Tell us how involved you are with your father's business."

"Not that involved." Jack was no longer amused, either. "Our dad is an entrepreneur, with his hand in a lot of pies. He's got several business ventures going on. We only handle the computer part of it."

"Yeah," Larry added. "We handle the online bookstore. Kind of like Amazon."

"Only with filthy products?" Mark's voice was raspy. "You make me *sick*."

Larry stubbed out his cigar. "Why don't you shut up, you little jerk? You don't know what you're talking about. You're just mad because we cut you out!"

Doug had had enough. Time was ticking on his daughter's life. "Tell us where they went, or so help me, I'll kill you both!"

The sheriff's eyes flashed. "Take him out of here!"

Doug fought the deputies. "Search their houses! Go through the files! Just tell me what towns the stores are in! I have to go after her!"

"Doug, I warned you not to interfere!" Sheriff Scarbrough's finger wagged in his face. "I told you to keep your mouth shut! Now, I don't want to arrest you—"

"Arrest *me*?" Doug couldn't believe what he was hearing. "*They're* the murderers! They're the ones who helped clean out the Abernathys' and Whitsons' houses!"

Larry sprang up. "*Murder?* Now, wait a minute."

The deputies wrestled Doug to the gate. He tried to break free before they could get him through it.

"Dad killed my next-door neighbors!" Mark shouted. "He broke into their house and murdered them for diamonds! They had children, grandchildren. They were decent people who didn't deserve that!"

"That's *enough*!" Sheriff Scarbrough took his handcuffs off his belt and clamped them around Mark's wrists. "Take him out, too," he said through his teeth.

Another set of cuffs clamped Doug's wrists, but he didn't give up. "Where is he? Where did he take her?" he yelled.

"Wherever she wanted to go!" Larry screamed back at him. "Little tramp's been itching to run off with him!"

Doug could have murdered him with his bare hands, had they been free.

"I'm gonna find your sleazy father, and when I do, if he's hurt my daughter, I'll kill him!" he shouted. "I'll tear him apart, limb from limb. And then I'll come back and do the same to you!"

The deputies wrestled him through the gate. "What is *wrong* with you?" one of them asked when they got him into the front yard. "This is a homicide investigation, and you're undermining all our efforts to get at the truth! I should lock you up."

"Oh, right!" Doug bit the words out. "Arrest me, when the whole town's swarming with criminals and lowlifes. Don't do anything about the killers and thieves, but make sure *I'm* behind bars!"

"We ain't lockin' you up, Doug, but you're not helpin' matters. We have a mess on our hands."

"It'll be less of a mess if you lock up those two and then go after their father."

"We can't lock them up. We don't have any evidence against them, and we can't go after Vic Green because we don't have the resources."

Anger shivered through him. "So he could just take my daughter against her will, rape and murder her, and leave her for dead—and *nobody* cares?"

"*You* care!" the deputy said. "You go after them. But we have to stay here. We have a community we have to protect."

"Well, you're not protecting it!" Doug shouted. "Evil is running rampant around here and you're sitting on your hands. My daughter could be dead by now—" The words rang through him, and he blinked back the tears in his eyes. This was useless. He was wasting precious time arguing with them.

"Go home, Doug." The deputy unlocked his handcuffs.

Doug jerked his bike up, threw his leg over it. "I'm going, but so help me, if you don't arrest those two, somebody else is going to wind up dead. Next time it might be *your* wife and children!"

FIFTY

DOUG RODE HOME, THE WIND OF HIS ANGER MAKING HIM FLY. He packed the provisions he would need to go after Deni, and Kay helped him get it all into a backpack he could carry on his bike.

"Jeff, it's going to be up to you to defend the family," he said as he checked his rifle. "The Green boys are still running free, and two of them have an axe to grind with me."

"I can defend us, Dad. You can count on me. I won't sleep at night."

"What about the daytime?"

Kay wiped the tears off of her face. "He and I will take turns. I can carry a gun as well as anybody. Besides, maybe it won't take that long. Maybe you'll find her right away."

Doug thought of his daughter, raped and beaten, murdered on the side of the road. He rode the bike on pure adrenalin, zigging and zagging through the stalled cars on the road, shining his flashlight in front of him, searching for the wagon.

Fortunately, his bike would go faster than a wagon ever could. He'd overtake them soon.

He prayed he wouldn't be too late.

FIFTY-ONE

DENI SLEPT OFF AND ON ALL NIGHT, CURLED UP ON THE backseat of that van, alternately resting and then waking, scared to death of the sounds of whispering leaves and croaking frogs.

Self-loathing pulsed through her. What had she done?

She pictured her mother pacing the floor, crying as though Deni was already dead and buried. Her father was probably out looking for her. Would it even occur to him to try this road instead of the interstate?

She thought of her little sister and brothers. What an example she had been for them. Jeff was probably full of *I-told-you-so*'s about Deni's lack of character. Logan probably enjoyed the drama. Beth was probably crying her eyes out and eating herself up with worry. Hadn't she been traumatized enough?

She wondered what Craig would think when he found out she had put her life into the hands of an alcoholic stranger. He would consider her childish, stupid. Would he reconsider her suitability as his wife? No one with political aspirations wanted a loose cannon in his life. He needed someone stable, strong, smart ...

But it couldn't be undone now. She was here. She'd gotten herself into this mess. Somehow she had to find a way out.

The sky cracked and lightning flashed, and she felt as if God stood in His heaven, arms crossed in judgment for her miserable choices. As the rain began to beat down on the ceiling of the van, she felt even more alone.

She sat up on the bench seat. Wrapping the plastic-covered dress around her, she tried to get warm. She stared out the rain-splattered window, catching glimpses of the road and woods with each flash of light, watching to make sure no more evil approached. The stalled cars reminded her of dread spirits with no homes. The dripping pines and mimosas were places for killers to hide.

And then there was Vic, camping out in the rain, no doubt trying to get his horses to shelter and find a dry place to sleep.

Unless he was passed out drunk.

She tried to make a plan for tomorrow. Should she try to make it to I-20 and head back home? Or should she keep going east? Maybe she could stop off in the next town, find work somehow, and earn enough to buy a bike or horse.

But if these towns were like Crockett or Birmingham, no stores were open and no one would be interested in selling her their transportation. Even her own parents had fought over letting go of some of their bikes.

Maybe she'd have to steal one.

The thought slipped into her mind, then quickly fled. But before she could banish it for good, it crept back.

What was wrong with a desperate person stealing out of necessity? She could target a family with several bikes. They could get by with one fewer. It was practically a victimless crime.

But it was still a crime.

No, as low as she'd sunk, she hadn't sunk low enough to steal. She still had her integrity. Vic Green wasn't going to drive her to crime.

Fatigue finally pulled her under, and she drifted into a shallow sleep, plagued by dreams of running and running, yet never reaching her destination. Then she dreamed she was strapped into a first-class seat in an airliner, sipping on orange juice when the plane plunged, crashed, and tumbled across the tarmac. Fire erupted around her, an inferno from hell.

The sound of her own screams woke her.

She sat up in the van, relieved that sunlight had broken. Morning had finally come.

The rain had stopped, and puddles glistened on the long stretch of road before her.

Her stomach rumbled, and her mouth was parched. Would she be able to find her way back to the brook without running into Vic?

If she'd just waited, maybe the lights would have come back on in a few days and she could have taken normal, civilized means of travel to get to Craig.

Already, it was at least eighty degrees, and the humidity had to be 100 percent. Yesterday she'd had the benefit of the tarp over the wagon to keep the sun from blistering her. Today she had nothing. She hadn't thought to bring sunscreen, or a hat to keep from being scorched.

She just hadn't thought.

She got out of the van, pulling her dress and suitcase with her. The thought of walking to the next town seemed absurd. No, she would go to I-20, and then maybe she could make up her mind whether to go east or west.

As she walked, tears stung her dirty face and the shoes on her feet rubbed blisters. And then she heard it.

Horses' hooves ...

"Deni! Hey, Deni!" Vic's voice carried on the breeze.

Her heart stopped, and she thought of running. But where would she go? There was nothing but woods on either side of the highway, and she couldn't pull her suitcase through.

Besides, Vic didn't sound angry. Maybe he'd slept off his drunkenness.

She stopped and waited, her chin thrust up defiantly, and her teeth ground together.

He laughed at her as he came closer. "You sure you want to do this on your own?"

She couldn't even answer.

"Look, I was drunk last night. I'm paying for it this morning. No reason you should have to pay for it, too."

She looked up at the wagon, hating it—but she hated it less than the long stretch of road, especially if she had to take it one step at a time. He *had* been drinking too much last night. Besides, what were her options?

"Come on, get in," he said. "I've got some water and a granola bar for you. Next time you march off in a huff, you might want to take some food with you."

Her anger withered. She was dying for food and a drink of water. She stood there a moment, staring up at him, wishing she had the strength to march right past him. But she didn't. Her face twisted, and she started to cry like a little girl. "I guess I have no other choice."

"Oh, you have a choice. I'm not gonna force you into this wagon."

She hated herself. She was such an idiot.

But she needed to eat and drink, so she stepped toward the wagon and handed him her wedding dress. He threw it in the back, then reached for her suitcase.

"Now get on up. We can make good time today."

Hope blossomed in her heart.

She stepped up into the wagon, sank into her captain's chair. She hated the smell of it, the smell of the horses, the smell of him, the smell of herself ... but she had no choice but to go on.

He handed her a bottle of water and the granola bar.

"Thank you," she forced herself to say.

"No problem." He tapped the reins.

And they were on their way again.

FIFTY-TWO

EXHAUSTION PLAYED A CLOSE SECOND TO THE FRUSTRATION Doug felt as he pedaled down I-20, stopping at every exit to ask if anyone had seen the bizarre wagon. So far, no one had. And something else disturbed him.

There were no horse droppings in his path.

If Deni and Vic had come this way, wouldn't he see an occasional pile on the road? With four horses, there would have to be some.

They must have gone another way.

He pulled off the road, trying to remember if there was a highway that ran parallel to I-20. There were other roads going east, but for the life of him, he couldn't remember what they were.

He needed a map, but where would he get one with gas stations and stores closed?

The stalled cars. Yes, he could find a map in one of the stalled cars!

He walked his bike to the nearest one, a white Cadillac. Someone had broken the window in and stripped it, so he got in and looked in the door pockets, over the visors, in the glove compartment. There wasn't one there.

He went to the next one, a Caravan, and searched for a map. Again, he came up with nothing.

Moving from vehicle to vehicle, his rifle swinging from its strap on his shoulder, he searched frantically. And then he found it.

On the backseat of a Buick Regal was an atlas with maps of every state. He flipped the pages, found Alabama, and sought out I-20. Yes, parallel to the interstate, was Highway 78. That must be where they were.

Tearing out that page, he stuffed it into his pocket. Then, mounting his bike, he rode like Lance Armstrong to the next exit, and found his way to Highway 78.

FIFTY-THREE

THE HORSES MOVED SLOWER THAN THEY HAD YESTERDAY, AND much to Deni's chagrin, Vic stopped to water them every hour. Their joints were showing signs of stress due to the hard surface of the road. They would do better on dirt or grass, Vic said, but the grass on the sides of the road wasn't flat or wide enough.

They reached the outskirts of Atlanta about midafternoon. The trip that would have taken two hours by car had taken them eleven.

Once again, she despaired of ever reaching her destination.

As the highway took them into town, traffic picked up. Bicyclers passed to and fro. Pedestrians seemed to be everywhere, and an occasional horse and wagon went past. Vic's wagon turned heads, and several walkers called up to them, asking how he'd built the axle holding the wheels on the wagon. Vic pulled over and showed them.

All the while, time hurried by.

While she waited, Deni scanned the stores along the road, looking for a place where she could go to the bathroom in privacy. And then she saw the Dairy Queen up ahead, and two men sweeping the glass in the parking lot.

When Vic got back in the wagon, she pointed up ahead. "Look! That Dairy Queen is open."

He followed her gaze. "No, it's not."

"There are people sweeping. No one would be there sweeping unless they were working there, would they?"

"That doesn't mean they have food."

"No, but maybe they'll let us use their bathroom."

He didn't seem convinced, but he slapped the rumps of his tired horses.

He pulled off the highway onto the frontage road that would take them to the DQ. As they grew closer, Deni could see that its windows had been broken out. Cars with smashed windshields—some stripped of their wheels—filled the parking lot. Two men swept up the broken glass.

Deni called to them. "Are you open?"

One of the sunburned men looked up at her. "If we were, what do you think we'd serve you? Ice cream?"

She hadn't expected such a surly reply. "Excuse me. When I saw you sweeping, I just thought—"

"I'm in charge of this store," the grumpy man cut in, "and somebody broke into it. When the lights come back on, I'm going to have to pick up the pieces. I'm just here trying to get a jump on it."

"Can I use the restroom?"

He looked up at her. "No. I don't have anything to flush with. Find another place."

She couldn't believe he was turning her down. "Come on, I just want a little privacy. We've come all the way from Birmingham."

The man perked up. "Birmingham? Is everything out there, too?"

"'Fraid so," Vic said. "It's out everywhere."

The man moaned and picked his broom up again, and swept the glass viciously into a pile.

"So do you know of anywhere around here we could get a hot meal?" Vic asked.

The man laughed bitterly. "No. And all I've got is a freezer full of spoiled food, no way to dispose of it, a lot of glass to pick up, and no paycheck."

Deni tried again. "Then what will it hurt if I use your restroom?"

He sighed. "All right. But you leave it clean. I got enough to do."

Deni hurried into the Dairy Queen and looked around, trying to breathe in the scent of normalcy, but all she smelled on the stale hot air was rotten hamburger meat. She kicked through the broken glass and made her way to the bathroom.

When she came back out and got into the wagon, Vic was asking the men where he could water the horses.

The man pointed. "Up the street. Go up to that stoplight and take a right. There's a small lake in that neighborhood there." The man stepped closer to the rig. "What you got in that wagon? Any food?"

"Just a few provisions. I'm coming this way on business."

"What business?"

"I own the Sneak Peak."

The man's eyebrows shot up, and for the first time he grinned. "Sneak Peak, huh?"

"That's right. I'm hoping to get my stores back open in the next day or two."

"What makes you think your stuff'll sell, what with everybody scraping for their lives?"

"Hey, people'll always dish out a few bucks for some good reading material."

The man laughed. Deni frowned and looked at Vic, wondering why that was so funny.

THEY FOUND THE LITTLE LAKE SOME TIME LATER, SITUATED AT the center of a circle of houses. They pulled the horses and wagon into an empty lot, and Vic jumped out, filled up a bucket full of water, and brought it for the horses to drink.

"I have to do some business here," he said as they drank. "It'll bore you to death. So I was thinkin' I could leave you here for a couple of hours and come back and get you later."

"A couple of hours?" She gaped up at him. "We'll lose so much time. Couldn't you do business here on the way back, after you've gotten me to D.C.?"

"No, darlin'. I need to get my store open today. We won't lose that much time. Go for a walk. Stretch your legs. I'll be back before you know it."

"How do I know you'll even *be* back? You could leave me stranded here."

"Now why would I do that? If I wanted to get rid of you, I would've let you keep walking this morning."

"Why can't I just come with you?"

He looked back at his wagon, as if trying to decide whether to take her or not. "I don't want to take you because I don't want to hear your yapping about my store."

"My yapping? What would I yap about? I don't care anything about your stupid bookstore!"

His lips compressed, and he took the bucket from the horses. "All right. You can come. But I'm warning you. You yap, and I'm putting you out."

As they rode the few miles to the store, Deni tried to imagine what he was so sensitive about. It must not be much of a store. She pictured an old broken-down building that smelled of mold and dust, with shelves and shelves of used paperbacks.

But then, how did he live in such a fine house and have so much cash?

As they made their slow progress through town, the clomp of those horses' hooves percussing through her, she longed for a *Cosmo* magazine, or *People*. Maybe they had some at his store. She wished she were in Starbucks sipping on a Grande Caramel Mocha Latte with whipped cream while she caught up on celebrity gossip. She longed to watch Regis and Kelly, and *Good Day Live*, to get her nails done, to eat in a restaurant.

But the longings only made her ride worse.

Vic was quiet as he turned the horses down a seedy-looking street, and the horses pulled them past several nightclubs and huge billboards advertising a strip club. A railroad track ran the length of the road they were on, and clusters of men loitered on the corners. They looked like drug dealers.

As they rode by, Deni grew uneasy at the attention their wagon drew. She hoped they wouldn't get curious about the things it contained.

As if Vic had the same thoughts, he pulled his revolver out of his pocket. That made her feel a little better.

"There it is," he said. "There's my store."

She looked up ahead and saw the sign— "SNEAK PEAK." Had there been electricity, the words would have been lit up in red neon on the front of the store, beneath the sign that said "ADULT BOOK STORE."

Deni caught her breath. "You're kidding me."

He shot her a look. "I warned you not to go yapping."

"An adult book store? You sell trashy books?"

"One man's trash is another man's treasure."

He pulled the wagon into the Sneak Peak's parking lot, and she saw a handwritten sign on the front that said "OPEN."

He laughed with delight. "My boy's already got the place open. I have good managers. You want to come in?"

She gave him a disgusted look. "No. I'll stay here, thank you very much."

"All right. I'll leave you the gun. It's loaded. Don't shoot yourself with it."

She took the pistol and watched as he went inside. Nervous, she craned her neck to make sure none of the loitering men approached the wagon. When she was satisfied it was safe, she stood up and reached for one of Vic's boxes. She pulled back the tape sealing it and ripped it open.

Filthy magazines and pictures were stacked there, carefully wrapped in cellophane to protect them, like rare art. She closed the box, feeling sick.

Vic Green was a pornographer. He got rich pedaling his evil in disgusting stores across the country.

And she had run away with him.

Nausea ripped through her. She couldn't go on with him. It was dangerous. She had known it last night and had escaped. Why had she accepted a ride from him again?

She should take her suitcase, her wedding dress, and his revolver, and leave right now, while he was distracted. But wouldn't those men on the street be even more of a threat to her than Vic?

No, she couldn't leave now. She'd have to stay with him until he got her someplace safe. But she would get away from him as soon as it was humanly possible.

She looked back at the loitering men. Business seemed to be good for them. Despite the shortage of food, she supposed drug addicts still found ways to buy drugs. And husbands and fathers spent their families' provisions to feed pornography addictions.

That self-loathing at her own stupidity threatened to smother her again. She closed her trembling hand over that pistol, and prayed for a way out.

FIFTY-FOUR

VIC TOOK BACK HIS GUN WHEN HE GOT INTO THE WAGON AND got the horses moving again. "I have good men running my stores. Key is to compensate them well. Give them a share in the profits, and they'll always put the store first."

Deni sat stiffly in her seat. "If you don't mind, I'd rather not talk about your perverted business. You should have told me the *kind* of bookstores you owned before we left home. I wouldn't have come with you. You misled me into thinking you were a legitimate businessman."

"I *am* legit. There's nothing illegal about selling adult pornography, depending on the city. And I'm legitimately rich. What I do doesn't hurt anybody."

"Tell that to the wives and children of your deviant customers. Does Mark know what you do?"

"Mark couldn't handle it. He has those trumped-up ideas of right and wrong. His mother made a pansy out of him. Much as I'd like for him to share in some of this wealth, he'd be nothing but trouble."

Deni closed her eyes. What was she going to do? Last night was enough to make her flee for her virtue—maybe even her life. Then her stupidity had refreshed itself this morning, and she'd accepted Vic's help again.

Her parents would say she had stinking judgment, and they'd be right. They'd say she was immature and irresponsible, that she wasn't ready to make decisions for herself. That she followed her emotions without a thought, putting herself at risk. That she did whatever she pleased, determined to manipulate things in such a way that they'd work out somehow.

It had always worked that way before. But now ... she was in over her head.

She had to get away from Vic. There was no way she would stay with him tonight. If she could just get help from someone, trade something for a bicycle, she could go back home. But she had nothing to trade.

She turned in her seat and looked in the back of the wagon, to the ridiculous suitcase she'd brought with her. It was full of useless things. A flat iron. A makeup mirror. A blow-dryer. They were worthless, like confederate dollars after the Civil War. They only weighed her suitcase down, made it difficult to carry. No one would want to trade a bicycle for them.

She looked at her precious wedding dress, still in its plastic bag. It, too, weighed her down. Why had she brought it? It was just dead weight, making it impossible for her to move quickly.

Anger rose inside her, at the government, at her parents, at Vic, at herself ...

But most of all, at Craig.

Why hadn't he come? Why had he left her there in Crockett, desperate to see him? Why hadn't he been her knight in shining armor, coming for his princess? Just this once, why hadn't he put her first?

It was *his* fault she had stolen away with this jerk who worked in that sleazy trade, and if anything happened to her because of it, that would be his fault, too. If he'd chosen his work over his bride-to-be, his senator over his fiancée, then he deserved whatever happened.

But it wouldn't happen to him ... it would happen to *her*.

She seethed at the thought of what his neglect might cost her.

Craig always put his work first. Ambitious to a fault, he'd often stood her up for dates without even an apology when Senator Crawford needed him.

She remembered one Sunday afternoon, not so long ago, when he'd promised to meet her for a picnic at the Washington Mall.

She packed fried chicken and potato salad from the local deli, and found the perfect spot to lay her blanket.

Craig forgot to come.

She had finally reached him on his cell phone, and he told her about some public relations crisis that threatened Senator Crawford's reputation. She was expected to understand completely.

So she did.

Even the night he asked her to marry him, he had cut the evening short and run back to the senate office building to work on a bill the senator was proposing. She accepted that, and spent the rest of the evening showing her friends the ring.

Now she hated herself and all she stood for, all she fell for, all she was.

She had to cut her losses and get out of this wagon. She determined that the next safe-looking house she saw would be her destination. She'd get off the wagon and tell Vic good-bye. Maybe some kind soul would show compassion and loan her a bicycle.

Her stomach signaled the dinner hour, but she didn't want him to stop to eat. She wanted to move on, until she could see a place where she could find refuge.

And finally she saw it. A farm off the highway, with a big white house on the other side of a plowed field. She saw people sitting on the porch of that peaceful-looking house, a family enjoying each other's company, children playing in the yard.

Her heart jumped. This was it. This was where she would get off.

"Stop the wagon," she said.

Vic glanced over at her. "Why?"

"Just stop!"

He reined the horses in, and the wagon rolled to a creaking halt.

Deni reached over the boxes of his sleazy books and magazines and pictures, and grabbed her suitcase.

"What are you doing?" Vic watched her throw her suitcase over the side.

"I'm getting off here."

"What? You can't just get off out in the middle of nowhere. What's the matter?"

"I just don't want to go any farther." She grabbed her wedding dress and jumped off the back of the wagon. Walking around to the front, she looked up at him. "Thank you very much for the ride, Vic. But I've changed my mind."

She grabbed up her suitcase, and lifted her dress to keep the bag from dragging the ground.

"Wait a minute. You think you're just gonna up and leave? I haven't done anything to run you off."

"It's not you," she lied. "I just realized this is too hard. I don't think I can handle it for several more days. I want to go home."

"Well, you're not gonna get there. What do you think you're gonna do? Prance back up the highway on foot?"

"I'll think of something. It's not your problem."

He gave her a disturbed, somber look. "If you go back home and tell them about my stores, I swear I'll make you regret you ever knew me. And I'll make your family regret it, too."

The threat hit home. "I won't tell them, Vic. I don't want them knowing how stupid I am."

It was then that the farmhouse caught his eye, and he saw the family sitting on the porch. "Oh, I get it. You think you'll get help from them."

Deni turned and looked at them. "So what? That shouldn't affect you at all. It's just a decision I've made."

"You scared of me now? Is that it?"

She swallowed. "No. I'm just tired and hot. I've had it. I regret coming in the first place."

He looked up toward the house with narrow eyes, and watched the people for a moment. Someone from that porch got up and walked down the steps, staring their way. It was an older woman, and she looked kind. She waved.

Vic waved back.

"I have to go." Deni got her suitcase, pulled out the handle, and tried to roll it through the soft grass, toward the barbed wire fence at the edge of their field. She glanced back, and saw Vic laughing softly. Let him laugh, as long as he left.

She heard him slap the horses with the reins, heard their feet clomping on the road again. It was too good to be true. He was leaving, and she would really be rid of him!

She took her suitcase, and with both hands, hefted it up and dropped it over the fence. Carefully, she dropped the dress over, letting it fall on the luggage. Then she pulled up the bottom wire and squeezed under it.

When she stood back up, she saw that the woman had come out into the yard, and seemed to be waiting for her. She didn't look angry that Deni had trespassed, or that she was crossing over their plowed field of beans.

Deni's feet sank into that soft dirt as she carried her wedding dress on one arm and the suitcase that felt as if it held cement blocks in the other.

By now that whole family had come off the porch and waited for her in the yard. One of the younger men came toward her.

She trudged forward as fast as she could, hoping they were as kind as they appeared.

Finally, the man approached her. He was young, maybe twenty-four or twenty-five.

"Hi," she said, out of breath. "I'm Deni Branning. I was hoping you could help me. I've been on the road for a couple of days—"

"Welcome, Deni." He took the suitcase out of her hand. "Mama saw you coming and told me to run out and help you."

"Thank you." She surrendered the suitcase, but held on to the dress.

"You look like you have a story to tell, and we need some entertainment." As they started back toward the house, he nodded to the dress over her arm. "Can I help you with that?"

"No. It's my wedding dress. I'll carry it myself."

He laughed then. "Well, that ought to make a doozy of a story." Calling up toward the house, he said, "She brought her wedding dress, everybody! And here I thought I was gonna have to go looking for a bride."

The family laughed as Deni and the young man came off the field, and she was suddenly surrounded by smiling, friendly people —the older couple who owned the farm, their two married daughters, sons-in-law, and grandchildren, and Michael, the handsome young man who had come to relieve her of her load.

She would be safe here, she thought as they invited her in. But as she started up the steps of the big house, she heard the sound of clomping hooves.

Her heart sank as she saw Vic in his wagon, coming up the long driveway from a side road.

FIFTY-FIVE

Frances Jones insisted that both Deni and Vic stay in their home for the night. Vic took her up on the offer right away, explaining that he and his "daughter" had had a little tiff out there on the road, and when they'd seen the house, Deni had huffed off. Frances seemed to understand the temper and mood of a young woman. She probably thought Deni was just a spoiled brat who didn't respect her father.

Before Deni could get away from Vic again, he took her aside. "You tell them one negative thing about me, little gal, and you're gonna see some wrath like you've never seen. Don't mess with me. You're way out of your league."

She shivered at the thought of what he meant by that.

Since the Joneses had a henhouse full of chickens, Frances cooked them a feast of scrambled eggs and gave them their fill of milk and water fresh from the well. As they ate, the family drilled them about the state of the world. Vic told them about Hank's message from Washington and what they'd seen on their trip so far.

As it began to get dark, the Joneses' children left to return to their own homes, leaving only Frances and Jim with Deni and Vic. Frances led Deni up to her room and lit a kerosene lamp. She'd had Jim bring up a bowl of water so Deni could wash. "You look tired, honey. I hope you'll be comfortable in this bed tonight."

Deni burst into tears. She sat down on it, careful not to get the dirt from her journey on the lavender bedspread.

"You have no idea how comfortable I'll be here. Last night I slept in a van with a smashed-out windows."

Frances picked up the wedding dress lying crumpled in its bag on a chair. "So you're trying to get to the east for your wedding?"

"I was. I'm not so sure anymore."

"Why not? Your dad made it sound like you were desperate to see your fiancé."

Deni looked out into the hall, making sure Vic wasn't nearby. "He's not my dad."

Frances just looked at her in the yellow light, then quietly, she went to the door and closed it. She came to sit beside her on the bed. "If he's not your dad, why did he say he was?"

"Because he's trying to seem presentable. Less threatening."

"Who is he, then?"

"He's a man who lived in my neighborhood in Crockett. He offered to take me east, and I was such a fool, I took him up on it. I didn't know that he deals in pornography."

Frances gasped. "Oh, my."

"His wagon is full of it. He owns a chain of sleazy stores. I have to get away from him." Tears rolled down her face, and she wiped them away. She looked down at her fingers and saw the dirt that had come off of her face. She must look awful.

Frances put her arm around her and pulled her close. "Well, honey, what can we do to help you get home?"

She swallowed and tried to think. "If you had a bicycle I could ride, then I could get away from him. And he wouldn't be able to catch up to me."

"Catch up to you? Why wouldn't he just let you go?"

"I don't know. I think he's afraid I'll go home and tell everyone what he really is. I thought I was rid of him when I got off the wagon. But now he's here."

A deep frown cut through Frances's forehead as she went to the window and looked out. Deni came to stand beside her. She saw Vic down at the wagon, talking to Jim, who seemed to be admiring his ingenuity in building it.

"What should we do?" Frances asked.

"I don't know."

"Do you think he's dangerous?"

"He has a gun. He seems dangerous to me. I don't want to be alone with him one more minute. But he's probably harmless as far as you guys are concerned." She looked at the woman. A thick vein ran from Frances' hairline to her eyebrows. "I'm so sorry I brought this on you. I thought he'd let me go, and that would be the end of it."

"I'll talk to Jim and see what he thinks we should do. Meanwhile, you can lock this door to make sure he stays away. Just relax and don't worry about a thing. My Jim will ask him to leave."

Alarm ran through Deni. "Please, don't make him mad. I don't know what he'll do."

"My Jim is a godly man with a lot of wisdom," she said. "He'll know how to handle it. As for you, we have three ten-speeds back in the barn. I'll give you one to get home."

Deni felt like she'd won the lottery. "Thank you. I knew you could help me."

Frances smiled and pushed Deni's hair back over her shoulder. The gesture made her long for her mother. "Just doing what I would want someone to do for my daughter if she was in your shoes. Consider it God's provision."

More tears rushed to Deni's eyes. "You remind me of my parents. They're good Christian people. They'd do the same thing. I miss them. They must be so upset."

"Then get home as fast as you can, sweetheart. Get a good night's sleep, so you can get a fresh start in the morning. Maybe you'll make it home by nightfall. Jim and I will be praying for you."

Deni felt better as Frances stepped out into the hall, and she locked the door. She closed the curtains over the open window, undressed, and began to wash herself. Then, pulling on a clean pair of jogging shorts and a T-shirt, she slipped into bed, listening for the sound of the wagon pulling away.

Tomorrow she would be rid of him. And with the bicycle, she would get home.

Her gaze drifted to that wedding dress. She got up and unzipped the bag. The dress was unsoiled and still intact. She pulled out the veil, and put it over her dirty hair.

She'd had such hopes for her wedding day.

Tears returned to her eyes as she looked down at that ring Craig had given her. It was beautiful. He'd picked out exactly what she wanted. He'd had genuine joy in his eyes as she'd accepted it.

So what if he'd gone back to work that night? Didn't she want someone with such a bright future? Wasn't she going to be just as ambitious when she started her job?

After all, she was an independent woman. She didn't need a man's undivided attention.

And so what if he hadn't come for her? Didn't the highways work both ways? If he'd had to stay to help the government solve these monumental problems, she couldn't fault him for that.

Yes, she'd told Frances she would go home. And she'd meant it ... then. But what if she *could* make it to Craig?

She thought of the joy she would see on Craig's face as she ran into his arms. He would lift her up and swing her around, and there would never be any doubt in his mind that she was the woman he needed to spend his life with. He liked her spunk, her independence, her courage—and he'd be proud of her for making it all the way.

Happy with her new plan, she drifted into sleep with that veil on her head, and dreamed about their sweet reunion.

FIFTY-SIX

KAY'S PRAYERS HAD NEVER BEEN MORE INTENSE — OR MORE desperate. She lay facedown on her bed, her sheets wet from her tears, and begged God to bring Deni and Doug home. Doug had left almost twenty-four hours ago, and she hadn't heard from him since.

Where were they?

Lord, please protect both of them!

She'd expected him to be gone a few hours. But that had stretched into the day, and soon it would be nightfall again. What could that mean? Possible scenarios drifted through her mind. He hadn't found Deni yet. Or he'd met with foul play of his own. Or he'd found her dead ...

That murderer who had her daughter might have killed them both. When would she know? How would anyone get word to her?

Panic rippled through her as she prayed, begging God to intervene. She hadn't eaten since yesterday, and couldn't remember if she'd fed the kids lunch or not. They hadn't asked about dinner, so she assumed they'd found something to eat.

If she could only talk to her parents, ask them to come and help her, have a few minutes of their wisdom. It had been a month since they'd spoken. Her mother would know exactly what to say. Just the sound of her voice would give Kay peace.

But that wasn't going to happen.

She'd have to handle it all herself. Somehow, she had to pull herself together enough to do what had to be done.

"Mom?"

Wiping her face, she looked up at Jeff, standing in the doorway of her bedroom. His shotgun had become like an extra appendage. She hadn't seen him without it since Doug left. "Yeah, honey, what is it?"

"Miss Eloise is here. Do you feel like talking to her?"

Kay forced herself to get up. She wiped her face and finger-brushed her hair. "Yeah, tell her I'm coming."

There had been a constant stream of visitors today, some trying to comfort her, others just getting information. Rumors about Vic Green had spread through the community like wildfire. She'd finally asked the kids to tell anyone else who came that she was sleeping.

But Eloise was different.

The frail woman was sitting on the couch when Kay came out of her room. Kay sat down next to her and they hugged. Eloise's arms felt like her own mother's, secure and confident.

"Still no word, huh?"

Kay shook her head. "Absolutely none."

"I've been praying, honey. You know God's in control. From where He sits, He knows exactly where Deni and Doug are. He has them in the palm of His hand. He has a host of angels at His disposal to surround and protect them. You believe that, don't you?"

In theory, she did. God was sovereign, and she knew that. He had promised never to leave or forsake them. But Deni was rebellious. Had she stepped out of God's protection when she launched out on her own? "I do believe it, but sometimes there are circumstances that cause God to take His hand away. And sometimes He allows disaster to come into our lives to do things in us. He did that with the outage. What if He's doing that with my child? What if He's going to take her? What if He's going to take Doug?"

Eloise patted her knee. "Those aren't the right questions, Kay. The question is, do you trust Him? Whatever the case, whatever

He has planned for you or your husband or children … Do you trust Him to do the right thing?"

Kay didn't want that to be the question, because she didn't know how to answer it. She regarded her neighbor through the blur of her tears. Eloise looked smaller, more sickly, than she had a month ago. Her cancer was taking its toll on her. "You've had to ask yourself that question, haven't you?"

The wrinkles on Eloise's face deepened. "I sure have, darlin'. Had to search deep in myself for the answer. But I realized I do trust Him. Whether He has healing in mind for me, or taking me home, I trust Him to do the right thing."

Kay wished she had that kind of faith. She breathed a laugh. "You may have noticed I'm not that good with suffering."

Eloise patted her hand. "Don't worry about it. It's a learned skill."

Kay pulled her feet up onto the couch, hugged her knees. "You make it look easy."

"Well, it is, if you trust Him." Eloise's hands trembled as she clasped them. It was clear she was waning. The cancer was winning the battle with her body. So why did Eloise still seem like the victor? "Funny, isn't it, that our problems are relative? Now you see why this outage hasn't shaken me like it has so many others."

Kay thought she understood. "You have much bigger problems."

"Oh, it's not that, dear. Not at all. I've been able to take it in stride because I started letting go of the things of this world months ago, when I first learned of my cancer. If God wants to take my technology, then so be it. If He wants to take my life, it's His."

Kay tried to absorb some of that faith, but she wasn't ready to let Deni go. And she didn't want to be a widow.

Eloise leaned forward and touched Kay's chin with her trembling hand. Kay looked into her wise eyes. "Darlin', I'm not telling you to get over it, or to stop praying your loved ones home. I'm not even telling you to stop worrying. You can't do that, no matter how hard you try, and God knows."

"Then what are you telling me?"

"I'm telling you to turn your focus from Vic Green's evil to Christ's love. Focus on His power."

The beginnings of peace crept into Kay's spirit. "I can do that."

"Of course you can. You're one of His children, aren't you? And so are your loved ones."

Tears rolled down Kay's cheeks, and Eloise wiped them away.

A knock on the back door startled them, and Kay looked through the french doors and saw Brad and Judith Caldwell. Brad held something in his hands.

Jeff stepped into the family room and glanced at her. "You want to talk to them?"

Kay hadn't spoken to them since the sheriff questioned Brad yesterday. They knew who their accusers were. They had every right to be angry.

"Yeah," she said, getting up. "I owe them an apology."

Slowly, she went to open the door. "Brad, Judith ... I should have come over to tell you how sorry—"

Brad held up a hand. "No need, Kay. Really, we're over it."

"Over it? You can't be."

There was no anger on Judith's face. "Kay, if I'd had the same evidence about you or Doug, I'd have come to the same conclusion. It's forgotten."

"We know who the killer is now," Brad said. "That's the important thing. And with all that's going on with Deni and Doug, you don't need to waste one more ounce of energy worrying about us."

Judith lifted the towel covering the platter in Brad's hand. "We made you dinner. Brad and the boys caught a lot of fish today over at Lake Bishop. We had extra. And they picked strawberries on the way back—way more than we could eat."

Extra? No one ever had extra. Kay's heart swelled with gratitude. God was providing. Smiling, she took the platter and hugged them both. "You're such good friends."

Brad's eyes glistened with compassion as he looked down at her. "Kay, let me know if you need anything. Whatever I can do ..."

"I appreciate that. But for right now, I think we're all right. Jeff's taking good care of us."

She glanced back at her son, who stood with that shotgun at his side. He'd grown up a lot in the last few days. Her affirmation seemed to give him strength, and he stood taller as he came and took the platter out of her hands.

He closed his eyes as he breathed in the scent of the meal. A poignant smile came over his face. "God is good," Jeff said.

"Yes, He is," Kay whispered. She knew she could trust in that.

FIFTY-SEVEN

DOUG'S LEGS STRAINED AGAINST THE PEDALS OF HIS ten-speed, and he wished he'd bought one that fit his body better. The year he'd bought it, he'd been on a health kick and resolved to ride forty miles a week. That lasted for about three weeks, and then he'd parked the bike and never gotten it out again.

Not until the outage.

Now his body was paying. He'd been riding since the wee hours of morning, and it was dark again.

Whenever he came to a town, or even a sprinkling of houses off the interstate, he stopped and asked if anyone had seen the covered wagon with the Goodyear tires and four horses. It was a slow process, but the few people who had seen the wagon affirmed that he was going the right direction.

He was making much better time than the horses and wagon could. But when he came to Atlanta, he realized he had no choice but to stop and rest.

He loaded his bike into a vandalized full-sized van, dusted the glass off of the seat, and lay down.

He would sleep for a couple of hours, then be on his way again. He was getting closer. He could feel it. But in the darkness, he feared he would pass them without seeing them.

Lord, protect Deni tonight, and protect my family back home. Please, God . . . He started to weep as he lay there, feeling the sting of his aching muscles, the pang of hunger, the ache of helplessness. *You're all I've got. My refuge and my strength. Please, help us all.*

He wiped his tears on his sleeve, and told himself that he didn't have time to cry. He had to take a nap—just a short one—so that he could get back on the road again.

FIFTY-EIGHT

DENI WOKE TO THE SOUND OF SQUAWKING CHICKENS. SHE SAT up, disoriented. It took her a moment to figure out where she was.

Oh yes. The Joneses' farm.

White lace covered her face. She lifted it up, realizing she'd fallen asleep in her veil. She sat up and examined it. It was wrinkled, but no harm was done.

She had slept deep and long, and she could tell through the curtains that daylight had taken its hold on the day.

She got out of the comfortable bed, stretched, and pulled back the curtain to see what the noise was.

Vic's wagon was still there.

Her heart plunged. Had Jim decided to let him stay last night?

She saw Vic coming off the porch. He was loading something into the wagon, something she couldn't see under the tarp roof. When he'd finished, he went back to the porch, and came back with a cage of chickens. As the birds cawed and cackled, he put them into the wagon, walked back to the porch, and came back with another cage.

Why was he taking the Joneses' chickens?

Maybe he'd bought them with all that cash he had.

She couldn't worry about it now. Somehow she had to sneak away without him seeing her. She got dressed, brushed her teeth, and packed her suitcase. She left out the hair dryer and flat iron, the makeup mirror, and all the useless things

that weighed the suitcase down. Maybe when the power came back
on, Frances could give them to her daughter.

She closed the suitcase and looked down at it, trying to figure
out how in the world she would carry it on the bike. There was no
place to put it. No, it would never work.

She looked around, trying to think of what to do next. Maybe
she should just leave it all here, and hope she got back home by
nightfall. But if she didn't make it, she would need a change of
clothes, her toothbrush ...

Even so, she wouldn't need nearly as much as she'd believed
she needed two days ago. The things she *really* needed would fit
into her wedding dress bag. Quickly, she unzipped it and threw
her necessities in with the silk gown and veil. She could drape that
around her shoulders and carry it on the bike.

Now if she could only get out of the house and to the barn
without alerting Vic. She thought of going downstairs and having
breakfast with the family, but then she'd have to talk to him. He'd
be waiting for her, and if she tried to shake him off, he would come
after her. No, it was better if she sneaked out the back way, and got
out of Dodge before he knew she was missing.

Quickly, she scrawled Frances and Jim a thank-you note.

Dear Frances and Jim,
  Thank you so much for being Good Samaritans to me.
You've saved my life. I'll never forget you. Please forgive me
for slipping away quietly, but I had to get away from Vic.
Hopefully, I'll be back home by nightfall. Some day I'll come
back and thank you properly for your kindness.

                                        Love,
                                        Deni Branning

She quietly slipped down the stairs. There was no sign of anyone in the house. They were probably out front with Vic.

She stole through the living room, and into the kitchen. No
one was there, either. She reached the back door, turned the knob.
Suddenly, she heard him bounding into the house.

"Come on, little gal!"

She swung around. Vic stood in the kitchen doorway, hands on his hips. "It's about time you got up. We've got to get going."

She clutched the wedding dress bag against her. "Where are the Joneses?"

"Out milking the cows. Come on now."

She looked through the window on the back door and saw no sign of them.

"Come on, time's wasting."

She realized she was caught. There was no way to slip off quietly, so she decided to be direct. "I'm not going, Vic. I'm staying here."

He stared at her for a moment. "I knew you were gonna pull this. But it won't work. You're not going back there to ruin me." His tone held a deadly calm, and she caught a whiff of whiskey on his breath.

She swallowed. "I'm not gonna tell anyone, Vic. I'm not even going home."

His eyes were like ice, and something in them terrified her. "That's not a chance I can take."

She backed away, looking out the window toward the barn. The cows were in the field. They weren't being milked. She wondered why he wasn't speaking in a quiet voice. It was as though he had no fear of being overheard—

A shudder went through her. Something had happened to the Joneses. That was why Vic was still here.

"I told you to get in the wagon. Now."

She couldn't catch her breath, and her heart pounded so hard it made her dizzy. What choice did she have?

She decided to feign compliance. "Okay, I'll come. You're right. I can't get to Craig by myself. Just let me get my suitcase." She moved away before he could grab her, and bolted toward the stairs.

"I'll get your suitcase. Get in the wagon now!"

Ignoring him, she ran up the stairs and through the hallway. She heard him following her, his feet bounding up the stairs.

"Deni, so help me!"

She ran to the Joneses' bedroom, threw open the door—

And there she saw them … lying on the floor.

Deni screamed.

She heard Vic's feet stomping up the hall, coming for her. She slammed the door closed, locked it.

"Let me in, or I'll kill you, too!"

She knew he would. He had to. He couldn't let her go and expose him as a murderer. Her mind raced as she stepped over the bodies, slipped in the blood. She dropped the wedding dress, and stumbled toward the window. There was no place to go, no place but out the window and two floors down.

He banged on the door, shaking it with his fury. Any minute it would burst open. She went to the open window, put her leg over the sill. She grabbed the curtain and hung on, hoping the rod was well secured to the wall. She let herself down slightly, caught her foot on some eaves over the bottom floor, managed to get her bearings …

Then jumped down the rest of the way.

She scanned the acreage behind the house. Off to her right was farmland with rows of green plants about knee high. No hiding place there. To the left was a pasture, where the cows grazed. The chicken coop and barn were on the other side of the pasture— surrounded by woods where she could hide.

She heard the bedroom door splinter open, heard Vic thundering her name. She took off across the grassy field, her feet sinking into the soft soil. If she could get to the barn and get a bicycle, maybe she could get away before Vic caught up to her.

She heard the backdoor to the house crash open, and looked back over her shoulder. Vic was racing after her, lifting his gun, aiming …

She reached the barn, threw the wide wooden door open. It smelled of hay and cow dung, and it took a second for her eyes to adjust to the change in light. She searched the junk in the corners, and found the bikes leaning against the wall. Grabbing the first one she came to, she dragged it to the back door and kicked it open.

"You can't get away from me, little gal." His voice was confident, bold, as he reached the barn's front door. She glanced back,
saw the revolver first as he cautiously came in.

Throwing her leg over the bike, she launched out the barn's
back door. Pushing the pedals with all her might, she made her way
across the soft pasture, straight for the woods.

God, help me!

A muffled *thwack* sounded behind her, and she felt the brush of
wind across her cheek. A bullet! He was shooting at her!

She reached the trees, and spotted a walking path. She turned
into it, thankful for the harder ground, the clear path.

He was coming after her, but she didn't dare look back. As she
picked up speed, putting distance between them, she saw a road
up ahead.

The minute the tires hit pavement, she shifted the levers into
the highest gear and took off down the road. She'd have to stick
to the back roads, hiding from him until he gave up. But she was
faster than he, thanks to the weight of the wagon and the horses'
sore joints. Even if he rode one of the horses after her, she'd gotten
a head start, and he didn't know which way she'd gone.

She cried as she rode, thinking of that evil man killing those
kind people. Michael would probably come up for breakfast and
find his parents there, murdered because they'd taken in two weary
travelers. They would think she was an accomplice. They would
consider her a killer, too.

Tears blurred her vision as she came to a crossroads, and tried
to decide which way to go. She looked up at the sun, trying to
gauge which way was east. Did the sun rise or set in the east? The
only thing that came to her was that balcony scene from *Romeo
and Juliet*, where Romeo had said something about the east, and
Juliet being the sun, but for the life of her, she couldn't remember
anything more.

She figured she'd left the farmhouse going south, so she took
the road going to the left, praying it would take her east. But was
that right?

Vic was probably beating the pavement to find her ... intent on killing her to keep her from talking ...

Slowly, she realized that he must be the one who killed the Abernathys and the Whitsons. *He* was the killer in her neighborhood.

As that thought occurred to her, she realized Larry and Jack, those sleazy lecherous sons of his, were probably his accomplices. Maybe even Mark.

If that was the case, then she had to tell her family. She *had* to get back home before Vic returned.

That meant she couldn't go east. She had to go west.

What *was* that line from Shakespeare's play? She tried to think. She had memorized it in school, even embroidered it on a handkerchief.

She'd thought it was burned into her memory. Why couldn't she remember it now?

Aloud, she tried to pant out the words. "But soft, what light through yonder window breaks? It is the east, and Juliet is the sun." Yes, that was it. What did that mean? Was the sun rising or falling in the east? She tried to think of the next line, and had to start over. This time, the line came back to her. "Arise, fair sun, and kill the envious moon."

The sun was *rising* in the east!

She looked at the sun. If she rode away from it, that should take her west. But she had to find another road, because backtracking was too dangerous.

She rode with all her might, searching for back roads that would take her back home ... and away from Vic Green.

FIFTY-NINE

MORNING SUNLIGHT WOKE DOUG FROM A DEAD SLEEP, AND he jolted upright. He'd slept too long. What had gotten into him?

If he'd gotten up when he planned, he might have overtaken Vic and Deni while they were stopped for the night. Now they were probably already moving, getting that much farther ahead of him.

He jumped on his bike, and rode until he came to Atlanta, where he got off the freeway at every exit, showing Deni's picture and describing the wagon. Finally, he ran into someone who had seen them.

"Yeah, I saw them yesterday, long about midafternoon," the man said. "I saw them pull in down there at the Dairy Queen. I remember because I thought it was real funny, them pulling up in a horse and wagon trying to go through the drive-thru like they were gonna order a Coke."

Relief burst through him. "Are you sure it was them?"

"Sounds like you described. A wagon with big Goodyear tires, a blue tarp for a roof, four horses pulling. Only one I've seen like that."

Doug's heart raced as he peered up the street to the Dairy Queen. "Do you know if the people they talked to are there now?"

"Doubtful. There's not much point in it. It's not like they can sell anything."

"Tell me about the girl," he said. "Could you tell if she looked like she was all right?"

"Looked fine to me."

Thank You, Lord!

"Which way did you see them go when they left the DQ?"

"Toward town. Little later they came back this way, got on the interstate, and kept trucking east."

Good. He was still on the right track. He thanked the man, then rode down to the Dairy Queen. Sure enough, it was empty.

As he got back on the eastbound interstate, he felt new energy seeping into his legs. Vic and Deni would have had to stop somewhere for the night, so they couldn't have made it that much farther than he had. He should catch up to them very soon.

And when he did, Vic Green would wish he'd never been born.

SIXTY

DENI RODE WITH ALL HER MIGHT, FIGHTING BACK THE nagging doubts that she was going in the right direction. She pedaled until the muscles in her legs burned and her back and shoulders screamed out for relief. *Help me get home, Lord! Help me get home.*

She had nothing to eat, and for miles she had ridden without any water. She needed to stop and rest, but she feared Vic would catch up with her.

She thought of the Joneses' children, wondered if they'd found their parents yet. When they did, grief like an infection would implant itself in their hearts and fever its way through the rest of their lives.

She never should have insisted on stopping there yesterday. But how could she have known?

She was such a fool, traipsing across that field with her clunky suitcase in one hand and that wedding dress in the other, bringing death to the Joneses' doorstep.

She hated herself and all the trouble she'd brought on others.

Now, here she was, pedaling for her life, with no food, no water, and no place to get either. She'd left with nothing. Her wedding dress still lay on the floor where she'd dropped it, like a banner proclaiming, "Deni Branning was here." They would think she'd been part of the killings. And if Vic was caught, he'd make sure they came after her, too.

As the temperature rose and her mouth grew as dry as cotton, helplessness boiled up inside her, growing so intense that she finally stopped, letting her bike fall to the ground under the shade of a huge oak tree. She stood there beside it, staring down at the bike that the police would think she had stolen.

God, please don't let them think I'm a killer.

If they did, they'd come after her, and she'd be thrown into some dark prison cell.

She sat down on the grass, leaning back against the tree trunk, and began to weep.

Oh, Lord, he's out there and he's going to kill somebody else. Anyone who gets in his way or has something he needs is dead. I've got to stop him, Lord. Please help me.

She covered her face, wishing with all her heart that her mother and father were here. Or that Craig would come riding up miraculously, her knight in shining armor.

But the only one coming for her was Vic. He was probably hot on her trail, figuring out ways to catch up to her. He'd probably stolen one of the other bikes in the barn. He could be watching her right now.

Or maybe not. He couldn't have left the wagon there. That would defeat his whole purpose in killing the Joneses. He'd want the loot, and the chickens, which would net a nice profit. He wouldn't want to leave such a red flag flying, pointing police to him. Maybe he was far behind her. Maybe she'd lost him entirely.

She closed her eyes and tried to pray some more, but she felt like God had turned His face from her. Why wouldn't He? She'd been rebellious and arrogant. Foolish. Irrational. Shouldn't He be disgusted with her?

Her father said God would provide. Didn't He provide for the birds of the field ... the lilies of the valley? If she needed a fish, would He give her a stone?

Maybe. If a stone was what she deserved.

She tried to pull herself together and get back on the road. But as a breeze whispered behind the trees, she thought she heard the sound of water.

She got up and listened, wondering if she'd conjured the sound in her mind. She heard it again.

Her heart pounded with new vigor as she grabbed her bike up. Rolling it beside her, she pushed through the trees and brush.

And there it was. A babbling brook, twisting through the forest.

Tears stung her eyes again. It was a miracle. A provision from God Himself.

She'd heard somewhere that rushing water, like that in a brook, was clean and safe. Living water, they called it. Just what she needed. But even if that myth was wrong, Deni didn't care. Getting a parasite and dying was better than dying of thirst.

She dropped the bike again and stumbled to the brook, knelt down and splashed some water onto her face. Cupping it in her hands, she drank it down. As the cool liquid filled her, her heart was overcome with gratitude. But that gratitude was followed by shame. God *was* watching over her, providing, even after she'd kicked dirt in His face.

She drank as much as she could, wishing she had some kind of container that she could take with her. But she had nothing. Maybe God would see fit to provide for her again when she needed it later.

But she couldn't stay here longer. There was still a lot of daylight left and she needed to move.

Reluctantly she walked her bike back through the trees, pulled onto the road, and continued her desperate journey.

SIXTY-ONE

DOUG SAW THE FARMHOUSE ACROSS THE FIELD FROM THE interstate. Maybe the residents had seen the wagon pass by. He stopped pedaling and tried to decide how to get to the house. Then he saw the road just past their property, hidden behind a grove of trees.

He turned onto the road ... and caught his breath.

There were tire tracks, laid there after the rain ...

And horse droppings.

His heart raced as he saw the turnoff to the farmhouse. *Please, God, let me find Deni.*

He stopped at the porch steps. The front door was wide open. Abandoning his bike, he trotted up to the steps and knocked on the door casing. No one came, so he called out, "Hello! Anybody home? Hello!"

Nothing. Taking a step inside the house, he called out louder. "Hello!" He went toward the staircase ... and froze.

A bloody footprint smudged the bottom stair.

Dread overtook him, and his heart began to sprint. He reached for the rifle hanging from its sling, readied it for action.

Sweat dripped in his eyes as he went from room to room, realizing the house had been robbed. The kitchen cabinets were open, and a few boxes of rice and macaroni lay on the floor as if they'd been dropped.

He ran up the stairs, keeping his rifle ready, and stopped cold at the first bedroom when he saw Deni's suitcase lying on the bed. Joy burst through him ... followed by stark terror.

"Hello? Deni!" His hands were shaking, and his throat was dry. His head had begun to throb. He took a few steps up the hall, and saw more bloody prints. They led out of the bedroom at the end of the hall. The door was partially open, but it looked like it had been kicked in. With his foot, he pushed the splintered door all the way open.

And there they were.

A man and a woman, lying on the floor ... just like the Abernathys ... and the Whitsons.

He stumbled back out, but as he did he saw the white dress bag lying on the floor. Forcing himself forward, he picked it up.

Deni's wedding dress! Had she fled and left it behind? There were small footprints in the blood, leading to the window. She must have climbed out.

He looked back at the broken door. Someone had clearly kicked it in. He imagined his daughter's terror as she fled, stepping over dead bodies, tracking through blood, jumping out a second-story window.

He turned back and ran down the stairs, his stomach bucking inside of him. Stumbling back outside, he vomited in the grass.

Dead people ... murdered ... Deni's dress ... *Where was she?*

Wiping his mouth, he tried to think. His chest was tight, and he couldn't breathe.

Think, Branning! Think!

He needed to tell the police. But first he had to find Deni.

Forcing himself to move, Doug ran out into the back pasture. There was no way to tell which way Deni had gone when she climbed out the window.

He scanned the landscape. The only places to hide were a barn and the woods behind it. He ran toward the barn, hope teasing him with feeble logic. He expected to find her there, hunched behind a tractor, alive but shivering in fear.

But his rapid search came up empty.

Two bikes leaned against the wall, and tire tracks on the dirt led out the back door. Had Deni taken one of the bikes?

Maybe she'd gotten away.

But if she had, Vic certainly would have gone after her. Where was his wagon?

Doug ran back to get his own bike, then followed the tracks to the woods. They led him to a small walking track threaded through the trees.

Yes, she had gotten away! But had Vic caught up to her?

He glanced back at the farmhouse. He should find someone at a nearby house and tell them about the dead couple. But there wasn't time.

So he followed Deni's trail, praying that he would find her alive.

SIXTY-TWO

THE SUN WASN'T FALLING RIGHT. DENI REALIZED WITH A sinking heart that she'd gotten west and east mixed up. The arc of the sun should go directly in front of her if she was going west, but instead, it was arcing off to her right. What did that mean? Was Highway 27 taking her south?

Dread fell over her as she rode, but she couldn't decide whether to turn around and backtrack. She decided to keep going until she came to a town, and then ask someone where this road led.

She rode for several miles without seeing anyone. Then finally, she saw a trio of bikers half a mile away, riding toward her. She slowed as they approached her. "Excuse me," she called up to them. "Could you help me?"

One of them slowed to a stop. Balancing his bike with a foot, he said, "Sure, what you need?"

"I'm trying to get to the Birmingham area. Am I going the right direction?"

The man laughed, and his buddies who had ridden ahead began to laugh, too. "What made you think 27 would take you west?"

Romeo and Juliet, she wanted to cry. Shakespeare *said* the sun rose in the east ...

She knew how ridiculous it would sound. "It looked like west when I started out, but the stupid road must have turned."

They laughed again.

She didn't even care that they found her so amusing. "Please ... is there some place where I can get some water?"

The man's humor faded. "You set out on a trip with no water?"

She didn't want to go into it. "It's a long story."

The man slung off his backpack and pulled a jug of water out. "Here, take this. I'm close to home, and you have a long trip."

Cautiously, she took the jug, and pulled the top off. Half expecting it to be something foul that would send them all into hysterical laughter, she took a sip. It was water, clear and clean. Gratitude seeped through her, and her eyes filled with tears. "Thank you. You're an answer to prayer."

The man smiled at that, then gave her directions back to I-20. "Get back there, and you'll get home faster."

The group rode on, and she sat there a moment, drinking more of the water, feeling life creep back into her bones.

The sun was about to set—in the wrong place—and it would be dark soon. There wasn't enough daylight to get back to I-20 before dark, and she didn't have enough courage to ride at night. No, she'd have to find a place to sleep. A place that was safe, where Vic couldn't find her.

When darkness finally came, she pulled her bike into another stalled van, and tried her best to sleep.

SIXTY-THREE

DOUG'S LEGS TREMBLED AS NIGHT FELL, AND HE FOUND
himself straining to pedal. Every fiber of his being told him
to pull over and sleep for an hour or two, but his best chance
of catching up to Deni was if he rode through the night. It
was a lonely ride, with no other cyclists on the freeway and
no streetlights or headlights. The night was darker than he'd
ever imagined. Loneliness fell over him like a thick fog he
couldn't evade.

Vic probably wasn't the only killer around. What if
someone came out of nowhere and murdered him for his
bicycle? What if he died here alone on this dark road and his
family never knew what became of him?

He forced his legs to pedal once more, twice more, three
times more, and then he realized he couldn't go another
foot. He wobbled to the side of the road and stumbled off
of the bike. His legs were so weak they could hardly hold
him up. He collapsed onto the dirt, laying the bike down
beside him.

Please, Lord, I can't sleep. There's no time. He had to
keep going. He'd tried to put himself in Deni's shoes. She
would have taken the back roads to avoid Vic, if he hadn't
caught her already. She'd head east, intent on reaching
Washington. But there had been no sign of her ... nothing
to indicate he was even on her trail.

His mind had taken him terrible places as he'd forced
himself on. What if Vic had caught up to her? He would

have to kill her to keep her from talking. He pictured Deni dead, in a heap in the back of that wagon, murdered and abused. Hatred rose up inside of him, curling its talons around his heart. The thought of revenge oozed like sweat from his pores.

Then he would think that maybe she was alive, that maybe Vic had her under his controlling spell, that maybe she cooperated with him to keep from being killed.

Yes, Deni, he thought, *cooperate with him. Don't fight! Just stay alive.*

Then his mind would stray again, and he would picture Vic digging a hole deep in the woods to drop her body in. They'd never find her, never know for sure whether she was dead or alive.

He pictured the hell his life would become after that and what it would do to Kay and the kids. None of them would ever be the same. Peace would elude them for the rest of their lives.

Now he sat on the dirt in the black of night, holding that bike in a paranoid grip. Rest would keep his mind from following destructive paths, but he couldn't let himself sleep. He had to keep going. He stretched out on the grass and sent up a plea to heaven.

Oh, God, please let her be alive. Take care of her. Send angels to protect her. Help her, Lord. I don't know what to do.

He wept out the agony of his fatherhood before the throne of God, but he was too weary to listen for an answer. Soon his tears drew the last bit of strength out of him, and he fell asleep there on the grass, one leg thrown over his bike.

DOUG AWOKE SOMETIME LATER. IT WAS STILL DARK AND HE SAT UP, realizing he had wasted time again. How long had he slept? He looked down at his windup Timex, but the moonlight wasn't bright enough for him to see the time.

He pushed to his feet, his aching muscles protesting. But he had a little more strength than before. The rest had done him good.

He got back on the bike. His bruised pelvis settled back into the seat, and his blistered hands gripped the handlebars.

He pulled the bike back onto the road and pedaled another mile, two miles, three miles, and then he smelled it ...

Something burning up ahead. Someone had built a fire. Hope flew up inside him, invigorating him with new strength. He pedaled faster until the scent grew stronger.

There was a rest stop up ahead, and when he reached the exit for it, he saw the light of a fire flickering inside. He turned toward it, riding more cautiously now, straining to see who the fire warmed.

There, silhouetted against it, he saw the infamous wagon.

He caught his breath, and a trembling started through his body.

He stopped, got off the bike, and hid it behind a tree. He didn't want the clicking of the wheels to alert anyone. Staying in the shadows, he moved closer to the wagon. The horses had been detached from it and were tied to a bicycle rack. One of them lay on the ground, its feet beneath it as it slept. The others looked at him as if they'd expected him.

Doug scanned the ground in front of the fire, but didn't see either Deni or Vic. He couldn't see into the wagon. Could Deni be in there? He didn't want to look for fear he would make a noise that would wake Vic up. Instead, he eased around the wagon and searched the ground around the fire.

And there he saw him, his enemy, sleeping soundly in a sleeping bag close to the fire.

Deni was nowhere around.

Doug's heart hammered as he turned on his flashlight and went to the wagon, and looked inside for his daughter. As he moved one of the boxes, a squawking erupted.

He shone his light on the cages of chickens.

He looked to see if Vic had stirred. The killer slept like a man with a clear conscience.

But where was Deni?

Had he already done away with her?

Something snapped inside him. With cool deliberation, he chambered a round, then went around the wagon and pressed the barrel to Vic's forehead.

The man jolted awake. "What the—?"

"Hands up. Over your head."

Vic lifted his hands, squinting to see his assailant.

"Where is she?" Doug asked through his teeth. "Where's Deni?"

Vic froze.

That rage that had been building for days erupted like hot lava, and Doug kicked him in the ribs. *"Where's my daughter?"*

Vic grunted and doubled over. "She's not with me."

Doug wanted to kill him right there.

"Where is she? Tell me now!"

Vic cowered with one hand over his head. "I don't know! She got away."

"You killed her, didn't you?" He spat out the vile words. "Just like you killed all those others."

"She's not dead!" he shouted. "I swear I didn't kill her. She took off, and I've been looking for her, but I haven't been able to catch up to her."

The words sank in, sending a flutter of hope up through Doug's heart. He wanted to believe it.

"What happened at that farmhouse?" Doug demanded. "I found Deni's wedding dress, her suitcase. And those people ... dead."

Vic squirmed like Gollum in *Lord of the Rings.* "It was self-defense. They attacked Deni, and I was protecting her. They turned on me, so I had to kill them. It scared Deni so much she took off, half crazed. I couldn't stop her."

Attacked Deni.

Self-defense.

The words echoed through Doug's mind. Could it be true? Had Vic been trying to protect his daughter ... ?

No. Deni wouldn't have run away from her protector. She would have stayed with him. Vic had killed the Abernathys and Whitsons. The man was a murderer.

Again, he thrust the barrel of the gun against the man's forehead. "Prove to me that Deni's alive, and I won't kill you."

"I can't prove it." His arms lowered slightly. "But I can help you find her. Maybe if we join forces ..." As he spoke, his arms came down, and one hand slid into his pocket.

"Hands up!" Doug shouted. Vic's hand came up with a gun.

Doug fired. The gun flew to the ground.

Vic screamed, clutching his bloody hand.

Keeping his rifle aimed at Vic, Doug moved around to where the revolver lay, and picked it up. The .22 was fitted with some kind of extension he'd never seen before. A silencer? Yes, it was the same one he'd used in the Abernathy and Whitson killings. He dropped the rifle, letting it hang from its sling. Slipping his finger over the revolver's trigger, he grabbed Vic's arm and twisted it behind him, jerking him to his feet.

He looked around for something to bind him with. Pulling Vic with him, he backed toward the horse that was lying down. With one hand, he unhooked the animal's bridle and worked it off over his head. The reins attached to it were long enough to restrain Vic until he could find something else.

Vic yelled when Doug tied his hands with the leather straps. The bleeding hand was limp, useless, and Vic fell to his knees in pain. Keeping that pistol on him and taking advantage of his weakness, Doug bound his feet.

Vic moaned. "I need a hospital. I'll bleed to death."

"Tell it to the police."

Using his flashlight, Doug searched the boxes until he found some rope and a box cutter. Cutting off a length of rope, he wound it around Vic's wrists and feet, next to the leather straps.

As the sun began to come up, Doug rebridled the horses and hooked them back to the wagon. He managed to throw Vic over his shoulder, and dropped him in the back of the wagon.

"You can't do this to me!" Vic shouted. "I can help you find her. You need me."

Doug riffled through boxes as the caged chickens squawked and fluttered. He found a rag and some duct tape. He stuffed the rag into Vic's mouth, then sealed it by wrapping the tape around his head. "That ought to keep you quiet."

The man grunted against the tape and squirmed to break free, but he was helpless. Just to make sure he didn't break free, he wrapped what was left of the tape around his wrists and ankles, reinforcing the rope.

Only then did Doug check Vic's bleeding hand. His bullet had shot right through it, shattering bones and nerve endings, leaving it maimed.

Despite his hatred for the man, the agony was hard to watch. He dug through Vic's duffel bag and found a shirt, which he used to wrap the wound. Then he went through the rest of the boxes, purging the wagon of all of the pornography, making more room for Vic to lie in the back. He tossed the filth into the fire, and watched the flames consume it, then he smothered out the flames.

Vic lay in a fetal position in the back of the wagon. Doug covered him with his sleeping bag, so no one would see him. If he could find a town that had police still working, and an active jail, he would take him there. But first, he had to find Deni.

The wagon would slow him down, and he couldn't waste time. He thought of tying Vic to a tree with a note that he was a killer. He could tell whoever found him about the murdered couple at the farmhouse, and point them to the evidence on his wagon. Warn the finder to turn him over to police.

But what if the person just robbed the wagon, taking the evidence? Weren't the chickens and food, and even the horses and wagon, coveted items? Why would any desperate soul pass up such provisions for the sake of justice?

And what if Vic managed to get free, or convinced someone to untie him? He might come after Doug and his family to shut them up. That would be his only hope for ever going home. After all, he wasn't aware that anyone back home knew he was the killer.

No, Doug couldn't take that chance. He would have to take Vic with him, and hand him over to the police himself.

He looked back at the bulky wagon. Wouldn't police be looking for it? Someone *must* have seen it at the farmhouse. There was no way he could chase after Deni in it, without drawing more trouble.

He sat in one of the captain's chairs, trying to think it through. *Lord, tell me what to do.*

He prayed for wisdom, guidance, forgiveness for his hatred ... and slowly, the fog of his uncertainty lifted.

He would have to take Vic back to Atlanta and turn him over to police there. Then he could go after Deni.

The thought sickened him. Deni would get farther and farther away.

But at least Vic wouldn't be on her trail.

As Vic fought and squirmed in his bonds, Doug knew he'd chosen the right course.

He would turn around and go west, back to Atlanta.

God would help him make up time later.

He loaded his bike into the wagon next to Vic, then hooked the horses back up. As daylight dawned, he pulled out of the rest stop onto I-20, and headed back to Atlanta.

SIXTY-FOUR

DENI FOLLOWED THE ROUTE BACK TO I-20 AND DECIDED TO chance returning home on the highway. Vic would expect her to go east, so he was probably searching the roads to D.C. Her skin felt tight and burned, and her lips peeled and cracked. If only she had a hat to shield her face from the ravages of the sun. She wished she hadn't left her sunglasses back at the Joneses' house.

Despair rode with her like a hostile passenger as her throat burned from thirst. Where would she sleep tonight? What would she eat?

The water jug the man had given her yesterday was almost empty, but she hadn't found a place to fill it up all morning. The sun was directly overhead when she huffed over a hill, beating down on her with relentless heat, sucking the energy from her bones. Tears rolled down her face as she pushed uphill.

When she reached the top, she knew she couldn't go on. She made it into the shade of a grove of trees, got off her bike, and laid it down beside her. Collapsing on the grass, she set her elbows on her knees and wept.

How had she come to this? Classy, sophisticated Deni Branning, who hadn't bathed in days, who wore a base coat of dirt on her face. Intellectual Deni, the college grad with a job to die for, who didn't have two pennies to rub together or even a safe place to sleep. Christian Deni, who had run off with a killer and pornographer, and was probably wanted for murder.

She was such a failure.

God must hate her. She didn't blame Him at all. She'd had such promise, but she'd turned into a loser. An embarrassment to everyone who knew her.

As she sat there crying, her sins paraded through her mind, mocking her, laughing at her.

You know everything, don't you, Deni?

Struck out on your own. Marched to your own drummer.

Oh yeah, Miss Independence, who left your family to grieve. Who's crying now?

She thought of her sins in college—all the things her parents would be appalled to know about. She'd been above obedience to God, too wrapped up in self-indulgence to deprive herself of anything she wanted. She had lied to her parents, and manipulated them. All the while, she thought no one would ever find her out. Her sins were secret.

But not from God.

And now they had brought her to this, wallowing in shame. Wasn't there a point at which He turned you over to your own devices? Let you launch away from Him to wallow in your own slop?

She'd called out to Him at crisis moments, begging for His help. But the second He got her out of her jams, she'd taken the reins back. And run her life right off a cliff.

Would He even listen to her prayers now?

God, don't turn Your back on me. I need You. Please help me. I've been such a fool.

She thought of Jesus, who'd died on the cross to pay for *her* foolishness. Look what she had given Him in return. It was as though she had kicked dirt in His bloody face, thumbing her nose at His tears. She was among the soldiers at the foot of the cross, gambling for His robe. She was the one who hammered the nails into His wrists. She was the one who stabbed the spear into His side.

How could He ever forgive her?

Some of Jesus' final words came back to her. *Father, forgive them, for they know not what they do.*

Were those words meant for her?

She took in a deep breath, and felt His answer.

Of course they're for you.

She wept harder as she felt His forgiveness, His redemption, His salvation.

And then she heard a sound, picking up on the breeze ...

"Come thou fount of every blessing ..."

Voices, lifted to the Lord. She wiped her face and got up, walked to the middle of the street.

The voices grew stronger.

A little white church stood not a hundred feet away, just on the other side of the trees. Deni's heart swelled with longing for the familiarity of church. She got her bike and rode to the door.

Through the window, she saw there were a couple dozen people inside. It wasn't Sunday, so she assumed this was their midweek service, held at noon since few were working, anyway.

The air was cooler in the shade of the pine trees, and the sound of singing soothed her soul. She wanted to go inside ... rest for a moment with people who weren't a threat ... bask in the comfort and protection of her Savior.

She got off her bike and walked it beside her, and stepped closer to the door.

"Prone to wander, Lord, I feel it ..."

Tears came to her eyes. She wanted to go in, but she didn't know what to do with her bike. She couldn't take the chance of anybody stealing it. It was all she had.

"Can I help you?"

She swung around at the sound of a woman's voice, and saw a girl who looked about her own age walking hand in hand with a young man.

"Uh, yes. I was traveling through and heard the singing."

The girl had big blue eyes and curly red hair, and freckles the size of raindrops all over her face. She looked kind. The man was a muscular brunette, dressed in a pair of jogging shorts and ratty T-shirt with John 3:16 on it. "It does sound nice, don't it?" he said. "Come on in with us."

"I can't. I don't want to leave my bike."

The song kept going as the girl reached out her hand. "I'm Rita, and this is my husband, Bobby."

Deni shook their hands. "I'm Deni Branning. I'm trying to get to I-20, so I can get back to Birmingham."

"Take a break and come on in," Rita said. "Bring the bike with you. Nobody will care."

"Are you sure?"

"Sure, I'm sure. Things ain't like they used to be. We all understand the need to hang on to our bikes. Just roll it over against the wall and slip in at the end of the aisle." She peered through the door. "Back row looks like it's empty. Won't be a problem at all. You can be our guest."

Grateful, Deni followed them in and rolled her bike to the wall, then slipped into the end of the row where she could keep her hand on it.

She looked up at the worship leader. He was smiling at her as he strummed his guitar.

"Looks like we have a visitor," he said.

The music stopped and everyone turned around to look at her. She smiled and waved.

"We're so glad to have you. Are you from around here?"

She touched her hair, wondering how bad she looked, but she gave them her name and told them where she was headed.

They all welcomed her. When they'd all taken their seats again, the preacher read to them from 1 John 2:15–17. " 'Do not love the world, nor the things in the world. If anyone loves the world, the love of the Father is not in him. For all that is in the world, the lust of the flesh and the lust of the eyes and the boastful pride of life, is not from the Father, but is from the world. And the world is passing away, and also its lusts; but the one who does the will of God abides forever.' "

She swallowed the sorrow in her throat. Boastful pride ... that was her downfall. It was her driving force ... her false god. She'd been so sure she could call her own shots, do things on her own terms. Her pride had brought her so low that she'd long ago crashed through the floor.

But God had forgiven her.

She melted in tears at His goodness. Basking in the comfort of familiarity, she surrendered to the restoration of her soul and spirit. The cool air of freedom swept over her, and joy replaced the fear.

When the service was over, Deni found herself embraced by the people in that place. Several invited her home, but she decided to say yes to Rita and Bobby's invitation, since they were the first ones she'd met.

They lived about a mile from the church, they said, but they had water to drink and food to eat, and they would be happy to share it with her.

She followed them back to the small trailer they lived in at the back of five acres his family owned. They mourned the fact that they hadn't planted anything last spring, but they had only been married for five weeks. They had just tied the knot before the outage.

Their trailer was quaint, decorated sweetly even though there was no light and very few windows. They served lunch—salad with homemade dressing—out on a picnic table under some trees, and they did their best to make Deni feel at home.

"I'm getting married, too," she told them as they ate.

"Really? When?"

"Supposed to be October," she said. "That is, if we ever see each other again. He was in D.C. when the outage hit, and I was in the Birmingham area visiting my family. I never dreamed I'd get stuck there."

She told them of the things she'd been through since she'd left home, and how she needed to get back to warn her family. She ended the story in tears, embarrassed to cry in front of strangers like this, but neither Rita nor Bobby were disturbed by her emotional display.

Rita just got a determined look in her soft eyes.

"Well, all I can say is there's no way we're letting you get back on the road today. You've got blisters on your blisters. You need to stay here overnight, get some rest, some food, some water. We have plenty of water in our well. We'll find something to put it in so you can take some with you. But you can't set out again without any kind of provisions."

"I had provisions," she said, "but I left them all when Vic killed those people. I brought the stupidest things with me from home. You wouldn't believe it."

"Try me."

"I brought a makeup mirror, a flat iron, and a blow-dryer."

Bobby laughed. "Rita would have done the same thing."

"Hey, you never know when the lights are gonna come back on." Rita winked. "A girl's got to have her equipment, don't she, Deni?"

Deni laughed for the first time in days. She thought of that man who'd given her the jug of water yesterday, when she'd been at her rope's end, desperately thirsty. God sent him at the perfect time, even though her heart was so far from Him.

And today, He'd given her Rita and Bobby.

He did provide, even when she didn't deserve it.

"You're welcome to stay and hide out here," Bobby said. "Stay as long as you want. That guy ain't likely to find you here."

"I'd love to stay. You have no idea. But I have to get back and warn my family. If Vic beats me home, everybody's in danger."

Bobby couldn't argue with that. "Then let's just make it our business to get you ready to go. But you have to stay tonight. You got to get some rest, get hydrated, get some strength back."

Deni was thankful to take him up on his offer.

AFTER A DINNER OF BOILED POTATOES AND BEANS, WHICH BOBBY and Rita got from her parents' garden, Deni slept for fourteen hours. She woke in the comfort of their guest bed, surprised to find the sun already high in the sky.

She had to get up and get going if she had any hope of getting home before nightfall.

When she pulled her covers back and got up, she saw her clothes folded neatly at the foot of her bed. Rita had washed them yesterday in the creek near their house, and loaned her some of her own clothes until they were dry. Deni pulled them on, wishing she could just stay here for a few more days.

She felt like a homeless waif.

But she *had* a home. A beautiful home with her own room and a soft mattress and a lake nearby. A home with people who loved her, who took care of each other and worked together to get things done.

She looked out the window. Rita and Bobby sat on the porch swing, the warm breeze floating through the trees around them. They were a sweet couple, she thought, not the kind of people that she and Craig would have chosen to spend time with. Bobby was an auto mechanic, whose job was now obsolete. Rita worked in a retail store for an hourly wage, but the store shelves were empty, so it hadn't been able to open since the outage.

Neither of them had gone to college.

A month ago, Deni would have turned her nose up at a couple like them and considered them losers. Today, she saw them as angels. Instruments of God Himself. So much for her Georgetown education, when she couldn't even tell west from south. So much for her abundant blessings back home, when she'd thrown them in her parents' faces, priding herself in her better judgment ... judgment that sent her into the hands of a killer.

These people with their simple lives would survive the outage just fine, and so would their marriage. They didn't need technology or high-class jobs to make them feel fulfilled or satisfied. Their love for the Lord and each other did that.

She sat down on the bed; pulled her socks on over her blistered, scabbed feet; and carefully slipped her feet into her shoes. Rita had given her some aloe for her blistered sunburn, so she rubbed the ointment onto the wounds, hoping it would ease the pain and the burn.

Her eyes strayed out that window again as she heard Rita laughing. She thought back to better times when she and Craig had hung out together in quiet, passing private jokes back and forth, staring out on the Potomac, laughing. It hadn't happened that often. Maybe a few times at first, when he'd been trying to win her over. But that hadn't taken long, and after that, he had the upper hand. His courtship had turned to simple maintenance.

When was the last time they'd sat holding hands, watching the leaves rustle in the trees, laughing like kids?

What would it be like to spend these dark days with Craig? He was already living in the house he'd bought for them—a three-bedroom townhouse in Georgetown. It had a steam room and a Jacuzzi and a state-of-the-art kitchen that she doubted she would ever use since she didn't know how to cook. There wasn't a yard to speak of, only a place to park out front and a little ten-by-ten enclosure in the back. Where would they grow food if the outage continued?

There were few windows in the place. The house would be dark, and miserably hot this time of year.

She wondered if the inactivity, the inability to get from one place to another, the lack of communication, had changed Craig in any way. She could hardly imagine what he might be like now, not getting up at the crack of dawn and rushing off to the senate building, not getting ten zillion cell phone calls a day, not slowing down until ten o'clock at night.

Was he enjoying the solitude, the peace and quiet, the slow pace? Or was he angry, bitter, frantic to get things restored?

Like she'd been.

She watched Bobby get up and stir the flames on the fire in the makeshift barbecue pit. Rita started to cook some eggs on the frying pan she laid on the grate.

They didn't know she was up yet, so she watched them as they scooped up the scrambled eggs, divided them into three bowls. They saved one for her, then sat down to eat their own. Before they did, Bobby put his arm around Rita, and they both bowed to pray. It wasn't just a "Thanks for our food" kind of prayer. This was a heartfelt, deep, falling at the Father's feet kind of prayer, full of praise and gratitude for all He had provided.

She couldn't imagine Craig ever praying like that.

But then, neither would *she*.

A deep sense of loss filled her as she realized how far she was from the person God wanted her to be. Since she'd left home and gone to college, church had been one of the lowest things on her priority list. She'd joined a church so she could tell her parents she was connected to one, but the only time she'd attended in the last four years was when her parents came to visit.

It wasn't surprising, then, that she wound up engaged to an agnostic who agreed with Karl Marx that religion was "the opiate of the masses." Since her own faith was so shallow, that hadn't bothered her at all.

Rita and Bobby would turn out like her own parents, loving and kind to each other and their families, imparting their values and insisting on their children being the best they could be for God.

She looked ahead twenty years, and imagined herself as a senator's wife, attending luncheons and dinner parties, waiting at night for her husband to come home. Maybe she would be a television anchor, with her own world to move and shake. Or maybe by then he would have decided that he needed her by his side during long, grueling campaigns.

Would she be fulfilled or lonely? And how secure would her children be with a father as busy as Craig? Sadness washed over her.

She finished dressing and went outside to join her hosts at the picnic table.

"Mornin'!" Rita's countenance made her feel as if she truly enjoyed seeing her. "I made you some eggs. They're probably still warm."

"Thanks." Deni got the bowl. "I'm sorry I slept so long. I meant to get up earlier."

Bobby waved off her apology. "You needed to sleep, after all you've been through." He finished his plate and leaned on the table.

"Deni, we prayed together for you this morning. I believe God's gonna get you home safe."

Tears came to her eyes at the poignancy of that. Her parents always said there was power in two or more praying together. She had never prayed with Craig.

"I really appreciate that," she said. "And everything else you've done for me. I was at my rope's end yesterday. I didn't know what I was going to do. And then ... God put you in my path." The words scratched her throat, and she started to cry.

Rita squeezed her hand.

"I'm sorry to start blubbering. I'm just feeling so ... so humbled that God would still watch over me like this, when I don't deserve it at all."

"Somebody must be praying for you."

"Yes, I'm sure they are. My parents, and my brothers and sister. God should have turned away from me. Left me to my own devices. But thankfully, He didn't." She took a few bites, relishing the taste, and looked back up at them again. "I look at you, Rita, and I see a useful person. You'll make it through this just fine. You can cook, and wash clothes, and Bobby can bring home food ..."

"You can do those things, too."

"No, I can't. I'm a terrible cook and never wanted to learn. Even since the outage, I've hardly helped my mother cook at all. I've whined and complained about everything she's asked me to do. If the outage had happened after my marriage instead of before, Craig and I would be at each other's throats. I'd be useless ... and so would he." Her soft laugh held no mirth. "We thought we were so important, setting ourselves up to have such significant, important jobs. But the fast lane has come to a screeching halt, and we don't have any skills to get us through this. What a nightmare it would have been. And he's not a Christian. Where would we have turned?"

"Maybe the outage will change him," Bobby said. "Maybe he'll see that he has to lean on somebody. Who else is there, if not Christ?"

Who, indeed? She felt that peace wash over her again.

"God got your attention," Rita said. "Maybe He'll get Craig's, too."

Deni hoped Rita was right.

They loaded her up with provisions she could carry in a backpack —two-liter bottles of sterilized water, paper sacks full of dry cereal, a few cans of kidney beans for much-needed calcium and protein, antibiotic ointment for her sores, and Solarcaine for her sunburn. Rita also gave her a big, yellow floppy hat to keep the sun off her neck and face, and sunglasses to protect her eyes. Then Bobby oiled the chain on her bike, making sure it was in good shape.

By the time she hugged them both good-bye and thanked them for the hospitality, she was in tears again. "I'm going to come back and repay you for your kindness," she said. "As soon as the outage is over, you'll see me again."

"Good," Rita said. "Then you can tell us how everything turned out with you and Craig."

The wind was at Deni's back as she rode away, helping her to make better time. She knew that was another provision from God. She thanked Him for it and, while she was at it, asked Him to protect her family from Vic and his sons.

She'd ridden about an hour, when dark clouds began to move across the sky. Thunder cracked some distance away. Rain began to sprinkle down.

She pedaled faster, hoping to get ahead of the storm, but the farther she rode, the harder it rained. When she finally reached I-20, just east of Atlanta, she was soaking wet.

She came to a closed convenience store just off the interstate and decided to wait the storm out under the shelter there. She pulled into that parking lot ...

... and heard glass crunching beneath her tires.

She jumped off her bike. A big shard of glass had punctured her front tire.

"No, Lord, please don't let it be so!" she cried. But it was. The tire was flat.

She had no choice but to walk to the next town, rolling the bike beside her and hoping she could find someone who could fix it.

The day had looked so promising, and now she was soaking wet and stranded.

As much as God had smoothed her path yesterday, orchestrating things to her advantage, it seemed He was turning His back on her again. But she knew better than that now. With God, things were never as they seemed.

Instead of cursing her misfortune, she thanked God that she had this big hat, the comfortable shoes, and the provisions Rita and Bobby had given her. And she spent the next hour talking to Him as she waited the storm out.

SIXTY-FIVE

THE RAIN BEAT DOWN AS DOUG RODE I-20 WEST BACK TO Atlanta, running the horses as fast as they could go on the pavement. The sooner he turned Vic over to the Atlanta police, the sooner he could find Deni.

Vic had been quiet and still as they rode. Doug hoped he was sleeping, but kept his rifle close at hand, just in case. He also carried Vic's pistol in the ammo case attached to his belt.

Oh, God, please ... I need divine intervention. Please take care of Deni.

As the rain started to pour, he saw something up ahead, a woman in a big floppy hat limping beside a bicycle that she rolled beside her. She was small, like Deni, and had a brown ponytail that reached halfway down her back. She walked like Deni ...

He slapped the reins on the horses. They sprang into a faster trot.

She must have heard the horses' hooves, because she turned around to look. He couldn't see her face in the shadow of the floppy hat, but suddenly the bike fell over, and he watched as she took off through the grass on the side of the road, into the trees ...

Running for her life.

It had to be Deni! Who else would run from a rig like this? Doug stood up on the wagon. "Deni! Deni! It's Dad! It's me! Deni!"

The pounding rain muffled his voice, and the thunder cracked overhead. Doug jumped out of the wagon.

He took off into the woods after her.

SIXTY-SIX

Deni tripped over a stump and picked herself up, kept running with a bleeding knee. The rain poured and the sky thundered, and she ran as if the very demons of hell were chasing her. Vic had found her!

She had to get away. She couldn't let him catch her. He would kill her for sure, and bury her in these woods, where no one would ever find her.

She ran, scratching her legs against a bush, slipping in the mud, stepping over logs and dodging branches ...

And then in the distance, through the rain and thunder, she heard a voice calling her name.

"Deni! Deni, it's me, Dad! Deni!"

Deni kept running. It sounded like her dad, but how *could* it be ...? No, it was a trick. Vic was imitating her father, trying to make her turn around.

"Deni! It's me!"

She wouldn't be fooled. It sounded like him, but why would her father be in Vic's wagon?

She tripped again, picked herself up, and searched frantically for a place to hide. A cave, a log ... anything!

"Deni, please! I've got Vic in the back of the wagon, tied up! He can't hurt you anymore. It's you and me, sweetheart, just like that day when the planes were crashing, and the guy stole our bike—"

She hadn't told Vic anything about that. How could he know?

She slowed and turned around, bracing herself as he emerged through the trees. It wasn't Vic but her own father, soaking wet in the rain, his rifle swinging on his back.

He had come for her.

"Daddy?"

"Oh, *honey!*"

She ran into his open arms. Weeping, he lifted her off the ground and swung her around. "Oh, baby! I'm so glad I found you! Thank You, God!"

"But the wagon! It's his. How did you—"

"I was looking for you and I found Vic. I know about the couple he killed. He's tied up in the wagon, baby. He can't hurt us."

"Is he dead?"

"No, he's alive. I'm taking him to Atlanta to turn him over to the police."

She slipped out of his arms and backed away. "But I don't want to go near him, Dad. He's evil."

"I know he is. But he's helpless now. Trust me."

She knew she had no choice. She let him lead her back out of the woods to the wagon where her enemy awaited.

"I have to see him, Dad. I need to make sure he can't break free."

"Of course, honey. I'll show you."

He pulled her up on the wagon. Taking hold of his rifle, he chambered a round, just in case. Then he grabbed the sleeping bag that covered Vic and pulled it off.

Vic sprang up and knocked the rifle out of Doug's hand.

It fell into the dirt.

And then she saw that Vic had his revolver, pointed right at her father.

Deni screamed.

SIXTY-SEVEN

DOUG STARED DOWN THE BARREL OF VIC'S REVOLVER AS THE rain pounded down. Thunder cracked over Deni's screams.

Deni leaped off the wagon and scrambled for the rifle. Vic's voice stopped her. "Don't move or I'll kill him."

She froze, looking up at him.

Doug knew Vic would kill him first, then turn the gun on Deni. He had to buy time, distract Vic somehow, and get that gun out of his grip. He was clearly still in pain, and held his wounded hand curled against his stomach, the severed duct tape still stuck to his wrists. Maybe Doug could use that injury against him.

Please, God, help us ...

It came to him in a flash. *Stroke Vic's ego.*

Doug swallowed hard. "Guess I underestimated you, Vic. How'd you do it? How'd you get the gun?"

Vic let out a bitter laugh. "Thought you could get the best of me, Branning?" His words rasped through his teeth. "Thought I was just gonna lay there and let you ruin me? You forgot that I'm the one who packed this wagon. I knew where another box cutter was. It took some doing, but I managed to back up against it and get it out. Cut myself free. Your second mistake was putting my revolver in the ammo pack on your belt. You never even knew when I pulled it out."

His thumb flipped the safety, and Doug knew the man was going to kill him.

How had it come to this? He'd come all this way to protect his daughter. God had laid out a path for him, and led him to her in spite of all the odds.

Was He going to let it end this way?

Vic would blow them away right here, then return home like nothing had happened, thinking he could resume his life as an upstanding citizen.

No, he couldn't let that happen. If he couldn't save his own life, he would die saving Deni's.

With all his weight, Doug lunged forward and grabbed Vic's injured hand. The pain knocked Vic back, and he screamed like a wounded dog. Doug went for the gun, but Vic pulled it away ...

Deni stood frozen in the line of fire.

"Run, Deni!" Doug yelled, but she just stood there as Vic's finger closed over the trigger.

The gun fired.

Deni dropped to the dirt.

Had he hit her? Was she dead?

Fury exploded in him with ballistic force, and Doug wrestled the gun over Vic's head, and knocked him to his back. "Deni!"

She didn't answer.

Dear God, he killed her!

Vic fought back, his teeth bared as he screamed in pain, but he lashed out with all the evil festering within him. Doug wrestled the gun over Vic's head, fighting for his daughter, for his family, for the Abernathys and the Whitsons and that dead farm couple ...

Doug closed his hand over the gun. He almost had it—

Suddenly Vic's teeth clamped on Doug's arm, sinking through the flesh. Doug lost his grip, and Vic got his bearings.

Before Doug knew what had happened, Vic was on top of him, pressing the gun between Doug's eyes.

Please, God. One more miracle.

Doug squeezed his eyes shut, bracing himself.

The gun fired. Doug's body went rigid.

The fight was over.

SIXTY-EIGHT

Vic's body dropped on top of him.

Doug pushed him off, and saw the bullet hole in his temple.

"Daddy?"

He swung around. Deni stood next to the wagon, his rifle trembling in her hands. He almost collapsed with relief. She was all right!

"Did I kill him?"

He took the pistol from Vic's limp hand and checked for a pulse. "Yes, honey. He's dead."

She lowered the rifle, her body quaking as the moment caught up to her. "Thank God. I thought he was gonna kill you."

He jumped off the wagon and took the rifle, and pulled her into his arms. Moments ago, when Vic fired his gun, Deni had dropped. But she hadn't been hit! God had given them that miracle. And he'd been certain the second shot had come from the revolver. But it was Deni who had fired. He crushed her against him, feeling her sob into his wet shirt.

She was okay. *Thank You, God.* The horses whinnied, and the chickens cackled. "It's okay, baby. It's all right now. He's gone."

"But, Daddy ...," her voice wobbled with despair, "...I killed him!"

"You had to."

She couldn't stop trembling.

"Come on. We have to find the police. We have to tell them what happened here, and about the couple at the farmhouse."

"What if they don't believe us?"

"They will. We'll convince them. God will vindicate us." He tried to coax her into the wagon, but the sight of Vic kept her back.

"No, I can't. Let's just leave him here. We can walk to town."

He looked at her bike lying on the ground, its tire flat. "Okay. You can ride my bike, and I'll walk yours."

He got his bike down, then covered Vic's body with the sleeping bag.

Then together, he and his daughter made their way to Atlanta.

SIXTY-NINE

DOUG AND DENI HAD BEEN GONE FIVE DAYS — AN ETERNITY in Kay's mind. She'd floated through the week in a fog, reminding herself to eat, to sleep, to breathe ...

Her thoughts ran in one long prayer, begging God for a miracle, despite the gnawing dread in her mind. If something happened to them, would she ever get word?

Her family did its daily duties the best it could. Logan hadn't complained even once this week, and Beth hadn't whined. Jeff had performed with little to no sleep, guarding their home with a vengeance. The neighbors brought them food and water, and Brad took care of some of the chores that needed to be done. Judith and Eloise comforted her like members of their own family, praying with her and reminding her that God was in control.

Why hadn't He brought them home?

She tried to shove that question to the back of her mind, and forced herself to get on with her work. She had to sterilize the water so they'd have something to drink. She set the pot on the grill and waited for the water to boil. For the twentieth time that day, sorrow lodged itself in her throat. Once again, she turned it into a prayer ...

And then she heard it. Logan's voice, calling from the front yard. "Mom! Mom! They're coming!"

Jeff, who'd been working in the compost pile at the back of the yard, dropped his shovel. Beth abandoned the water she'd been filtering.

"It's Dad and Deni!" Logan shouted, and Beth launched out across the lawn. Kay sucked in a breath and took off running. Jeff followed as they rounded the house.

It was true. Doug and Deni were riding up the street, their bicycles side by side.

They didn't make it to the driveway before Kay and the kids ran to embrace them, almost knocking them off their bikes.

Deni and Doug were both in tears as they hugged their family, all laughing and talking at once.

After a few moments, Kay pulled Deni into her arms and wept as she kissed her face. "I was so afraid Vic had killed you! I thought I'd never see you again!"

"He's dead," Doug said. "We left him with the police in Atlanta, with his wagon and all the evidence."

Relief flooded through her as she turned back to Deni. But her weary, sunburned daughter had a hollow, distant look in her eyes. And then she knew. Deni had been the one who killed Vic Green.

Seeing the pain in her face, Kay pulled her into a crushing embrace, as her daughter dissolved into tears.

SEVENTY

DENI LAY ON HER BED, KNEES TO HER CHEST, THINKING ABOUT the kick of the gun as she'd pulled that trigger. *I killed a man. God, can You ever forgive me?*

"Honey?"

She looked toward her doorway and saw her dad standing there. "Yeah?"

"There's somebody here to see you."

Deni sat up. "I don't want to see anybody, Dad."

He stepped inside. "It's Vic's son, Mark."

"No! Especially not him."

Her father came and sat down beside her. "I know it looks bad for him but I have to tell you, I don't think he was involved. He's the one who let me into Vic's house, took me around, and helped me discover all the stuff he had there. He was as surprised and shaken as any of us."

Tears came to her eyes. "It might have been an act. He learned from the best."

"I don't think so, sweetheart. He helped me look around the house for any sign of where Vic might have gone with you. He could have kept me out of certain rooms if he'd known about the stuff that was stashed there, but he didn't."

Deni got up and went to the window, looked out into the neighborhood. "Does he know I killed his father?"

"I'm not sure." He slid off the bed and came to stand behind her. "Honey, stop beating yourself up. You saved my life. You had no choice but to pull that trigger."

362

She wiped a tear rolling down her cheek. "I know. But it feels awful. Less than a month ago, I was joking with Jeff over the things I would kill for. A bike, a glass of water ... But I didn't mean it. Even in self-defense, it's hard to live with. Why did it have to come to this? So many people dead."

He shook his head. "I don't know. Seems like the world is a little more evil than it was a month ago. But there's still a lot of good in it. And we can do our best to represent that good."

She gazed up at him for a long moment. "God dealt with me, when I was on the road. He showed me what a wretch I'd been. He made me new."

Doug nodded. "I know. I can see that."

She was glad it was evident. "Dad, I'm so thankful you came for me."

He wiped a tear off her cheek. "Me, too."

"That first day, when the power went out, and we got our bike stolen ... I treated you like you were a coward."

He smiled. "You sort of did, didn't you?"

She breathed a laugh. "I was an idiot. You're not a coward. You're my hero. When I think of God's love for me, your face always comes to my mind."

Tears glistened in his eyes as he leaned over and hugged her. "I love you, sweetheart." He pulled back and wiped his eyes on his sleeve. "Now go talk to Mark. He's not having the same kind of warm fuzzies about his dad. Go easy on him, okay?"

What would she say? He was the son of her tormenter. But her father was right. Hadn't Mark tried to talk her out of going with him? And she'd known him for years. Mark had always had character and integrity, despite his father. In many ways, Mark was as much a victim as she. Maybe even more, since he hadn't brought any of this upon himself. "All right, I'll talk to him."

She went down the stairs and out the front door. Mark sat on the porch, waiting for her. His eyes were red, and his face held myriad emotions—anger, grief, shame, guilt.

She stepped toward him. "Hey."

He got up and tried to speak, but stopped, and only shook his head. Finally, he whispered, "I'm so sorry, Deni. So, so sorry."

She swallowed and nodded. "Yeah, me, too."

"You've got to believe me," he said. "I didn't know he was a killer. I suspected his business wasn't legal, but I never in my wildest dreams imagined—" His face twisted as he struggled with the words. "I had no idea my dad was capable of murder."

Deni's heart swelled with compassion. She reached up and hugged him, felt his body quaking with his sobs.

"He might have killed you," he whispered against her hair.

She let him go. "God protected me."

"I know He did. I was constantly praying for you. Praying that my dad would be stopped before he ... hurt anyone else."

Deni looked down at her feet. "Mark, did you know that I'm the one who shot him?"

He nodded. "I heard the story from the Caldwells. What else could you do? It was the two of you, or him."

She saw no anger in his eyes, not at her. "Your brothers ..."

"*Half*-brothers," he said bitterly. "I don't even know where they are. I haven't seen them since right after Dad left."

"Do you think they're involved?"

"Probably. Over the last few years, they've all made a lot of money, and nobody knew exactly how. One of their wives told the sheriff she knew they were dealing in pornography. The police are looking for them, but I have a feeling they might not be coming back. Once they heard Dad was wanted for murder, they probably hit the road."

"I hope the police find them."

"Me, too." He studied her face for a long moment. She felt as though he could see straight to her heart, and read her deepest thoughts. "Do you believe me, Deni? That I wasn't involved?"

She realized that she did. "Yeah, I believe you."

"Good," he said, "because a lot of people around here don't."

"I'll tell them."

"I'd appreciate that." He looked down at his feet, then shrugged. "Guess I'll go now."

She watched as he started down the steps. "Wait."

He turned back. His eyes were soft, fragile.

"You really prayed for me?" she asked.

"The whole time."

She stepped down, and looked up into his face. "Your prayers worked, Mark. God sent so many miracles. A babbling brook when I was dying of thirst. A church when I desperately needed to feel His presence. A couple to take me in at the right moment. Even a flat tire to slow me down, so Dad could find me. Things changed in my heart. He's gonna make me different from now on."

Mark smiled. "It's good when God does that before a person gets married. That way you can put Him at the center of your home."

Her smile faded, and she looked out into the breeze. Somehow, she couldn't imagine marriage to Craig having anything but politics at its center.

"So," Mark asked softly, "any thoughts of hitting the road again to get back east?"

"No. I need to stay here until the outage is over. I don't have the fortitude or the courage to take off like that again. I don't know how they did it in the old west." She smiled up at him. "We have a lot, you know? Even if we don't have air-conditioning and running water and electricity. We have nice homes, comfortable beds, people who love us."

"That's what I've been thinking, too," he said. "So what if we have to work a little harder? It won't kill any of us."

"We might even become better people."

He smiled, but it was short-lived. Grief shadowed his face again. "Just so you know ... I did love my dad. I prayed for him, too ... for years. But ultimately, the choice of giving his life to Christ was his. The choice to die in darkness ..."

His words choked off again. She wished she knew how to comfort him.

"Well, anyway ... I'm really glad you're okay. You get a good night's sleep tonight. Rest easy."

"Thanks," she whispered.

She watched as he made his way down the sidewalk back toward his own home, and said a silent prayer that the neighbors would go easy on him and not paint him with the same stripes with which they painted his father. Mark didn't deserve it, but it would take time for him to prove that to everyone. Such was the legacy his father had left him.

She went back upstairs and sat on her bed, and lit the candle on her writing desk. She got out her notebook, and started a letter.

Dear Craig,

I tried to get to you, but I almost got killed doing it. I ran away from everything I knew, bent on getting to the new life that waited for me. Tonight I feel like Dorothy in The Wizard of Oz, *who finally realized there's no place like home. I didn't make my way to you, and I didn't find a place where the lights were still on. Instead, I found good, giving people of simple means, rich in love beyond their own imaginings. And I found Christ where I least expected Him. I guess in a way, I found myself, too. I know more of who I am now than I did when I set out.*

I'm a woman who, for most of my life, has been spoiled and vain and selfish. I'm a woman who knows now what it's like to do without. To not have a home, or a family to lean on, or food or water. And it changed something inside me.

I'm also a woman who has fought great evil and lived to tell about it. I've seen good people killed for no good reason. I've looked a man in the face and pulled the trigger. I've watched a man drop to his death, of my own doing.

That changes a person.

I don't know if you'd like the changes in me. I hope you will. I miss you more than I ever dreamed possible, but I think I can live without you for a while now. I think I'm going to have to. The thought of getting far from my family during these hard times is more than I can bear. I need them. Now I know why families used to live so close together. When times are hard, you need people you can count on.

I think I can depend on you to be there, waiting for me when this is over. But if I can't, then it's good that I found out before the wedding. I hope you'll try to come to me. But if you don't, that will tell me things, too. I'm not sure what, quite yet.

For now, I'm just so thankful to be at home in my beautiful, dark house, on my soft, comfortable bed, with food and water—all things people who love me have worked so hard to provide. It's time I pitched in and contributed something more to this family.

My heart breaks for you ... but as I said, I'll wait until the lights come on again.

Love,
Deni

A NOTE FROM THE AUTHOR

You might say I'm delusional. I have that American virus, the one that says that all the trappings of this world, from prosperity to technology, from entertainment to security, from excess to extreme, will never pass away. I have that infection that makes me think that all this somehow has something to do with me, and that as long as I don't mess up really bad, things will keep going along just as they are.

When an ice storm hits my unprepared southern town, and the power lines are knocked down by tree branches heavy with ice, we leave our dark, cold houses and ride around in our cars to get warm. We drive to the homes of friends to shower and wash clothes, and we mark time waiting for the power company to get those lights turned back on, so McDonalds will be operational again and we can watch the latest reality show, since our own reality is a little too mundane to bear.

What if it never came back on? What if, in His sovereignty, God said, "That's enough. It's time for it to stop. I've tried for years to get your attention, but you won't look up. So I'm going to do something drastic."

What would that drastic thing be? Might it be a massive power outage like the one in my books? Might it be hurricanes one after another, or tsunamis, or mud slides, tornadoes, or terrorists? Might it be war on our own soil?

Or might it be more personal? Something closer to home. Something that hurts from the center of our being, in that place in our gut where we never quite recover.

In the severity of that thing, whatever it might be, would we see His gentle hand? Would we see compassion from the God who loves us? Would we see His love manifested in our crisis?

And how would we change?

Would He prepare us first? Is He preparing us even now?

I'll never forget the morning that my sweet mother-in-law was in a car accident that left her with a closed-head injury from which she would never fully recover. That morning, as I prayed, God prompted me to ask that I would be ready when tragedy hit, and that He would make my husband and me strong enough to sustain it when it came. Hours later, I knew why I'd prayed that prayer.

Over the next year, we watched that beloved woman suffer. She was never the same again, and spent the rest of her life in confusion and frustration, unable to do any of the things she'd done before, unable to even recognize her own home. She died of a secondary infection, but by the time she went, we had already said good-bye. In His gracious kindness, God had given us a year to release our hold on her. To realize that, in a way, she was already gone. In His compassion He made us ready for her passing home.

Sometimes He does that with our entanglements on earth. He tells us this is not our home, and He gently teaches us that the things here are just temporary. They're not ours, any more than the things in a European hostel are ours when we're traveling abroad. We have no ownership of that bed we slept in, or the table on which we set our things. The lamp in the corner belongs to someone else. When we return home, we will leave it behind.

The Bible says we are aliens in a land not our own, sojourners passing through, pilgrims on our way to a destination we haven't quite reached. We should look at the things in our lives as temporary pleasures, things for which to be grateful, but things that we can easily leave behind.

Our gaze should be set on our real home, for we are "aliens and strangers on earth" (Hebrews 11:13). God has prepared a city for us, and it's nothing like this one.

Sometimes the letting go is hard. We kick and scream and cry and plead with God to give it back. Our loved one who died, our good health, our home, our car, our bank account, our comfort.

But sometimes He loves us too much to do that. Sometimes His will is for us to look toward home, anxiously waiting for that day when we reach the gates of our own city. That place where all our ultimate comforts lie. That place where we will be welcomed in like dearly loved children long awaited.

Then I saw a new heaven and a new earth, for the first heaven and the first earth had passed away, and there was no longer any sea. I saw the Holy City, the new Jerusalem, coming down out of heaven from God, prepared as a bride beautifully dressed for her husband. And I heard a loud voice from the throne saying, "Now the dwelling of God is with men, and he will live with them. They will be his people, and God himself will be with them and be their God. He will wipe every tear from their eyes. There will be no more death or mourning or crying or pain, for the old order of things has passed away."

He who was seated on the throne said, "I am making everything new!" Then he said, "Write this down, for these words are trustworthy and true."

He said to me: "It is done. I am the Alpha and the Omega, the Beginning and the End. To him who is thirsty I will give to drink without cost from the spring of the water of life. He who overcomes will inherit all this, and I will be his God and he will be my son."

REVELATION 21:1–7

READING GROUP GUIDE

1. Discuss the family's initial reactions to the crisis. How are Doug, Kay, Deni Jeff, Logan, and Beth's reactions different? How are they similar?
2. How would you react to such a catastrophe? What would your first plan of action be?
3. Consider Jeff's rebellious night out to his friend Zach's house. What motivation would draw Jeff out in the middle of a dangerous night? How did his parents, Doug and Kay, react?
4. Imagine planning a shopping list for your first trip to the store after the disaster struck. What would be at the top of the list?
5. Who would you turn to in the event of a murderer in your midst? How would your community react?
6. What were some of the initial relationship barriers the Brannings had to work around within the family? When did those barriers begin to break down?
7. Mob mentality breaks down morals and values for many people. What morals and values did the Brannings abandon? Which are worth keeping? How much would you sacrifice to survive?
8. Doug Branning turned to the Bible to find answers, strength and hope. Where in the Bible would you turn during such times of disaster?

9. Hope interweaves Last Light as an important thematic thread. Where do you see hope in the lives of the Brannings and their community? When does hope seem absent?

10. What other common threads tie this book together? Where do you see these threads in different character's lives?

11. Miss Eloise calls suffering a "learned skill." Why would suffering be considered a skill? What aspects of suffering have the Brannings learned from?

12. Discuss the change in Deni's character throughout the book. What smaller events impacted her personality? How do you think she will continue to grow after her experience with Vic Green?

13. God's gifts abound in Last Light. What are some of the less tangible things God provided for the Brannings and their neighbors? What has God provided in your life?

ACKNOWLEDGMENTS

THE IDEA FOR THE RESTORATION SERIES HAS BEEN germinating in my mind for many years, but it's a subject that has required quite a bit of research, and help from several friends and experts. Special thanks to Randy Ingermanson, physicist and my fellow Christian author, who advised me on the kind of crisis that I needed for this book. Thanks also to banker Phil Posey, who advised me on the financial repercussions of an event like the one in the series. And thank you to my friend Beth Runnels, who caught the vision early in the process and encouraged me with stories from her childhood and ideas that I was able to use.

And as always, thanks to my readers. You're always on my mind as I write my novels. I hope I never let you down.

An Excerpt from *NIGHT LIGHT*

STEALING CAME EASY TODAY.

Most days, breaking and entering was harder than this for the boys, requiring hours of watching and waiting for families to leave their homes so the two of them could slip in and out, arms full of loot, without being noticed.

At nine and seven, Aaron and Joey Gatlin knew how to blend in. They had a system. They would case the ritzy neighborhoods while bouncing a basketball or tossing a Frisbee back and forth, looking like any other kids out playing on a summer day. No threat to anyone.

The massive power outage that had set technology back over a hundred years, knocking out everything from cars to electricity, had left millions hungry and desperate. But not Aaron's family. He made sure his brothers and sister had something to eat every day.

Some of those who lived in this neighborhood called Oak Hollow had begun plowing up their front yards, and vegetables were growing there instead of grass. Word around town was that they were digging a well, which meant they would have fresh water soon. The lake in the middle of the neighborhood already made them rich, since they didn't have to walk far to get water, and most of them had fancy barbecue pits in the backyard where they could boil the lake water to sterilize it.

"The Br-an-nings." Joey, Aaron's seven-year-old brother, sounded out the name on the mailbox. "They have a big family—they were all working out here in their garden yesterday. Bet they got a lot of food."

Aaron remembered seeing them. "Nobody around today. They're all at the lake, just like the message board said."

The big wooden message boards were a major source of information in every neighborhood around town, since there weren't any newspapers and people couldn't talk on the phone. According to the boards, Oak Hollow was having some kind of big-deal meeting. The mayor was coming to tell people about something. Most of the neighborhood would be there. There would be bicycle patrols up and down the streets during the meeting, but it was easy for the boys to work around them.

If they'd had more boxes and a way to carry them all off quickly, they could have swept a dozen houses clean in Oak Hollow today. As it was, they'd hidden their empty boxes in the woods surrounding the neighborhood. They would hit one house, fill the boxes to the brim, then roll their loot home in their rusty wagon. Then they would come back and do the same with the next house, and the next. The problem was that few of the homes had much of what they wanted, so it took a lot of hits to gather enough to call it a day.

The Brannings' house had two stories, with a double front door and a big porch with white wicker rockers and a cushioned swing. It was the kind of house Aaron's mother used to dream about on her good days. She would cut pictures out of magazines and tack them to the walls—glossy-paged shots of colorful rooms with soft, clean furniture and shiny floors. As if she had a chance of ever owning such a place.

There was no one around. The street was quiet. Aaron couldn't have timed things better. He hoped they'd left their windows open, inviting in whatever breeze there was in the sweltering month of August, as many families did since air-conditioning became a thing of the past. He and Joey had easily gotten into most of the houses they'd hit today and found treasures they hadn't expected. This morning, he'd even managed to find nearly new tennis shoes for Sarah and Luke, who'd been barefoot since they'd outgrown their own. His three-year-old sister had stepped on broken glass last month, and it had been a mess trying to get it healed. Now that it was, he didn't want to let her play outside till she had shoes. Luke, his five-year-old brother, was wearing an old pair that Aaron and Joey had both outgrown—they were so holey there was almost no point in wearing them.

They went around the house and through the wooden gate to the backyard. No one was there. The gate at the back of the property was open, offering a view of the yard behind them, but there was no sign of anyone there, either.

"Okay, Joey, I'll look for a way in. You run back and get the wagon. And watch for the bike patrol. Wait till they've gone by before you cross the street."

Joey complied, as always. Aaron glanced around again, then went to the back door and tested the knob. It was locked, as he'd expected. These people weren't stupid.

He backed up into the yard, stepping on some of the plants, and surveyed each of the windows. The ones on the ground floor were all closed ... but one on the second floor was open a few inches.

Perfect. There was a trellis with vines on it leaning against the house—as good as a stepladder to reach the second floor. He shook it to make sure it would hold him. Carefully, he climbed up, testing each foothold of the white lattice before moving higher.

At the top, he balanced carefully on the steep roof and stepped across the shingles to the open dormer window, pulled it up, and slipped inside. He looked back out—Joey was stealing back into the yard, two big cardboard boxes in the rattley wagon he pulled behind him.

Aaron grinned down from the window and flashed Joey a thumbs-up. His partner-in-crime grinned up at him, revealing his two missing front teeth.

The room looked like a teenaged boy's room, with a framed baseball jersey with Mark McGuire's number on it hanging proudly on the wall, an autographed picture beside it. Aaron lingered in front of it for a moment, wishing he could snatch that and hang it on his own wall. But it would be too hard to carry. No, he hadn't come for that.

The bed was unmade. Several pairs of large, muddy shoes lay on the floor. A computer sat in one corner on a desk, looking like it could boot up any time. A television with a DVD player and a PlayStation sat on shelves facing the bed, coveted items before the outage on May 24. But they were useless now.

He tiptoed out of the room and down the stairs, staying quiet in case they were wrong about no one being home. As he'd hoped, he saw and heard no one. Quickly, he opened the back door, letting Joey in. "Anybody see you?"

His brother shook his head. "Nope. They're all gone."

"Yeah, well, we better be fast. That meeting could break up any minute."

His brother rolled the wagon in behind him, its wheels rattling across the ceramic tiles. Aaron ran into the kitchen and threw open the cabinet doors. Worthless stuff: dishes and small appliances—a mixer, a blender, a coffeepot. He opened the dark refrigerator and saw nothing but recycled plastic containers, a stack of books, and some folded towels. He turned to the floor-to-ceiling pantry next to the fridge and opened it.

"Score!" Joey cried at the sight of the food on the shelves. The Brannings had a bag of apples and a loaf of homemade bread wrapped in plastic wrap. A paper sack full of potatoes sat on a shelf with a dozen or so jars of vegetables.

"We'll be eatin' good tonight!" Aaron began loading everything he could reach into the boxes in the wagon. He glanced at the kitchen counter. There were several jugs of water lined up there. Someone had written *drinking water* on the side of a plastic milk jug. They'd struck gold! "Go get that water," he told his brother.

Joey's grinning eyes widened. "Do you think they cooked it?"

"Prob'ly. Throw it in, quick."

Joey found the caps and snapped them on, then carefully placed them in the box. They'd have to remember this place, Aaron decided, so they could give the family time to restock and hit them again.

Joey helped him empty the shelves, then rolled the wagon around the open pantry doors.

"Careful, now. Those jars'll break."

"Mom?"

Aaron froze at the sound of footsteps coming through the back door. He grabbed his brother's hand and stopped him. The pantry door hid them as the footsteps entered the kitchen.

"That you?" It sounded like a girl or a young boy. Aaron looked down at his feet, wondering if she could see them under the pantry door. She was coming toward them.

He looked for somewhere to hide, but there was no place. Joey's eyes were huge, fixed on Aaron's, silently asking what they should do.

Suddenly, the door swung back. A blonde girl of about twelve faced them, her eyes wide with shock. She screamed, her voice an alarm that would resound across Oak Hollow. Any second a police task force would surround the place with AK–47s, gunning them both down and taking back the food.

Sarah and Luke would be twice abandoned.

Aaron couldn't let that happen.

TWO

BETH BRANNING GASPED AND STUMBLED BACK FROM THE two boys, her heart slamming against her chest. But the littlest one looked more afraid than she. His dark hair strung into his eyes, as he stared at her. These were kids, no older than her brother Logan. "What are you doing?" she cried.

The boys looked at each other and threw the box they'd been holding into a wagon, jars clanging. Their wagon rattled as they dragged it around the island at the center of the kitchen.

The little creeps had stolen their food! Beth's shock turned to anger as the fear of starving became greater than any danger. "Stop!" she screamed, trying to cut them off before they got out the door. "Give it back!"

"Run, Joey!"

The boys dashed out the door, but she caught up to the wagon and grabbed it to stop them. "That's our food! You can't have it!"

The oldest boy spun around and leveled a gun at her face. Sweat dripped from his dirty brown hair into his dark eyes. "Get back!"

She sucked in a breath and let the wagon go. The boys raced around the house and into the street, with Beth following at a distance. "Help!" she yelled. "Somebody stop them!"

Her brothers—part of the bike patrol—rounded the corner of their street, Jeff pedaling and Logan on back.

"Go after them, Jeff!" Beth called, pointing. "They broke in and stole our food!"

The boys were just disappearing into the woods, dragging their wagon.

"They won't get far!" Jeff yelled, turning up a neighbor's driveway and cutting through his yard toward the path into the woods.

Beth had no doubt her brother could stop those brats. He had to. If he didn't, the Brannings would go hungry tonight.

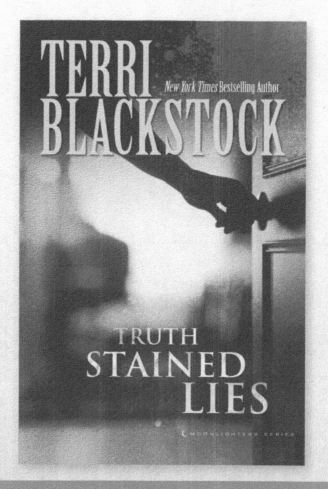

ABOUT THE
AUTHOR

Terri Blackstock is an award-winning novelist who has written for several major publishers including HarperCollins, Dell, Harlequin, and Silhouette. Her books have sold over 6 million copies worldwide.

With her success in secular publishing at its peak, Blackstock had what she calls "a spiritual awakening." A Christian since the age of fourteen, she realized she had not been using her gift as God intended. It was at that point that she recommitted her life to Christ, gave up her secular career, and made the decision to write only books that would point her readers to him.

"I wanted to be able to tell the truth in my stories," she said, "and not just be politically correct. It doesn't matter how many readers I have if I can't tell them what I know about the roots of their problems and the solutions that have literally saved my own life."

Her books are about flawed Christians in crisis and God's provisions for their mistakes and wrong choices. She claims to be extremely qualified to write such books, since she's had years of personal experience.

A native of nowhere, since she was raised in the Air Force, Blackstock makes Mississippi her home. She and her husband are the parents of three adult children—a blended family which she considers one more of God's provisions.

Terri Blackstock, a *New York Times* bestselling author, has sold over six million books worldwide. She is the author of numerous suspense novels, including *Intervention*, *Vicious Cycle*, and *Downfall* (the Intervention Series), as well as the Moonlighters Series, the Cape Refuge Series, the SunCoast Chronicles, the Newpointe 911 Series, the Restoration Series, and many others. (www.terriblackstock.com)

Share Your Thoughts

With the Author: Your comments will be forwarded to
the author when you send them to *zauthor@zondervan.com*.

With Zondervan: Submit your review of this book
by writing to *zreview@zondervan.com*.

Free Online Resources at
www.zondervan.com

Zondervan AuthorTracker: Be notified whenever your favorite
authors publish new books, go on tour, or post an update
about what's happening in their lives at www.zondervan.com/
authortracker.

Daily Bible Verses and Devotions: Enrich your life with daily
Bible verses or devotions that help you start every morning
focused on God. Visit www.zondervan.com/newsletters.

Free Email Publications: Sign up for newsletters on Christian
living, academic resources, church ministry, fiction, children's
resources, and more. Visit www.zondervan.com/newsletters.

Zondervan Bible Search: Find and compare Bible passages in
a variety of translations at www.zondervanbiblesearch.com.

Other Benefits: Register yourself to receive online benefits
like coupons and special offers, or to participate in research.

ZONDERVAN

ZONDERVAN.com/
AUTHORTRACKER
follow your favorite authors